英语畅谈
世界文化100主题

100 Topics On
World Culture

Nick Stirk 著　许卉艳　周维 译

外文出版社
FOREIGN LANGUAGES PRESS

Introduction

· ·

The dialogues

These dialogues are centred on world cultural symbols which not only give you information about these symbols but also enable you to have something to talk about with practically any foreigner you meet. This means that you will be prepared beforehand to talk with a native English speaker and that these dialogues will serve as an icebreaker before leading on to some great conversations that you can have.

These dialogues are also special in two ways. Firstly, they have been written by a native speaker who has had several years experience in China teaching at top universities. They are full of up-to-date natural expressions used by native speakers which mean that you will be using the same language that they speak. Secondly, there is an emphasis on collocations, phrases and expressions. This is because two, three, four and even five-word collocations, phrases and expressions make up a huge percentage of all naturally-occurring text, spoken or written. We are more likely to memorise and use phrases rather than single words. So get rid of word lists and replace them with lists of phrases.

How to get the most out of these dialogues

Role play dialogues are excellent opportunities for learners of English to practice English because they give students the chance to assume a role that is not their own. It does not matter if you make a mistake because it is not you who makes it. It is your character who does! You can totally assume the character and personality of your part and play it to the hilt and beyond! Role playing is a safe and enjoyable way to learn English. It is a good idea to find a partner to practice the following dialogues with. If you come across a dialogue with several different parts in it why not try (with your partner) speaking each part alternatively.

Tips on role plays

1. Don't be afraid to act the part;
2. Try to get into the character;
3. Explore different voices;
4. Use appropriate movements and gestures;
5. Change parts so that you can play a different character;
6. Don't be afraid to play a character of the opposite sex.

If you practice two dialogues a day then at the end of 50 days you'll be amazed at how your English has grown. Your confidence in speaking will be sky high and when a foreigner appears you will have plenty to talk about!

Acknowledgements

I wish to acknowledge the encouragement and assistance provided by my publisher Cai Qing and to thank Tori Waters-Wang for help with some of these dialogues.

Nick Stirk

前　言

．．

情景对话

本书的情景对话紧紧围绕世界各国的文化标志，不但能让你了解各国的文化特征，还能帮助你在遇到外国人时有话可说。如果你事先胸有成竹，交流中就能打破沉默的僵局，用英语进行愉快的交谈。

这些对话有两个特别之处。首先，作者来自英语国家，他在中国著名的高等学府授课数年。对话中的词句用法新颖、地道，这就意味着你学完本书后也能说一口原汁原味的英语。其次，对话大量选用了英语口语中的固定搭配和短语，这是因为在所有自然生成的文本中，无论口语还是书面语，由2至5个字组成的搭配和短语占了相当大的比例。他们往往比单个的词更容易记忆和使用。因此，我们应该记短语，而不是背单词。

如何充分利用这些对话

角色扮演是最好的口语练习方式，因为它能让学习者有机会扮演别人。讲错了不要紧，因为犯错误的不是你，而是你扮演的人物。你可以投入地演绎角色的品行和性格，甚至超越人物本身！可见，角色扮演既不让你出格，还很有趣。找个同伴一起练习本书的对话是个好方法。如果碰到对话中有几个不同的角色，那你和同伴可以从中任意选择一个进行练习。

关于角色扮演的提示

1. 别怕扮演角色；
2. 试着融入角色；
3. 尝试不同的声音；
4. 适当运用动作和手势；
5. 变换角色，这样你可以扮演不同人物；
6. 大胆扮演异性角色。

每天练习2个对话，50天以后，你就会惊讶地发现自己的英语已经进步了，讲英语的信心也会随之倍增。再遇到外国人时，你也可以滔滔不绝畅所欲言。

鸣谢

在这里，我想感谢我的出版人蔡箐给我的鼓励与帮助，同时也要感谢托里·沃特斯·王女士帮助我完成了部分对话。

作者　尼克·斯德克

学习指南

· ·

巧学活用本书能达到以一当十的效果，你至少可以做以下练习：

语音练习：选取你最感兴趣的课文，尽力模仿录音中的语音语调，把自己的朗读录下来和录音比较，找出差距反复模仿，直到乱真。

口语练习：利用书中对话做两人对练，或者和录音对练。就书中的主题换一个论点或谈话思路进行开放式对话创作。

听力练习：利用随书的 MP3 录音做精听和泛听练习。常用的内容精听，即反复听直到听懂每一个字并能流利跟读为止；其他内容泛听，能听懂大意并基本能跟读即可。

听写练习：听写能力表现在做课堂笔记和讲座笔记、会议记录等。利用本书 MP3 可以做听写练习，反复听写直到没有错误为止。

语汇练习：利用书中的词汇表，并摘录课文中精彩实用的句型或用法，建立自己的主题词汇库。

翻译练习：利用书中句型和对话做汉译英或英译汉练习，口译或笔译均可。

你可以根据自己的英语水平、工作需要和学习习惯将各种方法融会贯通，形成最适合自己的学习方法。当然，如果仅限于书本，再多的练习也只是纸上谈兵。如果你有找人开练的强烈愿望并付诸行动，离你的学习目标也就不远了。

Contents
目　录

· ·

英语畅谈
世界文化100主题

100 Topics On
World Culture

1. Maradona

马拉多纳

S: *Student*   *FS*: *Foreign student*

S: Hi, what are you looking at?

FS: It's a football website. I'm doing some research about famous players.

S: You should **look up** Maradona. Diego Maradona. He was a very famous player in the 1980s, played for Argentina. Have you heard of "The Hand of God"?

FS: Yes ... there's something about it here. In the 1986 World Cup in Mexico, Maradona scored a goal against England using his hand. The referee didn't **spot it** and awarded Argentina have the goal.

S: And later, when he was shown the illegal goal, Maradona said, "Even if there was a hand, it must have been the hand of God." That's how it got its name.

FS: I see. Let's look at his early career ... it says here that he was born in the slums of Villa Fiorito near Buenos Aires and was part of a very big family. Maradona entered professional football at the astonishing age of 15!

S: Very young! When he was 16, he played for the national squad of Argentina. Regardless of his talent, he was considered too young by the coach, who left him out of his selection for the 1978 World Cup.

FS: He must have been really disappointed, but I guess he **made up for it later**.

S: That's for sure. In the following four years, he dominated his country's domestic league and was eventually added to the Argentine squad for Spain 1982.

S: Although Argentina was unsuccessful, the brilliance of Maradona **did not go unnoticed** and after the World Cup, he was transferred to Spanish giants Barcelona.

FS: He went to the Italian club Napoli after that, in 1984.

S: What is he doing now? He must have retired, because he's pretty old.

FS: In 1991, he **tested positive** for doping and was banned from football for 15 months. That started the end of his international career.

S: It says here that in 1994 he tested positive for drugs again, that really must have been the end.

FS: It's a pity that drugs affected his career so much. He may not be a good man, but he was certainly an excellent footballer.

S: Yes, although I'm not sure about that "Hand of God"!

S：学生　　FS：外国学生

S: 你好，你在看什么？

FS: 看足球网站，我在研究著名的足球运动员。

S: 你应该查查马拉多纳，迭戈·马拉多纳。他是 20 世纪 80 年代的足球明星，为阿根廷效力。你听说过"上帝之手"吗？

FS: 听说过……这儿有一些相关信息。1986 年在墨西哥的世界杯比赛中，马拉多纳用手进了 1 个球，打败了英格兰队。裁判没有注意到，于是阿根廷队赢得了 1 分。

S: 后来，有人指出他违规进球，马拉多纳说，"就算是有一只手，那也一定是上帝之手。"这就是这个名字的由来。

FS: 我明白了。那我们看看他早年的情况……这里说马拉多纳出生在布宜诺斯艾利斯附近的维拉-费奥里托贫民区，他家是个大家族。他 15 岁就进入职业足球队，非常了不起。

S: 太年轻了！他 16 岁进入阿根廷国家足球队。当时不论他有多高的足球天赋，教练还是认为他年纪太小，不让他参加 1978 年的世界杯比赛。

FS: 他一定非常失望，不过我想他后来把这些遗憾都补上了。

S: 那是肯定的。接下来的 4 年里，他成了本国足球队的主力，最终在 1982 年参加了阿根廷队对西班牙队的比赛。

S: 尽管这次阿根廷队没能获胜，但马拉多纳的出色表现引起了大家的注意，所以世界杯之后，他就转到了西班牙绿茵豪门——巴塞罗那队。

FS: 此后，1984 年他加入意大利那不勒斯俱乐部。

S: 那他现在做什么？一定退休了，因为他的年纪很大了。

FS: 1991 年他因为服用兴奋剂，尿液检测为阳性，遭禁赛 15 个月。他的国际足球事业就这样开始走向终点。

S: 这儿还说他在 1994 年再次因为服药而被测试为阳性，这次一定是他的足球事业的终结。

FS: 遗憾的是，服药大大影响了他的足球事业。也许他不是个诚实的人，但他绝对是个出色的足球运动员。

S: 我也这么认为，尽管我不怎么相信"上帝之手"这个说法。

- look up　查询
- spot it　发现，判罚
- teste positive　测试结果为阳性
- make up for it later　后来得到了弥补
- do not go unnoticed　引起了人们的注意

2. Eva Perón

伊娃·庇隆

A: *Actress*   **F**: *Friend*

A: Oh, I wish I could be famous!

F: Maybe you could become famous for another reason, besides acting. What about Eva Perón?

A: What about Eva Perón? Or should I say "Evita", didn't Madonna play her in the movie?

F: Yes, she did. Evita was an actress, but she became famous for being the First Lady of Argentina. Maybe you could try another approach.

A: We are complete opposites, I mean she **grew up** very poor with five brothers and sisters, a mother, and no father.

F: Yes, I know your parents are rich and you are an only child. Did you know Eva's mother did not send her to school, but made her work in the kitchens of rich families?

A: Well, I'd never work in a kitchen. She **ran away** to Buenos Aires when she was 16 to become an actress. Good decision I say.

F: After that, in 1944, Eva met a young army colonel named Juan Perón. They were married in a year and she helped him **run for** the presidency in 1946. They won.

A: Then Eva started her own foundation that built hundreds of schools and hospitals in Argentina. What a wonderful woman!

F: Eva was also an advocate for the education of women. She also helped the poor workers of Argentina **gain a voice** and respect in the country that previously exploited them.

A: So you are saying that I should marry a politician? Or become a supporter of women's rights?

F: No, not exactly. I just think you could learn a lot from her. She was considered by many to be a politician, not an actress.

A: There had never been a female politician in Argentina before, but people believed in her. Hmmm ... maybe I could do something like that.

F: Unfortunately her political career only lasted for 4 years. In 1950 she was **diagnosed with**

cancer and died in 1952.

A：Evita's story can teach us all that it is possible to **defy fate**.

F：At that time a woman's place was in the home, not behind a desk.

A：Maybe I could do some volunteer work? I would like to help people. What an inspiring story!

A：女演员　　F：朋友

＊ 胡安·庇隆（1895－1974）：阿根廷总统，意大利移民后裔。曾任陆军部长、副总统，1946 年当选总统。任内赎买外资企业，增进劳工福利，提出"正义主义"（即"庇隆主义"）的政治主张。1955 年被军事政变推翻，此后侨居西班牙。1973 年回国再次当选总统，任内病故。

A：唉，我真希望自己能成为名人。

F：除了表演这一行之外，也许在其他方面你也能出名。像伊娃·庇隆那样怎么样？

A：伊娃·庇隆吗？或者我应该说是"埃维塔"，是不是电影中麦当娜扮演的那个？

F：是的，就是她。埃维塔是个演员，但她出名是因为她是阿根廷第一夫人。也许你可以试试其他途径。

A：我们俩完全不同，我是说她的家境贫寒，她和五个兄弟姐妹及母亲生活在一起，但没有父亲。

F：是的，我知道你父母很富有，你还是独生女。你知道伊娃的妈妈为什么不送她去学校，而是让她在富人家的厨房干活？

A：我可绝对不会干这样的活。她 16 岁就离家出走去了布宜诺斯艾利斯，后来就当了演员。我认为这个决定做得很好。

F：之后，1944 年伊娃遇到了年轻的陆军上校胡安·庇隆＊。一年后，他们结了婚。1946 年，她帮助他竞选总统，最终获胜。

A：然后，伊娃创办了自己的基金会，在阿根廷建了几百所学校和医院。多么了不起的女人！

F：此外，伊娃倡导妇女教育，还帮助阿根廷穷苦工人在曾经剥削他们的国家里争取到了发言权和应有的尊重。

A：那你是说我应该嫁个政治家了？要不就做妇女权利的维护者？

F：不，不全是这样。我只是想你能从伊娃身上学到很多东西。很多人认为她是个政治家，而不是演员。

A：阿根廷的历史上从来就没有女政治家，不过人们就是信任她。嗯……也许我可以那样做做。

F：不幸的是，她的政治生涯只维持了 4 年。1950 年她被查出患有癌症，1952 年去世。

A：我们从埃维塔的故事所能学到的是，与命运抗争并不是不可能的。

F：在当时，妇女的位置是在家里，而不是在办公室。

A：也许我能做些志愿者的工作？我愿意帮助他人。多么令人鼓舞的故事！

■ grow up　长大　　　　　　■ run away　逃跑，离家出走　　　■ run for　竞选
■ gain a voice　获得了发言权　■ diagnose with　诊断为　　　　■ defy fate　与命运抗争

3. Tango

探戈

M: *Man*   **W**: *Woman*

W: I wish you could find another hobby. Fishing is so boring! I want to find something we can do together.

M: Well, honey, you are going to love me even more! I have an idea ... what about dance classes?

W: Dance classes! How fabulous! But you said **"real men don't dance"**.

M: Maybe I've **changed my mind**. Now, let's decide which dance class to take.

W: There's ballroom dancing, disco, tap, jazz ... and tango. Tango sounds interesting, isn't it from Argentina?

M: Yes, I guessed you'd choose that one so I did some research on the Internet.

W: You know me too well. I took ballet when I was little but have never had the chance to dance in the past few years, because I thought you didn't enjoy it.

M: Did you know that Argentine tango was influenced by something called Tango Habenera?

W: I read that the knee flexing of the dance originated from African people living in Argentina. They danced with their knees bent to show off their skill.

M: It seems you are **a bit of an expert**. Have you been reading about it too?

W: Well, you know I've wanted to take dance classes for ages. Anyway, the tango they teach today didn't come about until the late 1930s, so it's probably very different to the original style.

M: The modern style is usually danced with flowers and a kind of musical instrument, those things you hold in one hand, they make a clicking sound.

W: You mean castanets. That sounds fun, my friend brought me some back from Spain when I was a child. Maybe I still have them somewhere. Did you know there are three different kinds of tango today? Which one do they teach?

M: The form known for stage, sometimes is referred as "for export", is aimed at English speaking people. So I suppose they teach that one.

M: I think tango is becoming more and more popular nowadays, some of these classes are already **fully booked**.

W: The Golden Age of Tango took place in the late 1940s and early 1950s, I guess it's having a revival!

M: What's the phone number? We should hurry up and book the classes.

M：男人　　W：女人

W：我希望你还有其它的爱好。钓鱼太没意思了！我想找点我们能一起做的事情。

M：这样吧，亲爱的，你会更爱我的！我有个主意……上个舞蹈班怎么样？

W：舞蹈班？太好了！可是你说过"真正的男人不跳舞。"

M：也许我改变主意了。现在咱们决定一下上哪个舞蹈班。

W：有交际舞、迪斯科舞、踢踏舞、爵士舞……还有探戈 *。探戈听起来很有趣，是从阿根廷传过来的吗？

M：是的。我猜你会选这个课，所以我上网查了一下。

W：你对我很了解嘛。我小时候学过芭蕾舞，可是过去几年一直就没有机会跳，因为我以为你不喜欢呢。

M：你知道阿根廷的探戈受过一种叫什么探戈·哈巴涅拉舞的影响吗？

W：我从书上看到过，舞蹈中膝盖弯曲动作源于生活在阿根廷的非洲人。他们跳舞时弯曲膝盖以显示自己的舞技。

M：你有点像个专家。你也一直看这方面的书吗？

W：是的，你知道这些年来我也总想上舞蹈班。不管怎么样，他们现在教的探戈是20世纪30年代末才出现的，所以很可能跟原始风格大不一样。

M：现代风格通常是跳舞时拿着一些花，一只手拿着一种会发出卡嗒声的乐器。

W：你是说响板吧。听起来很有意思。小时候，有个朋友从西班牙给我带回来一些响板。我应该还有，也许放在什么地方了。你知道如今有3种不同的探戈吗？他们要教哪一种？

M：舞台上常见的那种，有时被称作"出口货"，是针对讲英语国家的人们，所以我想他们会教这一种。

M：我觉得现在探戈越来越受欢迎了，有些班已经全部报满了。

W：探戈的黄金时代是在20世纪40年代末和50年代初，我想现在是复兴时期。

M：电话号码是多少？我们应该赶快预定课程。

> * 探戈：阿根廷的探戈、墨西哥的松、智利的库艾卡、秘鲁的圆舞曲等都是典型的拉美民间音乐歌舞体裁。拉丁美洲的文化是欧洲文化、印第安文化和非洲文化经过长期的碰撞、冲突、渗透、吸收后融合而成的。欧洲殖民者带来的西班牙、葡萄牙的伊比利亚音乐，结合印第安音乐和非洲黑人音乐，形成了拉美音乐丰富的色彩、独特的节奏、美妙的旋律和浓郁的和声，为世人瞩目。

■ Real men don't dance.　真正的男人不跳舞。
■ a bit of an expert　有点像专家
■ change my mind　改变主意
■ fully booked　全部订满

4. Sydney Opera House

悉尼歌剧院

D：Debbie   **G**：Glenn

D：What are you planning to do on your trip to Australia?

G：There are so many things to see, **I'm not sure where to start**. We're going to Sydney first.

D：If you're going to Sydney, the first thing you should do is to visit the Opera House. The architecture is **out of this world**!

G：Tell me some more about the Opera House, I'm a bit of an Australia novice!

D：Well, it's situated in Sydney Harbour at Bennelong Point. It was opened in 1973 but it wasn't built by an Australian.

G：Really? I've always thought it was built by a local.

D：Joern Utzon is the Danish architect who entered and won the international competition announced in January 1956 to design it.

G：Oh, I see. I wonder why I've never heard of him. So, was there a competition to select a designer? What did he win?

D：He's only known for that building. His prize for the winning design was 5,000 Australian pounds, this was before they had Australian dollars.

G：After winning the competition for the opera house design, he must have spent a long time planning the Opera House, before he started building it.

D：Actually, it took 15 years to build and the final cost was fourteen times the original estimate.

G：Wow! Why did it take so long to build?

D：I think one of the reasons was because the roof was so top-heavy and nothing so daringly inclined had ever been built before.

G：What happened to him later on?

D：In 2003, at the age of 85, Joern Utzon was recognised by his peers and awarded the prestigious Pritzker Prize, regarded as the Nobel Prize of architecture. But perhaps the most unusual thing about him was that he never actually saw the Opera House **in person**.

G: What if I want to watch something there, a musical or an opera, or something. What would you recommend?

D: Various theatre performances and other cultural events are held at the Sydney Opera House. You should look at the Sydney Opera House website and **check out** what's on during your visit.

G: That's a great idea.

D：黛比　　**G**：哥勒恩

D：这次澳大利亚之行，你计划做些什么？

G：要参观的地方太多了，我也不知道从哪儿开始。我们首先会去悉尼。

D：你们要是去悉尼的话，第一个要参观的应当是悉尼歌剧院，这是举世闻名的建筑。

G：给我多讲讲悉尼歌剧院吧，我对澳大利亚还真是不熟。

D：好的。歌剧院地处悉尼港的本纳隆角，于 1973 开放，但它的建筑师并不是澳大利亚本地人。

G：真是这样的吗？我一直都以为它是当地人建的。

D：丹麦建筑师杰恩·伍重参加了 1956 年 1 月宣布的澳大利亚悉尼歌剧院的国际设计竞赛，并最终获胜承担设计工作。

G：哦，是这样啊。我还纳闷怎么从没听说过他。这么说那时举办过一次设计师选拔赛，对吗？他的奖品是什么？

D：他只是因为这个建筑而出名。这次设计他获得 5000 澳大利亚镑的奖金，这事发生在澳元被使用之前。

G：赢得悉尼歌剧院设计大赛之后，他一定花了很长时间来做设计，然后才开始建设。

D：事实上，建这个剧院共花了 15 年的时间，而且最后的花费是最初预算的 14 倍。

G：哇，怎么花了这么长的时间？

D：我想其中一个原因就是在此之前从没有建过像歌剧院那样的建筑，顶部重得出奇，倾斜度也很大。

G：他后来怎么样了？

D：到了 2003 年，杰恩·伍重 85 岁时得到了同行的认可，获得了著名的普利兹克奖。这个奖被认为是建筑界的诺贝尔奖。但对他来说，最奇怪的是他从未亲自参观过悉尼歌剧院。

G：我要是想去歌剧院看点什么，比如音乐剧或歌剧什么的话，你有什么可推荐的吗？

D：悉尼歌剧院上演各种戏剧并举办其它文化活动。你最好到悉尼歌剧院的网站上看看，查查在你参观期间会上演些什么节目。

G：这个主意不错。

■ I'm not sure where to start.　我不知从哪儿开始。　　■ out of this world　世界闻名的

■ in person　亲自　　■ check out　检查

9

5. Aborigines

土著居民

S1: Student 1   **S2**: Student 2

S1: I'm writing a paper on early civilisations, I've decided to focus on the Australian **aborigines**.

S2: **Sounds good**. I'd love to do some extra reading on this topic.

S1: I'm not sure exactly what to write.

S2: **Let's begin at the beginning**. Australia may well be the home of the world's first people. Stone tools discovered in 1971 show that humans lived in Australia at least twelve thousand years before they appeared in Europe.

S1: I read that so far three early sites have been discovered in Australia, the Penrith one being dated about forty-seven thousand years old, a Western Australian site forty thousand years old and another in Lake Mungo, New South Wales, thirty-five thousand years old.

S2: That means there have been in excess of 1,850 generations of aboriginals!!!

S1: I never thought of it that way. Let's look at their culture, too. More than 30,000 years ago the population of the world was small, and people lived in family groups, hunting, fishing and food gathering.

S2: At that time there were no cultivated crops, animals were not herded for food and metalworking was yet to be discovered.

S1: Life must have been very different back then. At that time, known as the last great Ice Age, Australia was joined to New Guinea.

S2: So, they must have journeyed across the ice. As the ice flows of the Ice Age began to melt, the sea level rose, isolating Australia.

S1: **They were stuck there**, with no way to go back home. So, they made Australia their new home.

S2: The first Aboriginals found an Australia with a better environment than today. Large animals, now extinct, provided more meat than the animals with which we are familiar.

S1: Some parts of the continent were richer in vegetable foods, but the land contained no

10

cultivated crops, or animals that could be domesticated, such as cattle and sheep.

S2: Did you know they even have their own flag? It's divided horizontally into two equal halves of black (top) and red (bottom), with a yellow circle in the centre.

S1: Yes, it's flown or displayed permanently at aboriginal centres throughout Australia.

S1: 学生1　　**S2**: 学生2

S1: 我在写一篇有关早期文明的论文，我已经决定重点写澳大利亚的土著居民*。

S2: 就这个话题我也想多读点东西了解一下。

S1: 我不知道到底该写些什么。

S2: 那就从头说起吧。澳大利亚很可能是世界上最早一批人类的家园。1971年发现的石器表明人类在澳洲出现的时间比在欧洲至少早上12,000年。

S1: 我也从书上读到过，说至今在澳大利亚发现的3个早期遗址中，彭罗斯大概有47,000年的历史，澳大利亚西部的一个遗址也有40,000多年历史，而另外一个位于新南威尔士芒戈湖的遗址也有35,000年的历史。

S2: 也就是说生活在澳大利亚的原始居民已经超过了1,850代!!!

S1: 我从来没有那样想过。我们再来看看他们的文化吧。大约30,000年前，世界的人口总数还很少，人们都是以家庭为单位，一起打猎、捕鱼和采集食物。

S2: 当时人们还没有种植农作物，也没有圈养动物来获取食物，金属加工业也还没有发展。

S1: 那时生活肯定很艰苦。当时正好是最后一次大冰川时代，澳大利亚和新几内亚还连在一起。

S2: 所以他们肯定是从冰上走过去的。后来由于冰川时代冰河的溶化，海平面上升，把澳大利亚与其他地方隔离开来了。

S1: 他们被困在了那里，找不到回家的路，于是就把澳大利亚当成了自己的新家。

S2: 第一批土著居民所发现的澳大利亚环境比今天的要好。而且，与我们今天所熟悉的动物相比，那些已经灭绝的大型动物能给他们提供更多的肉食。

S1: 大陆有些地区有较丰富的植物可食用，但那时没有人在这片土地上种植庄稼。这里也没有能被家养的动物，比如牛和羊。

S2: 你知道吗？土著人还有自己的旗帜。旗子被分为均等的两部分，上面是黑色，下面是红色，中间是一个黄色的圆圈。

S1: 是的，这种旗帜在遍布澳大利亚的土著人中心陈列着，永远飘扬。

> * 澳洲土著居民：1788年英国殖民者侵入澳洲大陆时，当地约有26万土著居民，分属大小500多个部落，保持着原始氏族公社的生活。他们有各自的语言，没有文字，以采集、游猎为生，用石、骨、木制作器具，崇拜图腾。近200年来，澳洲土著居民遭受殖民者的驱逐，现仅存14.4万人（1983年），其中纯土著约占1/4，主要分布在西澳大利亚州、昆士兰州、北部地区，部分被驱入荒漠和保留地。

■ aborigines　土著居民
■ Let's begin at the beginning.　让我们从头开始吧。
■ Sounds good.　听起来不错。
■ They were stuck there.　他们被困在那里。

6. Kangaroos

袋 鼠

K：Karen   **C**：Charlotte

K：What's your favourite animal? I like koalas the most.

C：**Funny you should say that**, I like kangaroos. How very antipodean of us!

K：I think kangaroos are funny looking animals.

C：Kangaroos are part of a special category of animals, called marsupials.

K：Kangaroos usually have small deer-like heads with wide set eyes and binocular vision, prominent upright ears which rotate to hear in all directions.

C：Yes, and a moderately long muzzle with a split upper lip, short forelimbs with mobile grasping forepaws that can hold food, open its pouch and box just like a boxer!

K：They **are very skilled at** using their little arms! And when they have a little baby in the pouch it looks adorable.

C：A joey.

K：A what?

C：A joey, that's what a baby kangaroo's called. Another interesting thing about them is their long hind limbs, with the characteristic long narrow feet which gives them the name of "macropod" or "big-foot".

K：So, because they have short forelimbs and long hindlimbs, they can jump easily, quickly and for long distances.

C：Right. **Taking off** on their hind feet, landing on their fore limbs and tail, pushing off again with their hind limbs. The elongated and very strong fourth toe of the hind foot serves as a lever to propel the animal along and bears the animal's weight when it stands.

K：I see. Long legs increase the stride when hopping. Forelimbs and tails prop them up when they crawl slowly to feed. Powerful hind limbs and a large heavy tail serve for balance and support.

C：But tree kangaroos have shorter prehensile tails and climb rather than hop. Many kangaroo species are grazers and browsers adapted to living in dry desert habitats.

K：Just like me! I'm always eating and gazing at what's going on around me. The desert is so dry, what can they eat?

C: They usually eat any grass they can find, even very hard grass.

K: They must have good, strong teeth too.

C: Some, such as several tree kangaroos, my particular favourite, are **threatened with survival**, but others, like the grey and red kangaroos, have flourished and are now considered to be pests.

K: 卡伦　　C: 夏洛特

K: 你最喜欢什么动物？我最喜欢的是考拉。

C: 说起来还真有意思。我喜欢的是袋鼠。我们真是截然不同啊！

K: 我认为袋鼠的样子看上去很好玩。

C: 它是一种特殊的动物，叫做有袋动物。

K: 它的小脑袋像麋鹿，但眼睛大且双眼都有视力，耳朵高高竖起，还可以转动以便听到四面八方的声音。

C: 是的，它的口鼻长度中等，上唇裂开，前肢短小。它前爪灵活，可以抓食物，打开袋子，并且像拳击手一样打架。

K: 它们还很善于运用短臂！它们的育儿袋里放着小袋鼠时看起来非常可爱。

C: 一只幼兽。

K: 一只什么？

C: 一只幼兽，也就是小袋鼠。袋鼠另外一个有意思的地方就是它们的后腿很长，而脚是又长又细，因此又被称作"长脚"或"大脚"。

K: 正是因为袋鼠前肢很短而后肢又很长，所以它们才能跳得又快又远。

C: 没错。袋鼠用后脚起跳，用前肢和尾巴着地，然后用他们的后肢推动再次跳起。袋鼠后脚的第4个脚趾长而有力，作为向前跳跃时的支撑点，还承担着自己站立时的体重。

K: 我知道了。长腿使它们跳得更远，而缓慢爬行进食时，它们的前肢和尾巴又起着支撑作用。它们强有力的后腿和粗重的尾巴也起着平衡和支撑作用。

C: 但是树袋鼠的尾巴较短，有捕握力，适合爬而不适合跳。许多袋鼠都是食草和嫩叶的动物，喜欢四处觅食，适合在干旱的沙漠环境中生活。

K: 就像我一样！我总是一边吃东西一边注意观察身边发生的事。不过沙漠这么干，袋鼠都吃些什么呢？

C: 能找到的所有草类，它们通常都吃，哪怕是那些很坚硬难啃的草。

K: 它们的牙齿也一定都坚硬耐磨。

C: 有些袋鼠，比如一些树袋鼠，也是我最喜欢的那种，现在正濒临灭绝；但另外一些种类，比如红袋鼠和灰袋鼠，现在因繁殖过多而被当成祸害。

■ funny you should say that　说起来还真有意思　　■ be very skilled at　很善于
■ take off　起跳　　■ be threatened with survival　生存受威胁，濒临灭绝

13

7. Great Barrier Reef

大堡礁

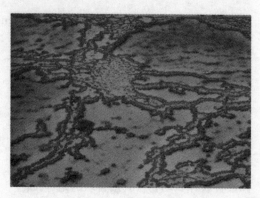

D: *David*   **V**: *Vicki*

D: Vicki, hello! **Long time no see**. Where have you been?

V: I spent the last six months in Australia. It was so great, I had a wonderful time. The best bit was snorkelling at the Great Barrier Reef. The sea life there is **out of this world**.

D: The Great Barrier Reef is the only living organic collective visible from Earth's orbit. It's one of the wonders of the natural world.

V: And it's the world's largest coral reef ecosystem. There are loads of beautiful islands scattered around and idyllic coral cays.

D: It's pretty big, isn't it? I think it covers more than 300,000 square kilometres.

V: Yes, it's huge. There are more than 3,000 reefs, which vary in size, the smallest is about 1 hectare. But the biggest is massive, over 10,000 hectares.

D: Wow! Unfortunately because many tourists go there, it's suffering. You know, because of the pollutants.

V: Unfortunately, that's true. Its protection is the responsibility of the Marine Park Authority, they have developed something called "The Reef Plan". This is a combined effort to protect the reef.

D: I believe they are **doing a good job** with that. How about the coral? Is it really as beautiful as they say?

V: Oh my god, yes! Coral consists of individual coral polyps—tiny live creatures which join together to form colonies. Each polyp lives inside a shell of aragonite, a type of calcium carbonate which is the hard shell we recognise as coral.

D: So, these polyps join together to create forests of coloured coral in interesting fan, antler, brain and plate shapes.

V: That's right. The ideal environment for coral is shallow warm water where there is a lot of water movement, plenty of light, where the water is salty and low in nutrients.

D: How many different kinds of coral are there?

14

V: There are many different types of coral, some are slow growing and live to be hundreds of years old, others are faster growing. The colours of coral are created by algae. Only live coral is coloured. Dead coral is white.

D: Have you got any photos?

V: Loads! **Come and have a look**.

D：戴卫　　**V**：薇琪

D：薇琪，你好！好久不见了。你去哪儿了？

V：过去半年我都待在澳大利亚。那里太好了，我玩得很开心。最有意思的就是在大堡礁潜水，那里的海洋生物是世界一流的。

D：大堡礁是唯一能够从地球同步轨道上看得见的生命有机体。它是自然界的一大奇观。

V：它也是世界上最大的珊瑚礁生态系统。那里四周都是漂亮的岛屿和田园般的珊瑚礁沙洲。

D：大堡礁很大，是吧？我想它的面积大概有 300,000 平方公里。

V：是的，相当大。它由大大小小约 3000 多个珊瑚礁组成，最小的大约一公顷大。但最大的却相当大，有 10,000 公顷。

D：哇，真够大的！可不幸的是，由于去那里参观的游客很多，大堡礁正面临毁灭之灾。你知道，这是由污染物造成的。

V：的确很不幸。保护大堡礁是海洋公园管理局的责任，他们制定了一个计划叫"珊瑚礁计划"，旨在号召大家共同努力保护大堡礁。

D：我相信他们是在做好事。对了，珊瑚怎么样？它们真的就像人们说的那么漂亮吗？

V：哦，天啊！真的非常漂亮。珊瑚由单个的珊瑚虫组合而成。珊瑚虫是一种微小的生物，聚合在一起而形成一个群体。每一个珊瑚虫都寄生在一个文石壳内。文石是一种碳酸钙，也就是我们所说的珊瑚硬壳。

D：也就是说，这些珊瑚虫聚合在一起形成了五颜六色的珊瑚丛，有扇形、鹿角形、大脑形和盘子形，非常有意思。

V：是这样，珊瑚生活的理想环境是海水流动较多的温暖浅滩，那里光线充足，水的盐分高、养分低。

D：大堡礁的珊瑚有多少种？

V：珊瑚的种类很多，有些生长缓慢，能存活几百年，而其它的生长较快。珊瑚的颜色是由海藻形成的。只有活着的珊瑚才是彩色的，死了的珊瑚都是白色的。

D：你有没有照片？

V：多的是。过来看看吧。

■ long time no see　好久不见	■ out of this world　世界一流的
■ do a good job　做好事	■ come and have a look　过来看看

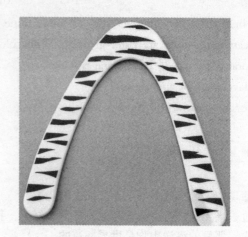

8. Boomerang

回飞棒

T：*Tim*　　*A*：*Alan*

T：I'm giving a lecture next week at the Australia Society, would you be interested in coming?

A：Yes, of course. What are you going to talk about?

T：Well, I'd thought of talking about boomerangs. What do you think?

A：A great topic! I know quite a lot about it too, so I can **give you a hand**. How are you going to start?

T：Like this ... the real question is where do they come from? Most people would say Australia, and they would be correct, for the most part.

A：Open with a question! Great! You must also establish the difference between a returning boomerang and a non-returning boomerang. Many people, even today, get the two confused. Non-returning boomerangs were used for hunting.

T：Yes, they are called "Kylies", like the Australian singer, Kylie Minogue. They are about three feet long and have a chord width of three to four inches across, being about one and a half inch thick and similar in shape to a banana.

A：And they don't return to the thrower. A thrown stick can fly great distances. One hundred to one hundred and fifty yard flights are not uncommon.

T：True. Then, I thought I'd go on to why they made boomerangs.

A：So, tell me, why did they make "the Kylie"?

T：The best thinking is that prior to throwing sticks people used clubs to settle their differences, but later they realized that a thin club flew further. At this point the basic concept of a throwing stick was established.

A：In Australia it was **handed down from generation to generation**. The oldest one is around 20,000 years old!

T：Next, I will talk about how the returning boomerang was developed. **The story goes** that an Aboriginal person was shaping a smaller, lighter slightly more bent throwstick than he

16

normally used. When he tested it he was very surprised to observe that it didn't fly straight at all, but came turning back to him.

A: Was it created by chance or skill? No one really knows. What we do know is they made it and passed the technique down through generations of time and we have it today, thankfully.

T: 蒂姆　　A: 艾伦

> *凯利·米诺格：人称"豌豆公主"的澳大利亚歌手凯利·米诺格（Kylie Minogue）在欧美的地位堪与麦当娜比肩。她拥有性感的舞台形象，被人们爱称为"美臀天后"。

T: 下周我会到澳大利亚社团做一次演讲，你有兴趣参加吗？

A: 哦，当然有了。你打算讲点什么？

T: 嗯，我想谈谈回飞棒，你觉得怎么样？

A: 选题不错！我对这个也很熟悉，所以我可以帮帮你。你准备从哪儿开始讲起？

T: 是这样的……真正的问题是回飞棒的发源地在哪里：大多数人说是澳大利亚，他们的说法基本上是对的。

A: 由问题入手，不错！不过你也要说明一下返回式回飞棒和非返回式回飞棒的区别。即使到今天，还有很多人把两者弄混。在过去，非返回式回飞棒是打猎用的。

T: 是的，非返回式回飞棒又被称为"凯利"，就像澳大利亚女歌手凯利·米诺格*的名字。它大约 3 英尺长，1.5 英寸厚，上面横放着一根三四英尺宽的弦，形状如香蕉。

A: 这种回飞棒并不飞回到抛出者身边。扔出的棒子可以飞出去很远，大约 100 到 150 码是很正常的。

T: 确实是这样。接下来，我想谈一下制作回飞棒的原因。

A: 那你给我讲讲，以前人们为什么要制作"凯力"？

T: 最恰当的解释是在此之前，人们用扔棍棒的方式来解决分歧，但后来人们意识到棍棒越细飞得就越远。由此，扔棍棒的这一基本想法就这样产生了。

A: 在澳大利亚，人们一代代地把这一发明传承下来。最早的回飞棒大约有两万年的历史。

T: 接下来，我会谈到返回式回飞棒是怎么产生的。故事是这样的：一位土著人正在做一根比他平常用的更小、更轻、更弯的扔棍，在试用那棍棒时却发现棍棒根本不是一直向前飞的，而是飞回他的身边。

A: 那这个发明到底是偶然发现的呢，还是依靠技术呢？没有人真正知道。我们所知道的是土著人发明了它，然后把这一技术世代相传，直到今天，我们因此幸运地拥有了回飞棒。

■ boomerang　回飞棒
■ hand down from generation to generation　一代代地传承

■ give you a hand　帮你的忙
■ The story goes ...　故事是这样的……

9. Mozart

莫扎特

U: *Uncle*   *N*: *Niece*

N: Uncle Jeremy, what's that beautiful music you're listening to? I mean, it sounds familiar, but I don't know what it is.

U: It's Mozart, Katie. Wolfgang Amadeus Mozart. This piece is called *Lucio Silla* and was written in around 1770.

N: Wow! That's a long time ago, I think it's unbelievable that we still listen to his music today. Didn't he start composing when he was 2 years old or something?

U: Actually he was 5 years old, but yes, he was very young indeed. When he was 6 he played for the Bavarian Elector and Empress.

N: That's amazing! When I was 6 years old, I was playing with dolls, not performing in public to famous people.

U: His father decided he should **cash-in** on Wolfgang's talents, so the family **set off** on a trip which took them to London and Paris.

N: So, his father wanted to make some money and took Mozart all over the world to play in public.

U: He played for the English and French royal families, who were astonished by his talents. After that, they **headed for** Vienna.

N: He must have had a very busy life as a child. Where was he when he wrote the piece we are listening to now?

U: He was in Italy at that time, acquainting himself with Italian styles. During that visit he also wrote *Mitridate*, which is also an opera and a serenata for performance in Milan.

N: He must have still been a teenager at that time, maybe a little younger than me. I was scared when I moved away to go to university, but he had been working around the world before he was 18.

U: Then, in 1773 he went to Vienna again, where he wrote a set of **string quartets** and, on his return, wrote a group of symphonies including his two earliest, *No. 25 in G Minor* and *29 in A*.

N: When did he die? Was he old?

U: He died in 1791 and was buried in a Vienna suburb, with little ceremony and in an **unmarked grave**.

N: He died young, must have been because his life was so busy.

U: 叔叔   N: 侄女

N: 杰里米叔叔，你在听什么美妙的音乐？我是说，听起来那么耳熟，可就是不知道是什么曲子。

> * 选帝侯：神圣罗马帝国（955-1806）中参与选举皇帝的诸侯。13 世纪时有 7 名，分别是 3 个教会诸侯：美茵茨大主教，科隆大主教，特里尔大主教，和 4 个世俗诸侯：萨克森公爵，勃兰登堡藩侯，普法尔茨伯爵，以及波希米亚国王。后数目有所增加。1806 年神圣罗马帝国灭亡，随之取消。

U: 凯蒂，这是莫扎特的曲子，沃尔夫冈·阿玛多伊斯·莫扎特。这是他的歌剧《卢齐奥·西拉》，大约写于 1770 年。

N: 哇，那是很早以前的曲子了。现在我们还听他的音乐，真太令人难以置信了。他是不是 2 岁左右就开始作曲了？

U: 实际上，那时他 5 岁了，不过年纪确实很小。他 6 岁时就为巴伐利亚选帝侯* 和王后演奏曲目。

N: 真了不起！我 6 岁时在玩洋娃娃，而不是在公共场合给名人表演节目。

U: 他父亲认定应该及时利用沃尔夫冈的天才赚钱，所以全家动身去伦敦和巴黎旅行。

N: 那就是说他父亲想要挣钱，于是就带着莫扎特去世界各地公开演出。

U: 他为英法两国的皇室演奏，这些人却被他的天才惊呆了。此后，他们又去了维也纳。

N: 对他这样一个孩子来说，日子一定过得非常繁忙。你现在听的这首曲子，是他在哪儿写的？

U: 当时他在意大利，正在努力熟悉意大利的风格。在那段访问期间，他还写了《米特里达特》，这也是为米兰演出而写的歌剧和合唱剧。

N: 那时，他一定还是个十几岁的孩子，也许比我的年龄还小一点。我离开家去上大学时还害怕呢，可是他却不到 18 岁已经在世界各地演出了。

U: 后来在 1773 年，他又去了维也纳，在那里写出了一组弦乐四重奏曲。回来后，又写了一组交响曲，包括他最早的两个曲目：《G 小调第 25 号交响曲》和《A 大调第 29 号交响曲》。

N: 他什么时候去世的？年纪很大吗？

U: 他 1791 年去世，当时没有举行什么仪式，就埋在了维也纳郊区一个不被人注意的坟墓里。

N: 他英年早逝一定是因为他生活节奏太快了。

- cash-in 及时抓住赚钱机会
- set off 出发，动身
- head for 出发，前往
- string quartets 交响曲
- unmarked grave 不被人注意的坟墓

10. Sissi and Schonbrunn
茜茜公主和美泉宫

F1: Friend 1   *F2*: Friend 2

F1: I picked up a biography in the bookstore, about Empress Elisabeth of Austria, you know "Empress Sissi"?

F2: Really, was it good? I've seen some of the films about her, but I've never read her biography.

F1: I would recommend that anybody who is enchanted by the myth NOT read it—reality might destroy the romantic illusion.

F2: Why? I think the story of her and her husband, Franz Joseph is extremely romantic. They seemed to be so in love.

F1: But that's it, it's just a story. In the biography it says that Franz was a workaholic and **spent most of his time** in his office.

F2: Really? I thought they were always together. Anyway, I know something about her. For example, she was born in 1837, in Munich.

F1: Right! But, I bet you didn't know this ... Franz Joseph was actually meant to marry her sister, Helene, but Franz fell in love with Sissi.

F2: I did know that, actually. It was in a film I once saw. The engagement to Sissi was a sensation.

F1: I bet. She later said that she regretted marrying him. Also, did you know she was murdered? A crazy anarchist stabbed her to death when she was 60 years old.

F2: I didn't know that! I did read that she went a little crazy though, because she dieted too much. Did you read anything about their castle? Schon ... something.

F1: Schonbrunn, yes. It was built in around 1700 and lots of famous people have lived there over the years, not only Sissi.

F2: It's in Vienna, isn't it?

F1: Yes, that's right. It was the Viennese **summer residence** for Austrian royalty for many decades, even Empress Maria Theresa, who give birth to 16 children there.

F2: I read that Marie Antoinette was born there, and lived there until she **married into** the French royal family.

F1: She was one of Empress Maria Theresa's many kids. Schonbrunn is huge and totally beautiful! It has 1,441 rooms and is decorated in the delicate **rococo style**.

F2: That is big. We should visit in the summer holidays, I hear the guided tour is great. It would certainly be an interesting holiday.

F1: 朋友1　　F2: 朋友2

> * 玛丽娅·泰瑞莎 (1717—1780): 奥地利女大公、神圣罗马帝国皇帝弗朗茨一世的妻子,皇帝约瑟夫二世的生母,哈布斯堡王朝最杰出的女政治家。
> * 玛丽·安东奈特 (1755—1793): 玛丽娅·泰瑞莎的女儿,法国国王路易十六的王后。法国大革命爆发后企图同路易十六逃往奥地利,被捕后押回巴黎囚禁,后被处斩。

F1: 我从书店买了一本传记,是关于奥地利伊丽莎白皇后的,你知道"茜茜皇后"吗?

F2: 真的吗? 书写得好吗? 我看过有关她的电影,但从来没读过她的传记。

F1: 我要建议所有对这一神话式人物着迷的人不要读这本书,因为现实可能会毁掉这一浪漫的幻想。

F2: 为什么? 我认为她和她丈夫弗朗茨·约瑟夫的故事很浪漫的。他们好像爱得非常深。

F1: 是这样,但这只是故事。传记中说弗朗茨是个工作狂,大部分时间都呆在办公室。

F2: 真的吗? 我原来以为他们总在一起呢。不管怎么样,我还是了解她一些情况。比如说,她 1837 年生于慕尼黑。

F1: 没错! 可是,我敢说你不知道这个……弗朗茨·约瑟夫原本是打算娶她的姐姐海伦,却爱上了茜茜。

F2: 这个我真的不知道。我以前在电影中看到过。弗朗茨与茜茜公主的订婚轰动一时。

F1: 的确是这样。她后来说后悔嫁给弗朗茨。那你还知道她被谋杀的事吗? 她 60 岁时被一个疯狂的无政府主义者刺死了。

F2: 这个我不知道! 我确实从书上读过,说她因为节食过度精神变得有点不正常。你读过有关他们住的城堡的书吗? 那个叫什么宫的。

F1: 是美泉宫。建于 1700 年左右。不只是茜茜公主,还有很多名人都在那里住过很多年。

F2: 是在维也纳,对吗?

F1: 对。这是几十年中奥地利皇室在维也纳的避暑圣地,玛丽亚·泰瑞莎女皇*还在那里生过 16 个孩子。

F2: 我从书上了解到,玛丽·安东奈特*就是在那里出生的,在嫁给法国皇室之前一直都住在那儿。

F1: 她是玛丽亚·泰瑞莎女皇众多孩子中的一个。美泉宫很大,非常漂亮,有 1441 个房间,采用洛可可式风格,装修得很精巧。

F2: 那是够大的。暑假我们应该去参观一下。我听说有团队游非常好,我们肯定会度过一个有趣的假期。

■ spend most of his time in his office 他大部分时间呆在办公室　　■ summer residence 避暑圣地
■ marry into 嫁给　　　　　　　　　　　　　　　　　　　　　　　■ rococo style 洛可可式风格

11. Pele

贝利

F1: Friend 1 *F2*: Friend 2

F2: Did you get the book I was talking about?

F1: Yes, ***Latino Sports Legends***. It's really interesting.

F2: Did you find the section on Pele?

F1: Edson Arantes Do Nascimento, to be exact.

F2: You've read it then! Yes, he is probably the greatest footballer in history, but he came from humble beginnings.

F1: Yes, from a very poor family and grew up in Tres Coracos, Brazil. His parents called him "Dico".

F2: I didn't know that. He has so many names!

F1: And it was his Dad that taught him football.

F2: Yes, I think his Dad could have been a great footballer too, but he broke his leg and that stopped him from making it into a career.

F1: It said in the book that he was discovered when he was 11 by another famous footballer, who took him to Sao Paulo. He started playing for a professional team when he was just 16 years old.

F2: Yes, and as he got older, he got even better! He represented Brazil in 4 World Cups, but in 1958 he almost didn't play because of a knee injury.

F1: He's lucky that the injury didn't significantly affect his career, many footballers have injured themselves and never play again.

F2: Well, in 1962 he actually couldn't play in the World Cup Finals against Chile, because of an injury.

F1: Oh, I see. Did you know that several European clubs offered him lots of money to move to their teams?

F2: Yes. I read that Brazil declared him an official "**national treasure**", to keep him in the country.

F1: But **his best was still to come**! In 1970, at the World Cup Finals in Mexico, Pele scored Brazil's 100th World Cup goal! He is now very well-known for that goal, which was scored against Italy.

F2: When did he retire? I think he must be really old now.

F1: He retired in 1974, but then played in America for a while.

F2: Also, in 1993 his name was entered into the **Soccer Hall of Fame** and in 2000 he was awarded Sports Person of the Century.

F1: Wow! He is definitely **a football legend**!

F1: 朋友1   **F2**: 朋友2

F2: 我说过的那本书，你买到了吗？

F1: 买到了，《拉丁美洲运动员传奇》，写得非常有意思。

F2: 你找到关于贝利的那一节了吗？

F1: 确切地说是埃德森·阿兰特斯·多纳西门。

F2: 那你肯定是读过了。是的，他也许是历史上最伟大的足球运动员，但他的出身非常贫寒。

F1: 是这样，他出生在一个非常贫穷的家庭，在巴西的特雷斯科拉松伊斯镇长大。他父母叫他"迪科"。

F2: 这些我不清楚。他有那么多名字！

F1: 是他爸爸教他踢的足球。

F2: 是的，我认为他爸爸本应该也能成为伟大的足球运动员，但不幸的是他的腿断了，导致他不能把踢足球当成职业。

F1: 书上说，他11岁时被另一个有名的足球运动员发现，并把他带到了圣保罗。他正式进入职业足球队时只有16岁。

F2: 是的，而且随着年龄的增大，他越来越棒！他4次代表巴西队参加世界杯比赛，但1958年由于膝盖受伤差点踢不了球。

F1: 幸运的是这次受伤对他的足球生涯没有太大的影响，而很多足球运动员受伤后都不能再踢球了。

F2: 到了1962年，由于受伤，在巴西对智利的世界杯决赛中他实际上已经踢不了球了。

F1: 噢，我明白了。有几家欧洲俱乐部给他丰厚的待遇让他加入他们的球队，你知道这些吗？

F2: 知道。我从书上看到巴西正式宣布他为"国宝"，要把他留在国内。

F1: 但是他最精彩的故事还在后面呢！1970年，在墨西哥的世界杯决赛中，贝利为巴西队在世界杯比赛中踢进了第100粒球！那是在巴西队对意大利队比赛时赢得的，他为此威名远扬。

F2: 他什么时候挂的靴？我想他现在年纪一定很大了。

F1: 他1974年挂靴，但后来又在美国踢了一段时间的球。

F2: 此外，1993年他的名字被列入了"足球名人堂"，2000年被授予"本世纪最佳足球运动员"称号。

F1: 哇，他的确是个足球奇人！

■ Latino Sports Legends 拉丁美洲运动员传奇　　　■ national treasure 国宝
■ his best was still to come 他最精彩的故事还在后面　　■ Soccer Hall of Fame 足球名人堂
■ a football legend 一个足球奇人

12. Rio Carnival

里约热内卢狂欢节

S1 : *Student 1*　　*S2* : *Student 2*

S2 : I'm doing something amazing. I'm going to the Rio Carnival!

S1 : You are so lucky. It's the world's most famous street party.

S2 : Yes, millions of people come from everywhere and it goes on for several days. But the best part is called "The Sambodromo Parade". The Sambodromo is a 700-metre long street surrounded by **spectator stands** and **luxury boxes** which are filled with over 60,000 people. Tickets are expensive and **sell out** quickly.

S1 : You had better get your tickets early, then. I heard it's famous for people dancing the samba and **goes on all night**.

S2 : Yes. They have **lavish floats** with women dressed in amazing costumes, and these are accompanied by marching bands. Then, all around is **a sea of people** who are also dressed in costumes.

S1 : They change the themes and costumes every year, don't they?

S2 : Yes, so **you'll never see the same thing twice**. Another interesting part is the "**Masquerade Balls**".

S1 : Oh, I've heard of these too. Lots of famous people attend, so ticket prices are **sky high**!

S2 : Yes, so I don't know if I can go to one. But, the street parades, apart from "Sambodromo" are all free. Everyone joins in together, with the real dancers and marching bands.

S1 : I think that sounds even more interesting. If you go to "The Sambodromo Parade", you can only watch. But, if you go to a normal street parade, you can be part of it!

S2 : I have heard some stories though, that it's pretty dangerous.

S1 : I think you must be careful of thieves, yes. But, so many people take part every year and only a few are mugged. I think it's worth taking a little risk to be part of something so amazing.

S2 : I guess you're right. There should also be lots of delicious food, because for 40 days after the Carnival the local people don't eat meat. During Carnival time they eat everything!

S1: How many days does it last?

S2: Erm . . . I think from a Saturday to Wednesday.

S1: Oh, so is Tuesday what we know as Mardi Gras?

S2: Yes, it means "Fat Tuesday", so that should be a clue about the food!

S1：学生 1　　　**S2**：学生 2

S2：我要去参加里约热内卢的狂欢节，这真让人兴奋。

S1：你太幸运了。这是世界上最有名的街道盛装游行聚会。

S2：是的，来自世界各地成千上万的人都来参加，活动要持续几天。但最精彩的部分是"桑巴大道"。桑巴大道是条长 700 米的街道，周围有观众台和豪华包厢，能装下 6 万多人。门票非常贵，但很快就能卖光。

S1：那你最好早点弄到票。我听说这条街道之所以有名是因为人们在那里跳桑巴舞，而且是整晚地跳。

S2：是的。他们还有非常豪华的彩车，上面有穿着奇异服饰的女郎，还有行进乐队伴奏。那时到处都是人的海洋，人人都穿着节日盛装。

S1：他们每年都变换主题和服装，是不是？

S2：是的，所以同样的东西你绝对不会看到第二次。另一个有趣的节目是"化装舞会"。

S1：哦，这些我也听说过。很多名人都参加，所以票价高得吓人！

S2：是这样，所以我不知道我能否参加。不过，除"桑巴大道"之外，其他街道的表演都是免费的。大家都可以加入表演队伍，还有真正的舞蹈演员和行进乐队。

S1：我想那一定会更有趣。如果你选择"桑巴大道"，那你就只能看看。但如果参加一般的街道表演，那你还能参与其中。

S2：不过，我听到过一些传闻，说那样做会很危险。

S1：是的，我想你一定要小心扒手。但是每年那么多人参加，也只有几个被偷。我觉得参加这么有意思的活动，冒点险还是值得的。

S2：我觉得你说得对。那里还会有很多美食，因为狂欢节之后当地人 40 天之内都不吃肉，所以狂欢节期间，他们什么都吃。

S1：这个活动要持续多少天？

S2：嗯……我想是从周六到周三。

S1：哦，所以星期二就是我们所知道的四旬斋前的狂欢节吧？

S2：是的，那意思是"肥美的星期二"，从这个称呼就能联想到那些美食！

- spectator stands　观众台
- sell out　卖光
- lavish floats　豪华的彩车
- Masquerade Balls　化装舞会
- You'll never see the same thing twice.　同样的东西你绝对不会看到第二次。
- luxury boxes　豪华包厢
- go on all night　持续整个晚上
- a sea of people　人的海洋
- sky high　高得吓人

13. The Mounties

加拿大骑警

S1: *Student 1*   **S2**: *Student 2*

S1: Hi. I'm doing some research about the police. I want to write something about the Canadian police force.

S2: You mean "the Mounties"? The Royal Canadian Mounted Police. That should be an interesting paper.

S1: Yes, I hope so. It says here that they began in 1873, and were called the North-West Mounted police. They have played a leading role in Canada's history.

S2: Yes, whenever I think of Canada I think of the Mounties. They were the only police that dared go so far north, but they had a special job in the beginning.

S1: I know. Their responsibility was to suppress an **all-too-prevalent** practice of **white traders** using alcohol as currency for buffalo hides.

S2: Absolutely, they were meant to protect the local people from the large increase of white settlers.

S1: They always ride horses, right?

S2: Well, in 1916 they actually began using cars, too.

S1: Throughout the early to mid 1900s they really enlarged their force. They made an air section and started using **German shepherds** as **sniffer dogs**.

S2: Did you know that the new policemen in 1966 were the last ones to be trained how to ride and care for horses? Since then, horses have only been used for ceremonial events or public relations.

S1: That's interesting, because we still think of them riding horses to work everyday!

S2: I think that the Mounties must be unique, I don't know of another police force like them.

S1: They are special, yes. The RCMP is unique in the world, since it is a federal, provincial, and municipal policing body.

S2: Oh, I see. Also, the force is organized into four regions, the Pacific, Northwestern, Central, and Atlantic.

S1: So, I guess they must cover all of Canada, then. It says here that in 2000, there were about twenty thousand members of the RCMP, including civilian members and public servants.

S2: That seems pretty big. But I guess Canada is a big place!

S1: The RCMP is truly a modern police force that is capable of handling many different types of crime. I think learning more about them is going to be interesting.

S1: 学生 1   **S2**: 学生 2

S1: 你好，我在做一些警察方面的研究，想写关于加拿大警察的文章。

S2: 你是说"加拿大骑警"？写加拿大皇家骑警，那文章肯定很有意思。

S1: 是的，我也希望如此。据说加拿大皇家骑警成立于 1873 年，当时叫做西北骑警。他们在加拿大历史上发挥了非常重要的作用。

S2: 确实是这样，我一想起加拿大就联想起骑警。他们是唯一敢于冲到最北部的警察，可是他们最初的工作非常特殊。

S1: 我知道。当时白人商人用酒来交换水牛皮的行为非常普遍，骑警的责任就是制止这种行为。

S2: 没错，就是这样。由于白人移民人数不断增加，他们就是要保护当地人民的利益。

S1: 他们总是骑在马上，对吗？

S2: 是这样，实际上到了 1916 年，他们也开始用汽车了。

S1: 从 20 世纪初期到中期的几十年间，他们的队伍的确壮大了，有了航空兵分队，也开始用德国牧羊犬做嗅探犬。

S2: 1966 年的新警察是最后一批接受骑术和养马训练的骑警，这些你知道吗？从那时起，马就只用于庆典或公关场合了。

S1: 这真有意思，我们还以为他们现在还是每天骑马去上班呢。

S2: 我想骑警一定很与众不同，据我所知再也没有像他们这样的警察。

S1: 的确，他们很特别。加拿大皇家骑警是世界上独一无二的，因为他们是一个集联邦警察、省警、市警于一体的警察机构。

S2: 噢，我知道了，这个警察机构还包括 4 个地区组织：太平洋地区、西北部、中部和大西洋地区。

S1: 那我想他们一定遍布加拿大全国。据说 2000 年时大约有两万名皇家骑警，包括文职人员和公务员。

S2: 队伍似乎很庞大。不过我想加拿大本身也是个大国家。

S1: 皇家骑警是真正的现代警察机构，能够处理各种犯罪活动。我认为多了解一下这方面的知识会很有意思。

- all-too-prevalent 到处盛行的
- white trader 白人商人
- German shepherd 德国牧羊犬
- sniffer dog 嗅探犬

14. Maple Leaf

枫叶

M: *Man*　　**W**: *Woman*

M: Well, Susan, it seems that you have **gone green**!

W: Yes, I'm trying to redecorate using a natural theme. You know, trees, plants and flowers.

M: Have you thought of using the maple leaf?

W: Isn't that on the Canadian flag? Oh, that's why you suggested it, because you are Canadian!

M: That's true. But the maple leaf has a very special history. It's more than just our flag.

W: OK, what else is it used for? Just **maple syrup**, which we put on our breakfast pancakes?

M: Not only that. Well before the coming of the first European settlers, Canada's native people had discovered the food properties of **maple sap**, which they gathered every spring. According to many historians, the maple leaf began to serve as a Canadian symbol as early as 1700.

W: That's a long time ago. I read that in 1957, the colour of the maple leaves on the arms of Canada was changed from green to red, one of Canada's official colours.

M: Yes, so nowadays we have a red maple leaf. The maple leaf used to appear on all of our coins too, but nowadays it's only on the penny.

W: Yes, I still have some of the Canadian coins you gave me. The modern one-cent piece has two maple leaves on a common twig.

M: That's right. They haven't really changed that one in years, it's been the same since 1937, I think.

W: What about the National Anthem? I mean, in England we sing about our Queen, do you sing about the maple leaf?

M: We do indeed. Alexander Muir wrote *The Maple Leaf Forever* as Canada's confederation song in 1867; it was regarded as the national song for several decades.

W: Oh, I see. It **seems funny** to sing about a leaf though. But nowadays you sing O,

Canada! don't you?

M: Yes, we do. I guess singing about a leaf is a little strange.

W: Well, I think I like the original green one better and the colour **blends well** with the others I've used. Thanks for the great decorating tip, I will use the maple leaf for sure.

M：男人　　W：女人

M：哎，苏珊，你好像很环保嘛！

W：是的，我想试着用自然的主题重新装修，就是用树木、植物和花。

M：你有没有想过用枫叶？

W：是加拿大国旗上的枫叶吗？哦，因为你是加拿大人，所以才会这么建议。

M：你说得没错。不过枫叶的历史很特别，不只是跟我们的国旗有关。

W：好了，那它还有什么用？就是我们早餐配煎饼吃的那种枫蜜吧？

M：不只这些。在第一批欧洲移民者来到这儿之前，加拿大的当地人就发现了枫树液的食用特性，他们每个春天都去采集。根据很多历史学家的说法，早在 1700 年枫叶就成了加拿大的标志。

W：那是很早以前的事了。我了解过，1957 年加拿大国徽上的枫叶从绿色改为红色，这是加拿大官方使用的颜色之一。

M：没错，如今我们有了红色的枫叶。过去枫叶也出现在我们所有的硬币上，但现在只印在分币上。

W：是的，我还有一些你给我的加拿大硬币。现在一分的硬币图案是一个枝杈上的两片枫叶。

M：是这样。真的，这些年一分硬币没有什么变化，我想从 1937 年以来一直就没有变。

W：那国歌呢？我是说在英国我们歌颂女王，你们歌颂枫叶吗？

M：的确是这样。1867 年，亚历山大·缪尔写了一首歌《永远的枫叶》作为联邦歌曲，人们把这首歌当作加拿大国歌长达数十年。

W：哦，我明白了。可是，歌唱枫叶似乎有点奇怪。不过现在你们唱《啊，加拿大！》，是不是？

M：是的，我们是唱这首歌。我觉得歌唱一片枫叶的确有点不可思议。

W：好了，我想我更喜欢原本的绿色，这个颜色和我用过的其他颜色搭配得非常好。谢谢你给我提了这么好的装修建议，我肯定会用枫叶的。

- go green　变得环保
- seems funny　似乎很奇怪，滑稽
- maple syrup　枫蜜
- blends well　搭配得好
- maple sap　枫树液

29

15. Spirit of Raven

乌鸦精灵

L: *Local*   *V*: *Visitor*

V: Hi, I wonder if you can help me. I'm trying to do some research about the spirit of the raven. I have some details already, but I would like to hear more.

L: Well, **you've come to the right place**. I'm somewhat of a local expert on the spirit of the raven.

V: Excellent. Well, I know that the raven stole the sun to light up a dark universe, but I don't really know the details.

L: That's true, the raven was a thief, but in a good way.

V: A thief! But this story is very old, isn't it?

L: Yes, the story **stretches back** thousands of years. We **native Canadians** tell this story to our children, generation after generation.

V: So, what do you know about the spirit of the raven?

L: This story tells, as you said, of the Raven who stole the sun to light up a dark universe.

V: But why did he need to light up the universe? I mean, didn't we have a sun then?

L: It is told by the elders that, at the beginning of time, the Trickster Spirit looked around and saw only darkness.

V: Right, so there was no sun. But why do we think of the raven? You said the Trickster Spirit stole it?

L: The Trickster Spirit transformed himself into the raven and then set out to find the light and bring it to the world.

V: So, is this a story used for teaching us lessons about life? What exactly can we learn from it?

L: Well, we can all identify with the Trickster Spirit, because he is **half-human**. He is creator and spoiler, hero and clown.

V: So, he is unpredictable, one minute inspiring awe for his creativity, the next moment provoking laughter at his foolishness.

L: Exactly. The moral teachings **are laced with** humour and an easy acceptance of the truth that nobility and foolishness can reside in the same person—and you can never predict which face will show itself next.

V: Thanks for giving me this extra information, I didn't realize that the spirit of the raven was so significant in Canadian culture.

L：当地人　　V：参观者

V: 你好，不知道你能不能帮帮我。我想研究乌鸦精灵*。我已经有了一些详细资料，但我想再多听听。

> * 乌鸦精灵：乌鸦被北美印第安人视为聪明和富有创造力的象征，主要根源于印第安神话故事"乌鸦偷日"。传说一只乌鸦从一个居住于高山之巅的储藏光明的老人那里偷来太阳和月亮，送给了长期在黑暗中生活的人类。许多部落都将乌鸦作为自己的图腾，图腾柱上乌鸦口中所含的球就是太阳的象征。

L: 好的，你算是找对地方了。我可以说是当地这方面的专家。

V: 太好了。我知道乌鸦把太阳偷走，照亮了整个黑暗的世界，但细节我就不太清楚了。

L: 是有这么回事，乌鸦是个贼，但，是个义贼。

V: 一个贼！不过这个故事很老了，是不是？

L: 是的，这个故事有几千年的历史。我们土生土长的加拿大人把这个故事讲给孩子听，就这样一代代流传了下来。

V: 那么，你对乌鸦精灵都知道些什么？

L: 正像你刚才所说的，这个故事讲述了乌鸦把太阳偷走照亮了整个黑暗的世界。

V: 但是，为什么他要偷太阳来照亮世界？我是说，那时我们没有太阳吗？

L: 据老人们讲，在远古时代，魔术师神下来到处察看，结果只看见漆黑一片。

V: 是这样，所以当时没有太阳。但我们为什么会想到乌鸦？你说是魔术师神偷的？

L: 魔术师神把自己变成乌鸦，然后动身去寻找光明，并把光明带给了我们这个世界。

V: 所以，这个故事就是用来教给我们一些生活经验吗？我们究竟能从这个故事中学到什么呢？

L: 是这样，我们大家都认同魔术师神，因为他是半人半神。他既是创造者又是毁灭者，是英雄又是小丑。

V: 所以他是不可预测的，他一发挥创造力就令我们对他肃然起敬，接着他一糊涂又引起大家对他的讥笑。

L: 一点不错。道德说教经常要带点幽默，这样大家更容易接受事实的真相。同样一个人也会同时有高贵和愚蠢的一面——而且你永远也无法预测接下来会出现哪张面孔。

V: 谢谢你给我那么多新信息，我不知道乌鸦精灵在加拿大文化中如此重要。

■ You've come to the right place.　你找对地方了。　　■ stretch back　追溯
■ native Canadians　加拿大当地人　　　　　　　　■ half-human　半人的
■ be laced with ...　用……装饰

16. The Great Wall
长城

T: *Tourist*   *L*: *Local*

T: Hi, do you speak English?

L: Yes, I do! What can I do to help you?

T: Well, I know very little about the Great Wall. Do you know anything about its history?

L: Of course!

T: Great. Could you tell me when it was built?

L: It has a history of more than 2,000 years, in the dynasties of Qin, Han and Ming.

T: 2,000 years! That's a long time!

L: Yes, some civilisations have long histories, especially China.

T: OK, how long is it exactly?

L: It's 6,700 kilometres long. But, unfortunately some sections are in ruins or **lost forever**. It **stretches across** deserts, grasslands, mountains and plateaus.

T: It sounds amazing. Where can I see an **untouched area**? I mean, an area where not so many tourists go.

L: You could go to Simatai. That area is **pretty untouched**, with few tourists. But I think the best place to view the Great Wall is here at Badaling because we have a museum here.

T: Do you know who built the wall?

L: It was a **team effort** of soldiers, prisoners and locals. We believe it shows the tenacity of the Chinese people.

T: Before, you mentioned that the wall was built during many dynasties. Which dynasty does the part we can see now come from?

L: Most of the wall we can see today comes from the Ming dynasty. It's a shame, but nowadays only 30% of the wall is **in good condition**. But, the Ming dynasty part is still very long. It **goes from** Shanhaiguan Pass in the east to Jiayuguan Pass in the west. It **passes through** Liaoning, Hebei, Beijing, Tianjin, Shanxi, Inner Mongolia, Ningxia, Shaanxi and Gansu.

T: Wow! I didn't realise it **ran that far**. I'd love to see another section.

L: As I said before, you **could try** Simatai. But it's quite difficult to get to, 110 kilometres north east of Beijing. But I can help you to find a way to get there.

T: Thank you so much. You have taught me so much already, but I can't wait to find out more!

T: 游客　　L: 当地人

T: 你好，你会讲英语吗？

L: 是的，我会！要我帮什么忙吗？

T: 是这样，我对长城了解很少。你知道它的历史吗？

L: 当然知道！

T: 太好了。你能告诉我长城是什么时候建起来的吗？

L: 长城有 2000 多年的历史，建于秦朝、汉朝和明朝*。

T: 2000 年！那历史很长了！

L: 确实是这样，有些文明的历史非常悠久，尤其是中国。

T: 好的，长城究竟有多长？

L: 有 6700 公里。但令人遗憾的是，有些地方已经成了废墟或永远不能修复了。长城绵延万里，穿过了无数的沙漠、草地、大山和平原。

T: 听起来很壮观。去哪儿能看到保存完好的长城？我是说游客比较少的地方。

L: 你可以去司马台，那个地方保存得很好，游客也很少。不过我认为游览长城最好的地方是这里——八达岭，因为这儿有博物馆。

T: 那你知道是谁修建的长城吗？

L: 这是士兵、犯人和当地人共同努力修建的。我们认为长城反映了中国人民不屈不挠的精神。

T: 你前面提到，长城的修建历经了很多朝代，那我们现在看到的长城是哪个朝代建的？

L: 我们今天看到的城墙大部分是明朝建的。说来惭愧，现在只有 30% 的城墙还保存完好。不过，明长城还是很长的，从东面的山海关一直到西面的嘉峪关，经过了辽宁、河北、北京、天津、山西、内蒙古、宁夏、陕西和甘肃。

T: 哇！我不知道长城绵延那么长。我很想再去看看其它部分。

L: 我刚才说过，你可以去司马台看看。但是去那个地方不太容易，它在北京的东北方向 110 公里的地方。不过我能帮你找到去那里的路线。

T: 太谢谢你了。你今天已经教了我不少东西，可是我非常想再了解一些。

> * 长城：长城的兴修始于战国时期。作为一种军事防御工程，长城在当时能有效地防止北方游牧民族骑兵闪电式的袭击。秦统一六国后（前 221 年），为防止匈奴南进，又将秦、赵、燕三国长城连接起来，筑起了西起临洮（今甘肃岷县）、东至辽东碣石，长达一万多里的长城。据记载，秦始皇使用了近百万的青壮劳力修筑长城，占全国人口的 1/20。当时没有任何机械，除用牲畜运砖土外，全部劳动都得靠人力，而工作环境又是崇山峻岭。长城的工程量，以明长城为例，若将其砖土筑成一道厚 1 米、高 5 米的大墙，可环绕地球一周有余。

■ lost forever　永远不能修复
■ untouched area　保存完好的地方
■ team effort　共同努力
■ go from ...　从……开始
■ run that far　延伸那么长
■ stretch across　跨过
■ pretty untouched　保存很好
■ in good condition　保存完好
■ pass through　经过
■ can try　可以试试

17. Dragons

龙

M: *Museum curator*　　**V**: *Visitor*

M: This picture we see here is of a very traditional Chinese dragon.

V: I'm sorry, but this dragon looks friendly unlike Western dragons which are fierce. Why?

M: Why? Well, in China dragons are not seen **in the same way** as in England. For example, they are not evil, but lucky.

V: Lucky, in what way?

M: Did you know we also connect dragons with the number 9? And 9 for us is a very lucky number.

V: In Western countries 7 is usually lucky and we think 13 is unlucky, but I don't think we have any special feeling about 9.

M: Although we don't know the exact origins, we are sure they **predate** history. We can find them in literature, poems, songs and architecture.

V: So they are very important to Chinese people, right?

M: Yes, they are part of our conscience.

V: In this display the clothing is decorated with dragons. Why are they so significant?

M: This is an imperial dragon robe from the Qing Court. We also have a very famous Dragon Dance which **dates back** to the Song dynasty, and nowadays the Dragon Boat Festival is celebrated internationally.

V: Yes, last year I was in Chinatown in London and we saw the dancing, but also a special type of boat race.

M: Yes, a Dragon Boat race. It is celebrated during the 5th month of the Chinese lunar calendar. It commemorates a great poet called Qu Yuan.

V: OK, so where else do we find dragons?

M: Well, there are many famous Chinese stories about the dragon. There is even a famous Chinese idiom "Lord Ye's Love of Dragons", which means an apparent love of something one really fears.

V: Really? **What's the story behind** the idiom?

34

M: Lord Ye had a fascination about dragons. He had dragons everywhere and he was thinking about dragons all the time. His love of dragons moved a real dragon, so the dragon came to visit him one day. When he saw the real dragon, he was frightened to death.

V: So you do agree that dragons can be scary, then?

M: For Lord Ye, yes!

M：博物馆馆长　　V：参观者

M： 我们看到的这张照片上是一条非常传统的中国龙。

V： 可是，打断一下，这条龙看起来很友好，不像西方的龙那么凶，为什么？

M： 为什么？噢，是这样，中国人与英国人对龙的看法是不一样的。比如说，龙不是邪恶的，而是吉祥的动物。

V： 吉祥的？怎么吉祥？

M： 你知道我们还把龙跟数字 9 联系在一起吗？而 9 对我们来说是非常吉利的数字。

V： 在西方国家，通常 7 是幸运数字，13 是不吉利的数字，但我想我们对 9 没有什么特别的感情。

M： 尽管我们不知道龙确切的由来，但我们确信那是很早以前的历史了。在文献、诗词、歌曲和建筑中都可以发现有关信息。

V： 所以龙对中国人非常重要，对吧？

M： 是的，它是我们意识形态的一部分。

V： 这次展览的服装上都饰有龙的图案。它们为什么那么重要？

M： 这是一件清朝皇帝穿的龙袍。我们还有个非常有名的舞龙表演，可以追溯到宋朝，还有，现在世界各地都在过龙舟节＊。

V： 没错，去年我在伦敦的中国城就看见了舞龙表演，而且还有专门的赛龙舟活动。

M： 噢，有赛龙舟。那是在中国阴历 5 月举行的庆祝活动，是为了纪念一个叫屈原的伟大诗人。

V： 好了，那么在哪儿还能找到龙？

M： 是这样，中国有很多关于龙的故事，甚至还有一个成语"叶公好龙"，意思是说爱上一个实际上害怕的东西。

V： 真的吗？这个典故是怎么说的？

M： 有个叫叶公的人非常喜欢龙。他每时每刻想着龙；生活的周遭环境里龙的形象也是无处不在。他对龙的喜爱感动了一条真龙，所以有一天这条龙就来拜访他。可是当叶公看见真龙时，却吓得要死。

V： 那你是不是也认为龙很可怕呢？

M： 对叶公来说是很可怕！

■ in the same way as ... 与……一样	■ predate 时间上先于
■ date back 追溯到	■ What's the story behind ... ……的来历，典故

China 中国

18. Spring Festival
春节

L: Local   **V**: Visitor

L: Spring Festival is the most important festival to us. Do you know anything about it?

V: Not too much. Just that it's the lunar calendar's New Year. It's different from New Year in the West.

L: Yes, that's right. It's the first day of the lunar month, and it originated in the Shang dynasty at around 1600 BC. It is based on the people's sacrifices to their gods and ancestors and the end of a year and the beginning of a new one.

V: The Shang dynasty? That's a long time ago. I had no idea it had such a long history. And it's always the first day of the lunar month?

L: **Strictly speaking**, it starts every year in the early days of the 12th lunar month and will last to the middle of the 1st lunar month of the next year. The most important days are Spring Festival Eve and the first 3 days.

V: I see that you and your family are all at home. Don't you have to work during Spring Festival?

L: No, we don't need to work. The government has made it **a 7 day national holiday**. We usually spend the time with family and friends.

V: Do you do anything special on the other days?

L: Yes, on the 8th day of the 12th lunar month we eat some very special food. It's called Laba Congee. We roll balls from the glutinous rice, fill them with berries or beans and boil them in water. Nowadays, you can even buy glutinous rice balls filled with chocolate!

V: Sounds delicious. Are there any other significant days?

L: The 23rd day of the 12th lunar month we call Preliminary Eve. At this time, people offer sacrifices to the kitchen god. But, to be honest, **in this day and age**, most families cook wonderful food, get together and enjoy themselves.

V: Well, I'm happy to be here for all of the celebrations. Someone told me we will watch an interesting TV show tonight.

L: Yes, CCTV has a special New Year variety show with all of our **top stars**. Singers, dancers, comedians, everything!

V: OK, let's watch it together.

L：当地人　　　**V：来访者**

L: 对我们来说，春节是最重要的节日。你知道有关春节的事儿吗？

V: 知道的不多。只知道是阴历的新年，与西方的新年不同。

L: 是的，你说得没错。春节是阴历1月的第1天，起源于公元前1600年的商朝。该节日主要是祭拜神仙和祖先，是前一年的结束和新一年的开始。

V: 商朝？那是很久以前的事了。我不知道春节有那么长的历史。它一直就是阴历1月的第1天吗？

L: 严格地讲，每年的春节从阴历12月的月初开始，一直到下一年阴历1月的中旬为止。最重要的日子是除夕和春节的前3天。

V: 我知道你和家人都要呆在家里。你们春节期间不上班吗？

L: 是的，我们不用上班。政府规定全国有7天的假日。我们一般用这7天走亲访友。

V: 其他日子你们有什么特别的活动？

L: 有，阴历12月初八我们吃一些特别的食物，叫腊八粥*。我们还用糯米滚元宵，里面装上果馅或是豆沙，然后再在水里煮。现在我们甚至可以买到巧克力馅的元宵。

V: 听起来很美味。还有什么其他重要的日子吗？

L: 阴历12月的第23天我们叫小年，那一天，人们给灶王爷上供。但说实话，在今天这个时代，大部分家庭都做些美味佳肴，大家聚在一起自己享用。

V: 真高兴，我能在这里参与所有这些庆祝活动。还有人告诉我，我们今晚可以看到很有意思的电视节目。

L: 是的，中央电视台有特别的新年晚会，我们所有的明星大腕都会登台演出。有歌手、舞蹈演员、喜剧演员等等，什么名人都有！

V: 好的，那我们一起看电视吧。

■ strictly speaking 严格地讲　　　　■ a 7 day national holiday 国家规定的7天假日
■ in this day and age 在今天这个时代　■ top stars 明星大腕

19. Confucius

孔子

FS: *Foreign student*   **S**: *Student*

S: Hi Zhang Ping. What are you reading?

FS: It's about Confucius and his rules for life.

S: Rules for life, like in a religion?

FS: Exactly! Confucianism is one of "The Three Ways", along with Buddhism and Taoism.

S: Oh, I see. When did he live?

FS: He lived from 551−479 BC. His life defines the end of The Spring and Autumn period in Chinese history. It wasn't until many years after he died that he became the dominant Chinese philosopher of morality and politics.

S: So, when did he become famous?

FS: In the Warring States Period from 390-305 BC, they extended and systematised his teachings, but they didn't become **what we know today** until the Han dynasty.

S: So, it was years and years after his death? I guess it's a little like Jesus, whose teachings became the official religion of the Roman Empire 300 years later.

FS: But Confucianism is all based on a terminology of morality.

S: What do you mean by that?

FS: OK ... for example, he believed in benevolence, charity, humanity and love. Or overall, kindness, which is called "Ren".

S: Be kind to each other, **that makes sense**.

FS: Yes, and right conduct, morality and duty to one's neighbour. It's called righteousness, or "Yi".

S: Yes, the *Bible* says we should love our neighbours, so that's a little similar.

FS: Most religions **have things in common**. Also, profit, gain and advantage, which are not proper motives for actions affecting others. It's called "Li", and it's why Confucius thought that commerce and industry were bad ideas.

S: I see. So are these the 3 main things?

FS: Yes. "Ren" is in the "Being" category, "Yi" the "Doing or Means" category and "Li" is part of the "Ends" category.

S: **Sounds complicated!**

FS: A simple way to remember is this ... to love others; to honour one's parents; to do

38

what is right instead of what is of advantage; to practice "reciprocity," or "don't do to others what you would not want yourself"; to rule by moral example, called "De" instead of by force and violence.

S：　OK, so be a nice, kind person, love each other and don't fight.

FS：　Yes, that's right.

FS：外国学生　　　S：学生

S：　张萍，你好! 你在看什么书?

FS：　关于孔子及其人生准则的书。

S：　人生准则，像宗教书吗?

FS：　一点不错! 儒教是"三教"之一，其他两个是佛教和道教。

S：　哦，我明白了。他生活在什么年代?

FS：　孔子生活在公元前551年至前479年，正是中国历史上的春秋末期。他去世很多年以后，才被认为是中国最有影响的道德家和政治哲学家。

S：　那他是什么时候出名的?

FS：　在公元前390年至前305年的战国时期，人们将他的学说扩充并进行系统整理，不过我们今天所了解的孔子学说是汉朝才成形的。

S：　那是他去世很多年以后的事了吧? 我觉得他与耶稣有点像，耶稣的教义在他去世300年以后才成为罗马帝国的国教。

FS：　可是儒教是以一整套的道德规范为根本的。

S：　这是什么意思?

FS：　是这样……比如，他信奉善心、慈爱、人性和友爱。或者说，最重要的是仁爱，叫做"仁"。

S：　互相友爱，这有道理。

FS：　是的。对自己的邻居要行为端正、讲道德、负责任。这就是道义，或"义"。

S：　是的，《圣经》也说我们要爱自己的邻居，所以这一点有点类似。

FS：　大多数宗教都有共通之处。此外，利润、收益和好处不能作为你妨碍别人的行为的正当动机，这叫"礼"，这也是为什么孔子认为工商业不好的原因。

S：　我明白了。这就是他的3个主要观点吗?

FS：　是的，"仁"是"本体"范畴，"义"是"行动或方式"范畴，而"礼"是"目的"范畴。

S：　听起来太复杂了!

FS：　有个简单的办法去记这些观点，就是爱他人; 尊敬自己的父母; 去做你认为正确的事而不是对自己有利的事; 实行"互惠"，即"己所不欲，勿施于人"; 以"德"服人，而不是靠武力和暴力压人。

S：　好了，所以一定要做个和蔼、善良的人，要互相友爱，不要争斗。

FS：　是的，就是这样。

■ what we know today　我们今天所了解的	■ that makes sense　这有道理
■ have things in common　有共同点	■ sounds complicated　听起来很复杂

20. Kung Fu

功夫

S: *Student*   *MT*: *Martial arts teacher*

S: Hi, I hope you can help me. I want to get fit, but I hate going to the gym. I want to try something different, any ideas?

MT: What about Kung Fu?

S: Like in a Jackie Chan movie? I don't know ...

MT: There's much more to Kung Fu than Jackie Chan or Bruce Lee. Kung Fu is an art form and also, very good for you.

S: OK, tell me more.

MT: Many styles of Kung Fu are based on the ideas of nature. Ancient boxing masters often developed their **fighting techniques** by **observing the world around them**. Animals, birds, and insects provided the basis for many systems of Kung Fu developed in the past.

S: So, I could learn to fight like a bird?

MT: Kind of ... there are many different styles but they take years to master.

S: What about Shaolin? How is that linked?

MT: Many of the hard forms of Kung Fu came from a Buddhist Monastery called "Shaolin". An Indian priest named Tamo came to live there nearly 1500 years ago. **According to legend**, Tamo arrived at the monastery where he found the monks in poor physical condition. Because they couldn't stay awake during meditation, Tamo introduced a series of 18 exercises designed **to feed both body and mind**. These movements are said to have **merged with** self-defense tactics studied in the Shaolin Temple.

S: I see. But I thought you said there were many types?

MT: Yes, later, in the 13th century, they were extended to 72 forms by Jueyuan the Monk. He traveled around China and met two other skilled fighters. They further extended the forms to 173 and classified them into 5 animal forms: dragon, tiger, leopard, crane and snake. That's how we get Shaolin Kung Fu's "Five Form Fist".

S: Sounds special. But I don't want to be too violent.

MT: Then I suggest a soft form of Kung Fu, called Tai Qi. It comes from Taoism and it's very good for your health. Through its training, you can get inner peace and a sense of physical and emotional well being. It's often called Chinese Yoga: the art and science of meditation through movement.

S: OK, great!

S: 学生　　MT: 武术老师

＊ 觉远和尚：金末元初，少林寺僧人觉远和尚离寺云游，欲访天下武功高手。他先后结识了兰州的李叟和洛阳的白玉峰。三人同回少林寺，一起对少林寺所演练的数百个拳械套路进行了系统整理。觉远和尚把少林寺镇寺之宝罗汉手增加到173手。白玉峰则撰写了《五拳精要》一书，并皈依少林寺为僧，法号秋月。

S: 你好，我希望你能帮我个忙。我想有个好身体，可是又讨厌去健身房。我想试试其他办法，有什么好主意？

MT: 功夫怎么样？

S: 像成龙演的电影里面那样？我不太懂……

MT: 功夫并不只是指成龙或李小龙，它是一种艺术形式，而且对你很有好处。

S: 好的，详细说说。

MT: 很多功夫招式来源于对自然界的想象。古代拳术大师常常通过观察他们周围的世界改进拳术技法。动物、鸟类和昆虫为过去很多功夫的系统发展提供了基础。

S: 那我能学像鸟那样的打架招势吗？

MT: 差不多吧……有很多不同的招势，但都需要很多年才能练好。

S: 少林武术怎么样？它跟什么有关系？

MT: 很多硬功夫都出自叫"少林"的佛教寺庙。大约1500年前，有个叫达摩的印度僧人来到这里。传说他来到寺庙，发现那里的和尚身体状况很不好。因为他们在坐禅时不能保持清醒，达摩就传授给他们一套十八手拳法，目的是锻炼他们的身心。据说这些动作融合了他在少林寺研究的防身术。

S: 我明白了。但是我记得你说过有很多种招势？

MT: 是的，后来在13世纪，觉远和尚＊把这些动作扩大到72手。他到中国各地旅游，遇到了两个武艺高强的人。他们进一步把招势扩大到173手，按动物种类分成5类形态：龙、虎、豹、鹤和蛇。这就是我们现在少林功夫中"五形拳"的由来。

S: 听起来很特别。不过我不想变得太暴力。

MT: 那我建议你学习一种温和的功夫，叫太极拳。它源于道教，对你的健康非常有好处。通过这种训练，你能达到内心的平和，以及身体和情绪上的安宁舒适。它经常被人们称作中国瑜珈：通过运动达到沉思冥想的一种艺术和科学。

S: 不错，太好了！

■ fighting techniques　功夫招势　　　　■ observe the world around them　观察他们周围的世界
■ according to legend　根据传说　　　　■ feed both body and mind　锻炼身心
■ merge with　与……融合

41

21. Zhang Yimou's Films

张艺谋的电影

S: *Shopper*   **F**: *Film memorabilia shop owner*

S: Hello. I'm looking for Zhang Yimou films. I just saw *Hero* and think he is a great director.

F: Yes, Zhang Yimou has become very popular in recent years. His recurrent theme is a celebration of the resilience, even the stubbornness, of Chinese people in the face of hardships and adversities. He is also well known for his sensitivity to colour. The first movie he directed was *Red Sorghum* in 1987 which won the Golden Bear at the Berlin Film Festival. The movie is full of dynamic edits, striking **close-ups**, and gorgeously photographed images.

S: Just like *Hero*, he seems to always make beautiful movies.

F: Also, in that year Zhang made two more movies, a movie called *Codename Cougar*, which I wouldn't recommend! And *Ju Dou* which won Best Film at the Chicago Film Festival and garnered an Academy Award nomination.

S: OK, so I won't watch *Codename Cougar*, then.

F: Then after a few years he made the amazing *Raise the Red Lantern* starring Gong Li.

S: Yes, I've heard of this movie. I will buy that one if you have it.

F: Here it is. Also, in 1992 he made this one, *The Story of Qiu Ju* about a pregnant lady whose husband has been beaten up by a village leader. This movie is very different from his others, there is no rigid style or sumptuous photography, it was filmed in a documentary style, which gives it a **gritty look**.

S: That one's very different, I'll take it too.

F: As for more recent films, in 1999 *Not One Less* won the coveted Golden Lion at the Venice Film Festival.

S: What about movies from the 2000s?

F: In 2002 he made *Happy Times* which was a seriocomic drama, then, of course *Hero*. And in 2004 *House of Flying Daggers*, which was set in the Tang dynasty and had **a flamboyant**

use of colour, very beautiful.

S：And most recently?

F：In 2006 he made *Curse of the Golden Flower*, an amazing **period epic**. It stars Gong Li, Jay Chow and Chow Yun Fat.

S：They all seem so different from each other, I guess I'll take them all!

S：顾客　　　F：电影纪念品商店店主

S：你好，我想找些张艺谋拍的电影。我刚看完他的《英雄》，觉得他是个了不起的导演。

F：确实，张艺谋最近几年非常走红。他导演的影片主题经常是赞美中国人民面对困难和不幸所表现出来的达观甚至是顽强的精神。他也因为善于运用色彩而闻名。1987 年他导演的第一部影片《红高粱》在柏林国际电影节赢得金熊奖。该片充满了富于变化的剪辑、惊人的特写镜头和炫丽的影像。

S：就像《英雄》一样，他似乎总能拍出精彩的电影。

F：此外，就在那一年，张艺谋导演了另外两部影片，一部叫《代号美洲豹》，我不会给你推荐这个。另一部是《菊豆》，在芝加哥国际电影节上获最佳影片奖，以及奥斯卡金像奖提名。

S：好的，那我就不看《代号美洲豹》了。

F：接着几年之后，他拍出了令人不可思议的《大红灯笼高高挂》，由巩俐主演。

S：是的，我听说过这部影片。你这里有的话，我买一张。

F：给你。除此之外，1992 年他导演了《秋菊打官司》，该影片讲述了一个丈夫被村长打成重伤的怀孕女人的故事。该片与他的其它影片大不一样，没有固定不变的模式或奢华的影像，而是拍成了一种记录片的形式，使得影片给人一种勇敢坚毅的感觉。

S：这个也很有特点，我也要了。

F：至于最近几年的电影，1999 年的《一个都不能少》在威尼斯国际电影节上赢得金狮奖。

S：那 2000 年以后有什么影片？

F：2002 年他拍了《幸福时光》，这是个既严肃又诙谐的剧本，再有当然就是《英雄》。2004 年，拍了《十面埋伏》，故事发生在唐朝，影片中大胆使用色彩，非常漂亮。

S：那最近有什么影片？

F：今年他导演了《满城尽带黄金甲》。这是部令人惊叹的史诗片，由巩俐、周杰伦、周润发主演。

S：这些影片似乎都各不相同，我想我就都要了吧。

- close-up　特写镜头
- period epic　时代片
- gritty look　勇敢坚毅的感觉
- a flamboyant use of colour　大胆使用色彩

22. Che Guevara
切·格瓦拉

B: Brian   **D**: David

B: Look at this, David. It's all about Che Guevara.

D: Ah, yes. He was a leader of revolutionaries who defeated the Batista dictatorship, right?

B: Right. Guevara was one of only **a handful** of foreigners who came to Cuba with the Castro brothers on the Yacht called "Granma" to fight against the Batista dictatorship.

D: Most of them were caught and killed upon arrival, though. Only 16 escaped into the Sierra Maestra mountains, where peasants and farmers aided them.

B: The peasants obviously wanted to overthrow Batista, too. By the time his troops marched on Havana with Camilo Cienfuegos' troops in January 1959, Guevara was very popular with the Cuban population.

D: Stories of his bravery and leadership **circulated widely**, and he was considered one of the most important figures in the Revolution.

B: What about his early years? We all know that he rode around South America on an old motorcycle at the age of 23. The journey was crucial for the awakening of his social conscience. What about before that?

D: Well, he was born in Argentina on June 14, 1928, and he studied medicine at Buenos Aires University.

B: So that must have been where he became involved in opposition to the Argentine leader Juan Perón.

D: I guess so. He was known as an intellectual and an idealist, able to speak coherently about Aristotle, Kant, Marx, Gide or Faulkner.

B: Wasn't he a poet too? I mean, he loved poetry, and was **equally at home** with Keats as with Sara De Ibáñez, his favorite writer. It is said that he knew Kipling's *If* **by heart**.

D: He enjoyed poetry, yes. But I don't know if he actually wrote any. Did you know he had a lifelong illness too?

B: I read somewhere that he had asthma, maybe that's why when he was a doctor he specialized in allergies.

D: What about his name, Che? Wasn't his first name Ernesto?

B: Yes, but "che" is the familiar diminutive for "you" in Argentina, as in "hey, you!"

D: Here it says that it was an affectionate term that became his "official" name and the one which he used for a signature, always with a lower case "c".

B: 布莱恩　　D: 大卫

B: 大卫，看看这个，都是有关切·格瓦拉的事情。

D: 哦，是的。他是古巴革命领袖，打败了巴蒂斯塔的独裁政府，对吗？

B: 是这样。格瓦拉是少数和卡斯特罗兄弟来到古巴的外国人之一，他们乘坐"格拉玛号"游艇向古巴进发，与巴蒂斯塔独裁政府展开斗争。

D: 不过，他们刚到那里时，大多数人不是被抓就是被杀。只有 16 个人逃出来，进了马埃斯特腊山区，那里的农民和农场主给他们提供了援助。

B: 显然，农民们也想推翻巴蒂斯塔政府。1959 年 1 月，当格瓦拉的军队和卡米洛·西恩富戈斯领导的军队向哈瓦那进军时，他受到了古巴人民的热烈欢迎。

D: 他的英勇善战和卓越的领导能力被广为传颂。人们认为他是古巴革命中最重要的人物之一。

B: 他早年的生活怎么样？我们都知道他 23 岁时骑着一辆老摩托游历南美大陆*。这次旅行激发了他的社会责任感。但在此之前他的情况又如何呢？

D: 哦，他 1928 年 6 月 14 日生于阿根廷，后来在布宜诺斯艾利斯大学学医。

B: 所以他一定是在大学期间就参与反对阿根廷领导人胡安·庇隆。

D: 我也这么想。人们认为他是一名知识分子，一名理想主义者，谈起亚里士多德、康德、马克思、纪德或福克纳这样的大家，他讲得头头是道。

B: 他不也是个诗人吗？我是说他喜欢诗，对济慈和他最喜欢的作家沙拉·德·伊巴内斯一样精通。据说他能默诵吉卜林的诗歌《如果》。

D: 是的，他喜欢诗。但是我不知道他是否真正写过诗。你知道他还患有终身疾病吗？

B: 我从什么地方看到过，说他得了哮喘，也许这就是为什么他行医时以过敏症为专业。

D: 那他的名字切是怎么回事？他的名字不是恩斯托吗？

B: 是的，可是"切"在阿根廷是指"你"的亲近称呼，就像"嗨！喂！"这样用。

D: 这本书上说这是个爱称，后来成了他"正式"的名字，他用这个名字来签字，经常用小写"c"。

> * 格瓦拉在这次旅行中所写的日记后来被好莱坞拍成电影《摩托车日记》(The Motorcycle Diaries)。1965 年，他辞去了古巴国家银行行长和工业部长的职务，先后到刚果和玻利维亚策动共产革命。1967 年 10 月 9 日被由美国支持的玻利维亚军队逮捕并杀害，年仅 39 岁。

■ a handful　少数的　　　　　■ circulate widely　广为流传
■ equally at home　同样精通　　■ by heart　默诵

23. Havana Cigars

哈瓦那雪茄

M: Man   **W**: Woman

W: Hey, Tom. You're a smoker, do you know anything about cigars?

M: Well, I do enjoy a nice Havana cigar on special occasions.

W: I need some info about cigars, particularly Havana's.

M: Did you know Cuba has a special climate? It's perfect for growing tobacco of very high quality.

W: Apart from these special climatic features, the chemical composition and agricultural properties of the soil in Cuba's tobacco-growing areas **couldn't be bettered**.

M: Also, the experience and care that Cuba's tobacco workers put into each of the many steps of cigar making.

W: The human factor is very important, not just the soil and climate.

M: Yes, for example, they **hand pick** the leaves between 45 and 80 days after planting and then sort them into different grades. This is done delicately and must be done by someone who is highly skilled.

W: I read that the vast majority of the workers in the **sorting house** are women. It must be true because I think women can do this job much better than men. We are better at doing things delicately.

M: Ha-ha! That's true. Anyway, in the factory they sprinkle the leaves that will be used as wrappers with water, to reduce their fragility.

W: There are many different kinds of leaves used as wrappers, though. I think it's between 18 and 20 different types.

M: But the most demanding job is that of the cigar maker. He places half a leaf of binder on his table, then picks up an assortment of different kinds of leaves and **shapes** them into a bundle. To cover the cigar, he smoothes the wrapper, trims the edges with his knife and wraps it around the bundle.

W: Then I suppose they trim them and store them somewhere. The quality control group takes samples of each cigar maker's work, to check the cigars' size, shape, appearance, texture and thickness.

M: Once their shape and size have been checked and approved, the Havana's are gently tied with a ribbon in groups of 50. They are very strict, every cigar must be perfect.

W: So, the whole process is done by hand. That is probably why Havana's are so expensive.

M：男人　　**W**：女人

W：你好，汤姆。你喜欢吸烟，那你对雪茄了解多少？

M：嗯，在某些特殊场合我确实抽过不错的哈瓦那雪茄。

W：我想了解雪茄烟的一些知识，尤其是哈瓦那雪茄。

M：你知道古巴的气候很特别吗？这种气候非常适合种植高品质的烟草。

W：除了这些特殊的气候特征外，古巴烟草种植区土壤的化学特性对于种植烟草来说是再合适不过了。

M：而且，烟草生产的每个环节都离不开古巴烟草工人的种植经验和细心照料。

W：不只是土壤和气候，人为因素的确也很重要。

M：是的，例如，工人要在烟草种植后的 45 到 80 天之间手工采摘叶子，然后分成不同等级。这个工作要做得非常细致，一定要由技术高超的人来完成。

W：我知道在分类车间的工人大多数是女性。肯定是这样安排，因为我认为女性做这项工作要比男人做得好。我们比较擅长做细活。

M：哈哈！你说得对。不管怎样，在工厂她们负责向卷雪茄的烟叶上洒水，以减少脆裂。

W：不过，可以卷雪茄的烟叶种类很多。我想有 18 到 20 种吧。

M：但是难度最大的是雪茄烟制作者的工作。他先把半张卷叶摊在桌面上，然后放上几种精选出来的烟叶，卷成整支。为了能包住雪茄，他要把包装叶弄平，用刀子把边缘修剪整齐，最后把烟卷包好。

W：那我猜他们应该在其他别的地方修剪和储存雪茄。质量检查小组负责抽取每个雪茄制作者的样品，检查烟的大小、形状、外观、质地和烟草密度。

M：一旦雪茄的外形和大小被检查通过的话，哈瓦那雪茄烟就按每 50 根一组，用一根丝带轻轻地捆好。质量检查非常严格，每根雪茄一定都要完好无损。

W：那么说，整个过程都是手工完成的。这也许是哈瓦那雪茄为什么那么贵的原因。

- couldn't be bettered　再好不过的
- sorting house　分类车间
- hand pick　人工采摘
- shape　定形

24. The Pyramids

金字塔

T: Traveller   **G**: Tour guide

T: Could you tell me about these pictures?

G: The pyramids were built at around 3000-2500 BC and are one of the most **impressive monuments** of the **ancient world**. They were built as tombs for the Pharaohs, the rulers of Egypt. The first Pharaohs built simpler tombs, called mastabas. These mastabas were square buildings with a room inside for the coffin and the mummy and some things to take with you to the afterlife.

T: Like this over here in the picture?

G: Yes. Then they began to build mounds of earth on top of their mastabas, to make them grander. Ordinary princes and other aristocrats went on being buried in mastabas. The Step Pyramid is one of the first of these new fancy tombs.

T: But, the pyramids we know all have filled in steps.

G: Yes, a short time after these were built, the Egyptians decided to fill in the steps, and then made them more pointed on top.

T: The ones in Giza are this style, right? I think they are the most well-known, everyone in the world must have seen a picture of them.

G: Yes, the ones in Giza were built following this design. Khufu's Great Pyramid was the tallest building on earth for almost five thousand years, until the Eiffel Tower was built in 1889.

T: That's amazing! How did they build them exactly? I've heard many stories about using slaves and even aliens helping them!

G: Yes, I've heard the ones about the aliens too! A pyramid is not hard to build, if you have plenty of cheap workers available. First they built a small mastaba-style tomb on the ground, in the ordinary way. Then one theory is that they **heaped up** tons and tons of dirt over the tomb, leaving a tunnel to the outside. Then they began placing huge stones

48

all over the outside of the pyramid. To raise the stones to the top of the pyramid, they built long ramps of dirt and then rolled the stones up them. They kept making the ramps higher and longer. When it was done, they took the earth ramps away again.

T: Still, it is unbelievable how they built such **massive structures** without machinery.

T: 游客　　G: 导游

T: 你能给我讲解一下这些照片吗?

G: 金字塔建于公元前 3000 年至公元前 2500 年左右,是远古世界最宏伟的历史建筑之一。它们是为埃及的统治者法老们修建

的陵墓＊比较简单,叫玛斯塔巴陵墓。这些陵墓是方形的建筑,里面有一个房间用来放棺材、木乃伊和一些来世所需要的随身物品。

T: 就像照片中的这一个吗?

G: 是的。陵墓建成之后,他们开始往墓顶上堆很多土,以便使这些墓看起来更壮观些。普通的王子和其他贵族就一直埋在这样的陵墓中。第一批奇特的新陵墓之一就是阶梯式金字塔。

T: 可是我们知道的金字塔都建有台阶。

G: 是的,这些金字塔建起来不久,埃及人就决定加上阶梯,然后使它们的顶部看起来更尖。

T: 吉萨的那些金字塔就都是这种风格,对吧?我想这些金字塔是最有名的,全球的人都一定见过它们的照片。

G: 没错,吉萨的金字塔是按照这种风格建造的。在 1889 年埃菲尔铁塔建成之前的 5000 年里,胡夫大金字塔是地球上最高的建筑物。

T: 真是了不起!他们究竟是怎么建起来的?我听说过很多关于使用奴隶甚至是靠外星人帮助建成的传说!

G: 是的,我也听说过外星人的说法!如果有大量廉价的劳动力,建一座金字塔并不难。首先,他们先在地上建一个小方形墓,很普通的样子。然后,有一种说法是,他们接着在坟墓上堆上很多很多的土,留出一个通向外面的通道。再接下来他们开始在整个金字塔的周围放上大石头。为了把石头抬到金字塔的顶部,他们修建了长长的土坡,然后沿着坡把石头往上滚。他们不断把土坡加高、加长。等一切完成之后,他们再把土坡清理掉。

T: 在没有机器的情况下他们建起这么庞大的建筑物,还是很令人难以置信。

■ impressive monument　宏伟的历史建筑	■ ancient world　远古世界
■ heap up　堆积	■ massive structures　庞大的建筑物

25. The Nile

尼罗河

T：*Traveller*　　*G*：*Tour guide*

T：The Nile. I know it begins in the south of Egypt and stretched about 4,000 miles north to the Mediterranean Sea. It's the longest river on earth, right?

G：That's right. It gets its name from a Greek word, "Neilos" which means "river valley". It gave water for growing food, drinking and for transportation. In fact, the Egyptian calendar of three seasons was based on the yearly cycle of the Nile.

T：Really? I never knew the Egyptians only had three seasons. It says here that the Egyptian year began in July, when the floods came.

G：It was also the main road of ancient Egypt, because roads couldn't be built on sandy desert or places that flooded each year.

T：So it was like a river road?

G：Exactly. Travelling was easy, going north, boats just **drifted along** with the flow of the river. And, because **prevailing winds** blew south, they helped travellers going in that direction, too.

T：That must be why there were so many traders in ancient Egypt. It must have been really easy to transport goods up and down the whole country.

G：The Nile also helped the Egyptians to survive in another way: food. Every year, the Nile flooded, spreading rich soil across the land. Without this annual flooding, the Egyptians could not have grown so many crops.

T：We think of **extreme weather** destroying crops, not helping them!

G：But, in the desert it's very different. Water is of utmost importance, because there is so little of it.

T：Yes, of course. How about the wildlife of the Nile?

G：There are many different types of animals living in or near the waters of the Nile, including crocodiles, birds, fish and many others.

T：But not just the animals depend on the Nile for survival, but also even nowadays, people who live there need it **for everyday use** like washing, as a water supply, keeping crops watered and other jobs.

G: Yes, and it's also a tourism resource. Many tourists come from all over the world and go on a Nile cruise, perhaps **a dream holiday** for most people.

T: That's my plan for next summer, now that you've **whet my appetite**! Thanks for explaining everything to me.

T：游客　　G：导游

T：尼罗河，我知道它起源于埃及南部，一直向北延伸 4000 英里到地中海。它是地球上最长的一条河，是这样吧？

G：是这样。这条河的名字源于希腊词 Neilos，意思是"河谷"。它是粮食种植、饮用和交通的水源。事实上，埃及的三季历法就是根据尼罗河的年周期制定的。

T：真的吗？我从来不知道埃及人只有三个季节。历法上说埃及年从七月开始，那时正是洪水泛滥之时。

G：尼罗河还是古埃及的交通要道，因为道路不能建在每年发洪水的沙漠或其他地方。

T：尼罗河就是条水路了？

G：一点不错。向北行非常容易，船只只需顺着河水的流向漂就行。同时，由于常年刮北风，所以对去南边旅游的游客也非常有利。

T：古埃及的商人那么多一定跟这个有关。在整个埃及来回运送货物肯定相当方便。

G：尼罗河还帮助埃及人以另外一种方式生存，即种植粮食作物。每年尼罗河泛滥，给周围带来了肥沃的土壤。没有每年一次的洪水，埃及人就不可能种植那么多的农作物。

T：我们认为恶劣的天气会毁坏农作物而不是对农作物有利！

G：但是在沙漠地区就不一样了。水是至关重要的，因为那里的水太少了。

T：当然，是这样。那尼罗河地区的野生动物怎么样？

G：在尼罗河水域或附近地区有很多种类各异的动物，包括鳄鱼、鸟、鱼和很多其他动物。

T：但是不只是动物要靠尼罗河生存，哪怕是现在生活在那里的人也需要把尼罗河作为日常生活的水源，如洗衣服，灌溉庄稼或干其他活。

G：确实如此，尼罗河还是一种旅游资源。很多游客从世界各地来这里航游尼罗河，也许对大多数人来说，这是个梦寐以求的假日。

T：既然你把我的胃口吊起来了，那我明年夏天的旅游计划就安排去尼罗河！谢谢你给我讲的一切。

■ drift along　顺着漂	■ prevailing wind　常年刮的风
■ extreme weather　恶劣的天气	■ for everyday use　供日常使用
■ a dream holiday　梦寐以求的假日	■ whet my appetite　吊我的胃口

26. Pharaohs

法老

S: *Student*　　**P**: *Professor*

S: Professor Thomson, do you know anything about when the pharaohs lived, in ancient Egypt?

P: **As a matter of fact** I do. They have a long history, from the Pre-Dynastic period, 5500-3100 BC to the Late Kingdom period, 664-332 BC. Pharaoh is the ancient Egyptian name for king.

S: That is a long history! Too long for my project, I think. What about famous pharaohs?

P: There were certainly many of those. Sneferu was a pharaoh during the Old Kingdom period, he reigned for around 30 years. He is famous because he was the first pharaoh to build pyramids.

S: He's very important then. Another?

P: OK, next is Khufu, who reigned during the 4ᵗʰ dynasty. He was famous for building The Great Pyramid at Giza, one of the most well-known throughout the world. This pyramid shows us how Khufu was able to lead and co-ordinate his people, who helped him to build the pyramid **in exchange for goods and services**.

S: Why didn't he pay them? After all, they were construction workers.

P: At that time, there was no **monetary system** in Egypt.

S: Oh, I see. OK, who's next?

P: Amenhotep III is next, he was king during the 18ᵗʰ dynasty and he reigned for almost 40 years. He's well known for being a prolific builder and **a benevolent ruler**. He built many splendid temples and statues of himself, but his greatest achievement was the Temple of Amun. It shows a relief which served to establish the legitimacy of his rule by depicting his birth directly from the god Amun.

S: He was king for 40 years you say? That's a long reign, he sounds like a great king. Are there any more famous pharaohs?

P: Yes, next I will tell you about perhaps the most famous of all the pharaohs. He was known as "The Boy King". Have you heard this before?

S: Yes, I think so. Was it Tutan . . . something?

P: Indeed! Tutankhamun, or "King Tut", he reigned for a very short time and died in his teens.

S: In his teens, well "The Boy King" is definitely the right name for him, then. Thanks so much for your help, I think my project will be a great success.

S: 学生　　P: 教授

S: 汤姆森教授，你知道古埃及的法老们大概生活在什么时代吗？

P: 我还确实知道。他们生活的年代很长，从公元前5500年至前3100年的前王朝起，一直到公元前664年至前332年的王国末期。法老是古埃及君主的称号。

S: 这段历史真的很长！我想，对我的研究计划来说也太长了。研究些著名的法老怎么样？

P: 有名的法老也有很多。斯尼夫鲁是古王国时期的法老，统治王国大约有30年。他是第一个修建金字塔的法老，因此而出名。

S: 那么他是很重要了。其他著名的法老呢？

P: 下一个是胡夫，是第四王朝的法老。他以修建吉萨的大金字塔而出名，这是世界上最有名的金字塔之一。该金字塔向我们展示了胡夫是如何领导和协调他的臣民，让他们帮助他修建金字塔以换取商品和公共服务的。

S: 他为什么不付给他们工资？毕竟他们是建筑工人。

P: 当时埃及没有货币体制。

S: 噢，我知道了。好了，下一个是谁？

P: 下一个是阿蒙霍特普三世，他是第18王朝的法老，统治王国约40年。以建筑众多和仁慈统治而闻名于世。他建了很多富丽堂皇的庙宇和他自己的雕像，但他最伟大的业绩是修建了阿蒙神庙。里面有个浮雕描述他是阿蒙神投胎转世，以此来巩固他合法的统治地位。

S: 你是说他当了40年的国王吗？统治时间那么长，似乎像个伟大的国王。还有什么著名的法老吗？

P: 还有，下面我要给你讲可能是所有法老中最有名的一个。他以"男孩国王"而闻名。这个你听说过吗？

S: 是的，我想我听说过。是不是叫图坦什么的？

P: 没错！是图坦卡蒙＊或"图坦王"，他统治的时间很短，十几岁就死了。

S: 十几岁，那"男孩国王"的称号对他来说再确切不过了。谢谢你的帮助，我想我的研究计划会很成功的。

■ as a matter of fact 事实上　　■ in exchange for goods and services 换取商品和公共服务
■ monetary system 货币体制　　■ a benevolent ruler 仁慈的统治者

27. The Eiffel Tower

埃菲尔铁塔

S1: Student 1 *S2*: Student 2

S1: What's that you are looking at?

S2: It's a postcard of the Eiffel Tower, my friend went to France last month.

S1: Do you know its history or anything at all about it?

S2: I'm sorry to say, I only know the history written on the back of this postcard.

S1: Well, I was born in France and I can tell you anything you need to know.

S2: Well, that's great. When was it built? It looks like a modern building.

S1: The Eiffel Tower was built for the International Exhibition of Paris of 1889 commemorating the centenary of the French Revolution

S2: So it has a big political idea, French folks feel the Eiffel Tower made them free?

S1: Yes, but they invited the Prince of Wales, later King Edward VII of England, to attend the ceremony. Of the 700 proposals submitted in a design competition, Gustave Eiffel's was unanimously chosen.

S2: But, it's also pretty to look at! I think that he was **a man of vision** and **ahead of his time**.

S1: Yes, I agree! Eiffel was an excellent designer and **the perfect choice** for a project so large. However it was not accepted by all at first, and a petition of 300 names—including those of Maupassant, Emile Zola, Charles Garnier who was an architect of the Opera Garnier, and Dumas the Younger—protested its construction.

S2: But why? Didn't they think he was good enough?

S1: Oh, I think they all thought he was a good architect but they saw the Tower as "useless and monstrous".

S2: I think the construction of the Eiffel Tower is important for all French people.

S1: Also, during its lifetime, the Eiffel Tower has also **witnessed a few strange scenes**, including being scaled by a mountaineer in 1954, and parachuted off in 1984 by two Englishmen.

S2: Oh yes, and I read that in 1923 a journalist rode a bicycle down from the first level. Some accounts say he rode down the stairs, other accounts suggest the exterior of one of the tower's four legs which slope outward.

S1: Well, whatever he did, he must have been crazy! Anyway, the Eiffel Tower doesn't have a really long history, but it's an interesting one.

S1: 学生1   S2: 学生2

S1: 你在看什么呀?

S2: 是一张埃菲尔铁塔的明信片。我朋友上个月去了法国。

S1: 你知道它的历史或其他相关信息吗?

S2: 很遗憾,我只知道明信片背面印的历史简介。

S1: 我在法国出生,可以告诉你任何你想知道的东西。

S2: 那就太好了。它是什么时候建的? 看上去像现代建筑。

S1: 埃菲尔铁塔是 1889 年为了召开巴黎国际博览会而建的,是为了纪念法国大革命一百周年。

S2: 所以它具有伟大的政治意义,是不是法国人觉得埃菲尔铁塔使他们获得了自由?

S1: 是的,但是他们却请了威尔士王子,也就是后来的英国国王爱德华七世来为开幕盛典捧场。在此塔的设计大赛提交的 700 多个方案中,居斯塔夫・埃菲尔的设计最终受到一致推选。

S2: 不过埃菲尔铁塔看上去也很漂亮。我想居斯塔夫・埃菲尔不仅有眼光而且走在了时代的前面。

S1: 是的,我赞成你的说法。居斯塔夫・埃菲尔是一个出色的设计师,也是这个大项目的最佳人选。不过,他的最初设计并没有被一致通过,有 300 人联名请愿反对采用他的设计,其中包括莫泊桑,埃米尔・左拉,加尼叶歌剧院的设计者查尔斯・加尼叶,以及小仲马。

S2: 这是为什么呢? 难道他们认为他不能胜任吗?

S1: 哦,我认为他们都公认他是个优秀的建筑师,但这座塔常被嘲笑为"毫无用处"和"怪异丑陋"。

S2: 我觉得埃菲尔铁塔的建设对所有法国人民都非常重要。

S1: 而且埃菲尔铁塔自建成之日起,也见证了很多奇闻逸事。例如 1954 年有一个登山运动员曾经攀登过埃菲尔铁塔,1984 年又有两个英国人带着降落伞从塔顶上往下跳。

S2: 是的,我还读到过 1923 年有一个记者从埃菲尔铁塔塔顶骑自行车下来。有些报道说他是从楼梯骑下来的,另外一些说他是从向外倾斜的 4 个塔柱之一下来的。

S1: 不论他从哪里下来的,我都觉得他肯定是疯了。不管怎么说,埃菲尔铁塔的历史并不算长,但挺有意思的。

■ a man of vision 有眼光的人　　■ ahead of his time 领先于时代,有前瞻性
■ the perfect choice 最佳选择　　■ witness a few strange scenes 见证很多怪事

28. French Food

法国美食

J: *Jane*   **M**: *Michelle*

J: I'm starting a new course, French cuisine, do you think you could help me?

M: Of course! I'm French, so I know all about French cooking.

J: I want to start with the basics. What is a béarnaise sauce?

M: Well, it's a butter based sauce with added egg yolk with the distinct flavoring of tarragon, shallots, and chervil.

J: So, it comes from the mayonnaise family, right?

M: Yes, just like Hollandaise sauce.

J: Every time I try to make it, it ends up lumpy. I never know why, what am I doing wrong?

M: It's a difficult sauce to perfect because **it requires special attention to** avoid separation and curdling. When prepared properly, it is a smooth, creamy sauce.

J: So what can I do to stop it from going lumpy?

M: If you follow the usual recipe, egg, butter, white wine vinegar, tarragon, shallots, and chervil, you shouldn't go wrong.

J: And should I whisk it constantly?

M: Yes, that's why you get your problem with lumps.

J: OK. So I must keep whisking. What was your favourite dish as a child?

M: My favourite dish was always "moules a la mariniere". With bread, of course! Made with mussels, shallots, garlic, white wine and cream.

J: I guess that's beautiful with a big crusty bread loaf! On a cold night, sitting around the fire.

M: Yes, it's perfect. But I do enjoy many other famous French foods. For example, did you ever try a "croque monsieur"?

J: No, I don't think I have. It's a kind of sandwich, right?

M: Not just any sandwich. It's the most amazing toasted cheese and ham sandwich in the world!

J: Really? Why is it so great, I mean a sandwich is just a sandwich? **It's nothing special.**

Why is French food so **highly acclaimed** throughout the world?

M: I think it's because French chefs **slave away**, for many years to perfect the best dish. That's why their food is excellent. And because the menu are written in French, it sounds delicious too!

J: OK, so tonight you are taking me to a French restaurant. I want to try everything!

J: 简　　**M**: 米歇尔

J: 我正开始学一门新课程,法式烹饪*,你可以帮我一下吗?

M: 当然可以,我是法国人,所以所有的法式做法我都知道。

J: 我想从最基本的学起。蛋黄酱是什么?

M: 哦,那主要是一种黄油酱,外加蛋黄以及风味独特的龙蒿、大葱和山萝卜做成。

J: 那么,这也是一种蛋黄酱了?

M: 是的,就跟荷兰辣酱油一样。

J: 每次我试着做蛋黄酱时,最后总是结成块状。我一直不明白为什么,我哪里做错了呢?

M: 要想做好确实不容易,需要特别注意避免分馏和凝结。准备得好,蛋黄酱就会柔滑、呈乳脂状。

J: 那怎样才能防止它凝块呢?

M: 如果你用平常的配料,鸡蛋、黄油、白酒醋、龙蒿、大葱和山萝卜,应该不会有问题。

J: 那我是不是应该不停地搅拌呢?

M: 是的,我想这可能就是你凝块的原因吧。

J: 好的,那我必须不停搅拌了。你小时候最喜欢吃什么菜?

M: 我最喜欢吃的一直都是"葡萄酒炖贝类汤",当然得外加面包。这是由贻贝、葱、蒜、白葡萄酒和奶油做成的。

J: 在寒冷的夜晚,坐在炉火边,再配上一大条法式长棍面包,我想那真是妙不可言!

M: 是的,简直是完美极了。不过许多其它有名的法国食物我也很喜欢,比如,你吃过"火腿干酪夹心面包片"吗?

J: 没有,好像没吃过。那是一种三明治,对吗?

M: 不单单是三明治,它称得上是世界上最美味的火腿干酪三明治。

J: 真的吗?为什么这么有名?我是说三明治就是三明治,没什么特别的啊。法国菜为什么还会在全世界享有盛名?

M: 我想是因为法国厨师们不辞辛苦,多年来不停地完善菜肴,所以才会有这么棒。而且他们的菜单是用法语写的,念起来感觉更好吃。

J: 那好,今晚你就带我去法国餐厅吧,我什么都想尝尝。

> * 法式烹饪:酒和香料是调制法国菜的两大法宝。香槟酒、红白葡萄酒、雪利酒、朗姆酒、白兰地等,是做菜常用的酒类。什么菜用什么酒有严格的规定,如红葡萄酒煮牛肉、白葡萄酒调奶酪、白兰地调牛排、白葡萄酒炖贝类和鱼汤。法国菜的香料包括大蒜、欧芹、迷迭香、百里香、茴香等,香料的搭配和比例也有定规。因此,无论是菜肴或点心,闻之香味浓郁,食之醇香沁人。

■ It requires special attention to . . .　需要特别注意……　　■ It's nothing special.　没什么特别。
■ be highly acclaimed　享有盛名　　■ slave away　不辞辛苦

29. The Cancan

康康舞

M: *Man*　　**W**: *Woman*

M: Hi Tina. I watched a great documentary yesterday, all about the history of the Cancan.

W: I watched it too, it was fabulous. I love the special costumes they wear.

M: Yes, me too. But what I didn't realise is that it started as a dance for the **working classes**. I thought that only rich people could afford to go to watch shows.

W: I think it's a dance that everyone can enjoy, men as well as women, rich and poor.

M: From the 1840s to the 1860s even men danced the cancan!

W: Really? That would be a funny sight! I can't imagine men doing the cancan.

M: Me too. Did you know the word "cancan" actually means scandal?

W: Well, I guess the dance is pretty scandalous!

M: Have you seen the movie *Moulin Rouge*? That's where the cancan was invented, in the club.

W: Yes, I think the documentary said it was invented there in the 1830s.

M: But by the mid-19th century it was **incredibly popular**, so people started to incorporate it into other stage shows.

W: There was also a famous artist, Henri Toulouse-Lautrec, he painted some wonderful cancan-themed pictures.

M: Yes, he made lithographs, too. I saw some in the gallery near the park, they were extremely beautiful.

W: It was so popular everyone wanted to see it, everywhere, in every type of show. I've only ever seen it on television, but I'd love to **go to a show**, too.

M: Maybe we can find a theatre here that has cancan shows. I'll look in the newspaper for a number to call.

W: Good idea. I think cancan music is also very special, very recognisable. Maybe we can buy a CD of it.

M: The most well-known cancan music composer was Jacques Offenbach, have you heard of him?

W: Not before I watched the documentary, no. But if he is so well-known it should be easy to find his music.

M: I've found something, it says here that the cabaret club has cancan nights on the first Tuesday of every month.

W: Let me see … next Tuesday is the first Tuesday of this month, **do you fancy going**?

M: Definitely!

M: 男人   **W**: 女人

M: 嗨，蒂娜，我昨天看了一个很棒的纪录片，是关于康康舞历史的。

W: 我也看了，真是令人难以置信。我喜欢她们穿的特制服装。

M: 我也是。但我不知道它最初是为工人阶层跳的舞蹈。我原以为只有富人才有钱去看演出。

W: 我认为这种舞蹈每个人都有权观赏，不分男女，也不论贵贱。

M: 在19世纪40年代到60年代间，甚至男人也跳康康舞。

W: 真的吗？那肯定很好看。我想象不出男人们跳康康舞的样子。

M: 我也是。你知道吗？康康舞的原意是指流言、丑闻。

W: 是吗，我猜是这种舞蹈名声不好。

M: 你有没有看过电影《红磨坊》？康康舞就是从红磨坊那样的夜总会起源的。

W: 我看过，有部纪录片也说康康舞是19世纪30年代在夜总会出现的。

M: 但是令人难以置信的是，到了19世纪中期康康舞变得非常流行，所以人们开始把它融入到其它舞台表演节目中。

W: 曾经还有一个艺术家亨利·图卢兹·罗特列克，他以康康舞为主题画了很多精美的作品。

M: 是的，他也画石版画。我在公园附近的一个美术馆看到过一些，画得特别漂亮。

W: 康康舞非常流行，每个人都想去看看，无论是在哪里，或是什么样的演出。我曾经在电视上看到过，不过我还是想去看一次现场演出。

M: 也许我们能在这儿的某个剧院看到康康舞的演出。我从报上找个联系电话问问。

W: 好主意，我想康康舞的音乐也很特别，与众不同。也许我们可以买张CD听听。

M: 最著名的康康舞作曲家是雅克·奥芬巴赫，你听说过他吗？

W: 在看这部纪录片之前从没听说过。不过他要是非常有名的话，应该不难找到他的乐曲。

M: 我找到了，上面说每个月第一个周二的晚上在歌舞夜总会有康康舞表演。

W: 让我看看……这个月的第一个周二就是下周二了，你想去吗？

M: 当然想去！

■ incredibly popular 非常流行	■ go to a show 去看现场演出
■ working class 工人阶级	■ Do you fancy going? 你想去吗？

30. Joan of Arc

圣女贞德

R: *Researcher*　　*L*: *Librarian*

R: I'm looking for some materials about Joan of Arc, where might I find them?

L: I'll show you. Are you doing some research?

R: Yes, I'm writing a book about famous figures in history.

L: Well, Joan of Arc is certainly famous. She was the most famous fighting woman in European history.

R: On the battlefield, she motivated her troops to drive the enemies from her homeland.

L: Although she knew nothing about warfare, she claimed to be guided by visions of saints. Few people believed her and many thought she used sorcery.

R: Yes, that's why when she was captured, she **was declared a witch** and burnt at the stake. I don't really believe she was a witch.

L: Maybe she was schizophrenic. She started to hear voices and have visions at the age of 13.

R: Yes, I suppose so. Seeing things is a symptom of mental problems. These visions, they were of saints, weren't they?

L: St. Michael, the captain-general of the armies of Heaven, and St. Catherine and St. Margaret who were both early Christian martyrs.

R: Well, nowadays Joan of Arc is a saint herself. I bet she never believed she would **end up** in such company.

L: I think all that she cared about was **fighting for king and country**, she probably never even considered the fact that many years later people would admire her and make her a saint.

R: Around the time she was born, France was at war with the English. I guess she couldn't have been born at a better time!

L: This conflict was not really a war, it lasted for more than 100 years. That's why we call it "The Hundred Years War".

R: A hundred years is certainly a long time to be fighting. A victory here would have **allowed** the English **a chance to** control all of southern France.

L: Yes, but they were stopped by the French, who were led by a seventeen-year-old peasant girl—Joan.

R: It's hard to think that someone so young could have led an army. This particular battle took place in Orleans.

L: Now Joan is known as "The Maid of Orleans".

R: 研究员　　**L**: 图书管理员

R: 我在查一些关于圣女贞德的资料，哪儿能找到呢？

L: 我指给你看吧。你在做研究吗？

R: 是的，我正在写一本有关历史上著名人物的书。

L: 嗯，圣女贞德的确很有名，她也是欧洲历史上最著名的女英雄。

R: 在战场上，她激励她的士兵们把敌人赶出国土。

L: 虽然她不懂战术，但她声称受了圣徒的指引。很少有人相信她，很多人还认为她使用了巫术。

R: 是的，这就是为什么她被捕时被宣称是个巫婆，最后被烧死在火刑柱*上的原因。我真的不相信她是个巫婆。

L: 她可能得了精神分裂症，从13岁起她就开始幻听、幻视。

R: 是的，我也这么认为。出现幻觉就是精神疾病的症状。这些幻影都是圣徒，对吧？

L: 是的，圣米歇尔，他是天堂里军队的统帅。还有圣凯瑟琳和圣玛格丽特，她们都是早期的基督教殉教者。

R: 哦，如今圣女贞德自己也成了一个圣徒*。我敢说她从没想过自己会加入这个行列。

L: 我想她最关心的是为国王和国家而战。她可能从未料到很多年以后人们会赞美她，把她当作圣人。

R: 在她出生前后的那段时间里，法国正与英国交战。我想她生得正是时候。

L: 这次冲突并不是真正意义上的战争，它持续了一百多年，所以我们把它叫做"百年战争*"。

R: 打了一百年，时间的确不短。要是英国人胜了，他们就有机会控制整个法国南部。

L: 是的，但是他们却遭到法国军人的阻挡，被一个17岁的法国农村女孩贞德所率领的队伍击退了。

R: 很难想象一个如此年轻的人可以带领军队。这次特别的战役发生在奥尔良。

L: 如今，贞德也被称为"奥尔良少女"。

> * 火刑柱：13至19世纪，天主教会设立宗教裁判所侦察并审判异端。异端包括不同于罗马正统教派的言行和思想。苦行、鞭打等皆属轻罚，严重者被处以徒刑或火刑。
>
> * 圣徒：1456年，贞德牺牲20余年后，教皇卡利克斯特三世为贞德平反。1920年，教皇本尼迪克十五世封贞德为"圣女"。
>
> * 百年战争：英、法两国间于1337年至1453年的战争。起因于两国争夺富饶的弗兰德斯和英王在法国境内所占据的领地。战争最后以英国失败告终，除加来港外，法国收复了英王在法的全部领地。

- be declared a witch　被宣称是个巫婆
- end up　结束；死亡
- allow ... a chance to　给……机会
- fight for king and country　为国王和国家而战

31. Napoleon

拿破仑

S1: Student 1   *S2*: Student 2

S1: I'm doing a paper on great figures in military history, who do you think I should choose?

S2: How about Napoleon?

S1: That's a good idea. He was known as "The Little Corporal", did you know that?

S2: Yes, because he was so short! It's hard to think that such a little man could lead an army.

S1: I know what you mean, but he may have been **little in stature**, but he had a very powerful mind.

S2: He was one of the greatest military commanders and a risk taking gambler, he was also a workaholic.

S1: And a genius. He was also very impatient, he couldn't wait for anything. He was also a vicious cynic who forgave even his closest betrayers.

S2: He sounds like a pretty amazing guy. After all, he was emperor of France twice. His military endeavors and sheer personality dominated Europe in person for a decade, and in thought for a century.

S1: He wasn't born in France though, was he?

S2: He wasn't born in mainland France, no. He was born in Corsica, an island owned by France.

S1: And he moved to mainland France after he completed his studies at the École Royale Militaire de Paris.

S2: Yes, but he talked to **people in high places** and managed to stay in Corsica most of the time. Did you know that he completed his course in just one year? It should have taken three!

S1: Well, he certainly was **strong willed**. While he was in Corsica he **played an active part** in political and military matters, initially supporting the Corsican rebel Pasquale Paoli, a former patron of Napoleon's father, Carlo Buonaparte.

S2: The French Revolution was an important time for Napoleon. By December 1793 Bonaparte was the hero of Toulon, a General and favourite of Augustin Robespierre.

S1: Yes, but shortly after Napoleon was arrested for treason. He got out of it because of tremendous political flexibility. He was saved by Paul de Baras, who would later become one of France's Directors.

S2: It's a good thing that he was saved. Military history as we know it would be very different indeed!

S1: 学生 1   S2: 学生 2

S1: 我在写一篇关于军事史上伟大人物的论文，你认为我该选谁呢？

S2: 写拿破仑怎么样？

S1: 好主意。拿破仑有个绰号叫"小下士"，你知道吗？

S2: 知道，那是因为他长得太矮小了。很难想象一个如此矮小的人能统率大军。

S1: 我明白你的意思。不过虽然他身材可能是矮了点，但他却很有头脑。

S2: 他是最伟大的军事将领之一，也是个敢于冒险的赌徒，还是个工作狂。

S1: 而且还是个天才。他性情急躁，对任何事情都没有耐心。他还是个自我矛盾的愤世嫉俗者，当他最亲密的人背叛了他时他原谅了他们。

S2: 听起来他还真了不起。毕竟他在法国两次称帝。他靠军事行为和独特个性统治了欧洲十来年，其思想影响了欧洲近一个世纪*。

S1: 但他并不是在法国出生的，是吧？

S2: 是的，他不是在法国大陆出生的。他生在科西嘉岛，法国一个附属岛屿。

S1: 在巴黎皇家军事学校完成学业后，他就去了法国大陆。

S2: 是这样，但他跟高层的人有了沟通，并设法在科西嘉岛度过了很长一段时间。你知道吗？他只用了一年时间就学完了所有课程，那本来是要 3 年才能学完的。

S1: 嗯，他的意志肯定很坚强。还在科西嘉岛的时候，他就积极参与政治和军事活动。最初，他支持科西嘉岛起义者帕斯奎尔·保利，拿破仑的父亲卡罗·波拿巴以前曾经追随过保利。

S2: 法国革命时期对拿破仑来说非常重要。到 1793 年 12 月他就成为了土伦战役的英雄，也成了奥古斯汀·罗伯斯庇尔跟前最受重用的将军。

S1: 是的，但不久之后，拿破仑就因叛国罪而被捕。但由于变幻莫测的政治变动，他被后来成为法国执政官之一的保罗·德·贝洛斯救出。

S2: 他获救是件好事，否则军事史真的将要改写。

> * 拿破仑执政时期制定的《拿破仑法典》又称为《法国民法典》，于 1804 年公布施行，经过多次修订，现仍在法国施行。它是资产阶级国家最早的一部民法典，对德国、西班牙、瑞士等国的立法也起到重要作用。随着 200 多年来法国政治、经济、社会情况的变化，该法典也经过 100 多次修改，以不断适应新的情况。

- little in stature　身材矮小
- people in high place　高层人士
- strong willed　意志坚定的
- play an active part in　积极参与

32. Champagne

香槟酒

K：*Kevin*   **D**：*Debbie*

K：I'm glad you **talked me into** coming to this wine tasting.

D：Tonight is special, we are tasting champagne.

K：Where's this one from?

D：It's from the Champagne region of France, **that's where it gets its name**. Only grapes grown there can make true champagne.

K：I see, so this one which is called brut must have been made from grapes grown in a different region?

D：That's right. The Champagne region has a cool climate, which has an effect on the wine making process.

K：What's this one, Dom Perignon. Didn't a man named Dom Perignon invent champagne?

D：No, he didn't invent it, but we owe a lot to him for improving it. Pierre Perignon was a Benedictine monk who, in 1688, was appointed treasurer at the Abbey of Hautvillers in Champagne.

K：So, his job was the management of the cellars and wine making. But why does champagne have bubbles? You said something about climate ...

D：The bubbles in the wine are a natural process arising from Champagne's cold climate and **short growing season**, so they pick the grapes late in the year.

K：Right, so this doesn't leave enough time for the yeasts present on the grape skins to convert the sugar in the pressed grape juice into alcohol.

D：The cold winter temperatures **put a temporary stop to** the fermentation process, but it starts to ferment again in the spring, but this time it ferments in the bottle.

K：So, the refermentation creates carbon-dioxide which now becomes trapped in the bottle, thereby creating the sparkle?

D：Exactly! But Dom Perignon didn't like the sparkle, he wanted still wine. He was not able to prevent the bubbles, but he did develop the art of blending.

K: You mean blending different grapes and different juices? It says here that champagne is made from black grapes, how can that be?

D: Dom Perignon developed a method to press the black grapes to yield a white juice. He also improved the clarity of wine, so his wine was the best ever made.

K: Nowadays, champagne is very popular. It's not just seen as a luxury anymore.

D: Yes, everybody drinks it now.

K：凯文　　D：黛比

> * 香槟区：香槟省位于法国北部，气候寒冷且土壤干硬，阳光充足，其种植的葡萄适于酿造香槟酒。此外，位于法国西南部的波尔多地区是法国最大的葡萄酒产地。其他著名酒区包括罗讷河谷、勃艮第酒区、卢瓦尔河谷等。

K：很高兴你劝我来参加这个品酒会。

D：今晚很特别，我们要品尝的是香槟酒。

K：这种香槟是哪儿产的？

D：产于法国香槟区*，并因此而得名。只有那里出产的葡萄才可以酿制出真正的香槟。

K：我明白了。所以这种低糖香槟肯定是由另外一个地区种植的葡萄酿造的。

D：是这样。香槟区的气候凉爽，这会影响到香槟的酿造过程。

K：这种又是什么？堂·培里侬。是不是由一个叫堂·培里侬的人发明的香槟？

D：不，不是他发明的，但他却对这种酒进行了大大的改良。皮埃尔·培里侬是个本笃会修士。1688 年，他被任命为香槟区奥特维雷修道院的司库。

K：所以，他的工作是管理酒窖和酿酒。但为什么香槟酒里有气泡呢？你刚说到了气候因素……

D：香槟里的气泡是由香槟区的寒冷气候和短暂的生长期自然产生的，所以他们年底时才采摘葡萄。

K：没错，这样一来，葡萄皮上的酵母就来不及把压出来的葡萄汁糖份转化成酒精。

D：冬天寒冷的天气使得发酵过程暂时停下来，但到了春天又开始发酵，不过这次发酵是在瓶子里进行了。

K：所以说，再次发酵产生的二氧化氮就封在了瓶子里，由此就产生气泡了，对吗？

D：一点不错。但是堂·培里侬不喜欢这些气泡，他想要没有气泡的葡萄酒。虽然他不能阻止产生气泡，却发明了调合葡萄酒的方法。

K：你是指把不同的葡萄和葡萄汁混合在一起吗？这里提到香槟是由黑葡萄酿制的，这又是怎么回事呢？

D：堂·培里侬发明了一种方法，挤压黑葡萄获取一种白色汁液。此外，他还提高了葡萄酒的纯度，所以他酿造出来的葡萄酒是最好的。

K：现在，香槟很流行，不再被认为是一种奢侈品了。

D：是的，现在每个人都能喝到。

■ talk me into 劝说，说服　　　　　　　　　■ that's where it gets its name 因此而得名
■ short growing season 短暂的生长期　　　■ put a temporary stop to ... 使……暂停

65

33. The Louvre

卢浮宫

M: Man   **W**: Woman

M: I've just finished reading a magazine article about museums of the world. Which museum do you think is the best?

W: The Louvre in Paris, **no contest**. I've been there many times and always enjoy it.

M: Why do you like the Louvre so much?

W: Well, it's a combination of things, really. It's one of the largest palaces in the world, a former residence of kings of France and one of the most illustrious.

M: They have a **massive selection of art**, too. Both ancient and modern.

W: Exactly. **What more can you ask for** in a museum? It has Oriental antiquities, Egyptian antiquities, Greek and Roman antiquities, sculpture from the Middle Ages to modern times, furniture and objets d'art, and paintings representing all the European schools.

M: It's a very old building, too. The first Louvre was a fortress built at the beginning of the 13th century by Philip II to defend the Seine below Paris against the Normans and English.

W: Yes and then, in 1564 Catherine de Médicis had her architect, Philibert Delorme, build a little chateau in a neighboring field to the west called the Tuileries. These were joined together to make a big royal residence.

M: After that, in the 17th century Louis XIII and his minister Richelieu extended Lescot's west wing northward by adding the majestically domed Pavillon del'Horloge, or Clock Pavillion by Jacques Lemercier.

W: Then, under Louis XIV and his minister Colbert, the Cour Carrée, a great square court, was constructed by Louis Le Vau.

M: So many changes! It must look completely different now to how it looked originally. Later on, Napoleon I began a wing parallel to that of Henry IV along the Seine. Napoleon III finished the wing, thus closing the great quadrilateral.

W: The quadrilateral shape is what makes it special. I think one of the most innovative additions was the great **glass pyramid**.

M: I agree. It was built by the Chinese-American architect I. M. Pei and opened in 1989.

Initially, some people thought it was a very strange idea.

W: Well, it has proved to be very effective in accommodating all of the visitors, I think it looks good too.

M：男人　　W：女人

M: 我刚在杂志上读到一篇关于世界博物馆的文章，你认为世界上最棒的博物馆是哪一个呢？

W: 巴黎的卢浮宫是独一无二的。我曾去过那里很多次，而且每次都很开心。

M: 你为什么那么喜欢卢浮宫？

W: 哦，原因真的有很多。卢浮宫是世界上最大的宫殿之一，也是法国国王以前的居所，而且还是最辉煌的地方之一。

M: 那里还收藏有大量艺术精品，古代的和现代的都有。

W: 真是这样。博物馆里的东西应有尽有。那里有来自东方、埃及、希腊以及罗马的古董文物，有从中世纪到现代的雕刻品、家具和艺术品，还有欧洲各流派的绘画作品。

M: 它也是一座非常古老的建筑。卢浮宫最初是在13世纪初由菲利普二世建起的城堡，用来防御巴黎塞纳河下游的诺曼底人和英国人。

W: 是的，但后来到了1564年，王后凯瑟琳·德·美第奇＊让她的建筑师菲利波特·迪罗门在西边的邻地建了一个小宫殿叫做杜伊勒里宫，这些合在一起就构成了一个大型的皇家居所。

M: 此后，17世纪路易十三和他的大臣黎塞留通过加建宏伟的圆顶钟塔，也叫做时钟长廊，向北扩建了建筑师勒柯修建的西翼，设计者是雅克·雷蒙西尔。

W: 后来，路易十四和他的大臣科尔波特又任命路易·勒沃建了一个巨大的方形庭院，即卡利庭。

M: 这么多的改建啊！它现在的样子肯定跟最初完全不一样。后来，拿破仑一世开始加建一条长廊，与亨利四世沿塞纳河建造的长廊平行。拿破仑三世完成了这一翼的加建，至此卢浮宫四大翼的建筑群体全部完工。

W: 正是这四翼的外形使得卢浮宫独具一格。我认为其中最富有创意的亮点要数巨型的玻璃金字塔。

M: 我也这么认为。它是由美籍华人建筑师贝聿铭设计的，于1989年开放。最初有些人认为这个设计理念很怪。

W: 但后来证明这个设计有效地吸引了各方游客，我也认为它很不错。

■ no contest　无可比拟的
■ what more can you ask for　没有比这更好的了
■ massive selection of art　大量艺术精品
■ glass pyramid　玻璃金字塔

34. Cannes Film Festival

戛纳电影节

T: *Teacher*   *S*: *Student*

T: What are you doing, Annie? Homework?

S: No, I'm reading about film festivals. At the moment I'm looking at Cannes.

T: I think it's perhaps the most famous film festival. For the rest of the year Cannes is just a small, sleepy town in France.

S: Yes, but during festival time **it really comes alive**, it gets totally packed.

T: How often is it held, annually?

S: Yes, usually in May. It was first held in 1946, but it was founded in 1939. Obviously they didn't hold it during the war years.

T: Also, the festival wasn't held in 1948 or 1950 because of **budgetary problems**. I guess they must have overspent the year before with too many **lavish parties**.

S: It was also halted in 1968. Louis Malle, who was the president of the jury, Francois Truffaut, Claude Berri, Jean-Gabriel Albicocco, Claude Lelouch, Roman Polanski and Jean-Luc Godard took over and interrupted the projection of films in solidarity with students and labor on strike throughout France.

T: I see. It has many awards, too. I think the most prestigious award given out at Cannes is the Palme d'Or, or "Golden Palm" for the best film.

S: The jury of the festival, **made up of** a small international selection of movie professionals, grants other awards, including the Grand Prix, or "Grand Prize"—the second most prestigious award.

T: The films can only win one award, right? However one award from the list may be awarded jointly to more than one movie, with the exception of the Palme d'Or.

S: That's right. There are loads of awards, such as Best Director, Jury Prize, Golden Camera, Best Screenplay, Best Actress, Best Actor, Un Certain Regard Award and the International Federation of Film Critics Prize.

T: They also have awards for short films, don't they?

S: Yes, there are two other awards for short films.

T: Given massive **media exposure**, the non-public festival is attended by many movie stars and is a **popular venue** for movie producers **to launch** their new films and attempt to sell their works to the distributors who come from all over the globe.

S: I'd love to go and see all the film stars. Who knows, I might even get discovered!

T: 老师　　**S**: 学生

T: 安妮，你在做什么呢？写作业吗？

S: 不，我在看电影节方面的书。现在我正看到戛纳电影节。

T: 我认为戛纳电影节应该是最著名的电影节。除了电影节以外，平时的戛纳只不过是法国一个静寂的小镇。

S: 是的，但在举办电影节期间，它又充满生机，而且人流拥挤。

T: 电影节多久举办一次呢？一年一次吗？

S: 是的，每年五月举办。第一次举办是在 1946 年，但戛纳电影节始创于 1939 年。显然，二战期间停办了。

T: 此外，1948 年和 1950 年也因为预算问题没有举办。我想肯定是因为他们前一年的宴会太多太奢侈了。

S: 到 1968 年又停办了。当时评委会的主席路易斯·马勒，以及弗朗索瓦·特吕福，克洛德·贝里，吉恩·加百利·埃比科可，克劳德勒·鲁什，罗曼·波兰斯基，让·吕克·戈达尔联合全法国的学生和工人罢工，接管并阻止了电影节的举办。

T: 我知道了。电影节还有很多奖项。我认为戛纳电影节颁发的最著名奖项就是最佳影片棕榈奖，也叫做"金棕榈奖"。

S: 电影节的评委会是由一小组从国际上精挑细选的电影职业艺人组成，他们负责颁发其它奖项，包括评委会大奖，或者说"戛纳大奖"，也就是电影节的第二著名奖项。

T: 一部电影只可以获得一项大奖，对吗？不过，同一项奖可以颁发给多部电影，金棕榈奖例外。

S: 是这样。奖项很多，比如最佳导演奖，最佳评委奖，最佳摄影奖，最佳剧本奖，最佳女演员奖，最佳男演员奖、特别关注奖和国际联合电影评委奖。

T: 还有电影短片奖，是吧？

S: 是的，有两项奖是针对电影短片而设立的。

T: 假如媒体对戛纳电影节再多关注一下的话，这一民间的电影节会有更多电影明星出席。同时，这也是许多电影制片人喜欢的聚集地，他们在此发布新片，并试图向来自世界各地的发行者出售影片。

S: 我很想去看看所有的电影明星。谁知道呢，说不定我也有可能被星探发现呢！

■ it really comes alive　充满生机
■ lavish party　铺张奢侈的晚会
■ media exposure　媒体曝光
■ launch　发行
■ budgetary problem　预算问题
■ make up of　由……组成
■ popular venue　受欢迎的聚集地

35. Perfume

香水

K: *Katherine* **J**: *Jeanne*

K: What's that incredibly beautiful smell?

J: That's my new perfume, I bought it in France.

K: The French weren't the first to use perfume, though. It was the Egyptians, they used it in a pre-love making ritual. I guess they wanted everyone to smell nice. They used frankincense.

J: They may have been the first, but they are certainly not the most famous. The French **beat everyone** when it comes to perfume. Did you know that perfume is made from twenty two percent essential oils?

K: I didn't know that, no. That's not the highest percentage, though. Eau de parfum is made from twenty three percent essential oils. It says so on the bottle.

J: Eau de toilette is eight to fifteen percent essential oils and eau de cologne is just five percent. I always go for the **alcohol free** eau de parfum, I've found it lasts longer.

K: But there's one with even less essential oils than eau de cologne. It's called eau fraiche, it only has one to three percent essential oils.

J: That one must be only for those who crave super subtlety. It would be too light for me, as I said.

K: There must be many different types of scent, I don't think I've ever found two perfumes that smell the same.

J: There are Floral, Oriental, Floriental, Chypre, Green Marine and Fruit. I usually **wear** a floral **fragrance** with notes of lemon. It's a fresh smell, which reminds me of summer.

K: Where should we put perfume? I think most women **spray** it **on** their necks and wrists, but there must be a special rule about where you should spray it.

J: Actually, there is. It should be applied to the body's pressure points which are inside the elbows and wrists, the backs of the knees and the neck. After spraying we should never rub our wrists together, it crushes the fragrance.

K: I think the most famous perfume is Chanel No. 5, even Marilyn Monroe wore it. She even put it on before she went to bed!

J: Chanel No. 5 is definitely the most popular, one bottle sells every thirty seconds.

K: My goodness! That's a lot of perfume.

K: 凯瑟琳   J: 珍妮

K: 这是什么味？香得出奇。

J: 是我新买的香水。在法国买的。

K: 不过最先使用香水的并不是法国人，而是埃及人。他们在示爱仪式之前使用。我猜他们是想让大家都闻起来舒服些。他们用的是乳香*。

> ＊古埃及历来被认为是香料的发源地。在古代，人们常把鲜花掺在动物脂肪中造出香油涂抹在身上。后来，阿拉伯人发明了从花的浸出物中析出液体制成香水的方法，开始向世界各地输出有名的戈雷香水。18 世纪出现了酒精与香料混合调制的香水，人们对香水表现出异常的热情。法王路易十五的宫廷被称为"香宫廷"。使用香水的习俗也从宫廷流传至民间，使整个巴黎变成了"香都"。

J: 埃及人可能是最先使用的，但肯定不是最有名的。说到香水，没人能与法国人相比。你知道吗？香水是由 22% 的香精油制造而成的。

K: 这个我还真不知道。不过，这不是浓度最高的香水。浓香水是由 23% 的香精油制成的，瓶子上就是这么写的。

J: 淡香水是由 8% 到 15% 的香精油制成的。古龙水只有 5% 的香精油。我一直喜欢不含酒精的香水，我发现这样的香水味道能保留更长久。

K: 但还有一种香水比古龙的浓度还低，叫做清淡香水，只含有 1% 到 3% 的香精油。

J: 那种类型的香水肯定只有那些喜欢特别淡雅味道的人才用。对我来说，我觉得香味可能太淡了。

K: 香水肯定有很多种不同的香味，我想我还没有发现有味道一模一样的两种香水。

J: 有花香、东方调、花香东方调香、柏香、海洋植物香和水果香。我经常用植物型带点柠檬味的香水。它味道清新，让我想起夏天的感觉。

K: 我们应该怎么用香水呢？我想大多数女性都把香水喷洒在脖子和手腕上，但是往哪儿喷香水肯定还有些特别的讲究。

J: 是的，确实有。香水应该洒在人体压力点位置，如胳膊肘和手腕内侧，膝盖和脖子后部。喷洒香水后，不要摩擦两个手腕，因为那会使香味消退。

K: 我想最有名的香水是香奈儿 5 号，连玛丽莲·梦露都用它。她甚至连睡觉前都要喷洒。

J: 香奈儿 5 号的确是最流行的，每半分钟就能卖掉一瓶。

K: 我的天啊，那要卖掉很多了。

■ beat everyone　战胜所有人，无人能与之相比
■ alcohol free　无酒精的

■ wear ... fragrance　用……香型
■ spray on　喷洒在

36. The Brandenburg Gate

勃兰登堡门

T1: *Tourist 1*   *T2*: *Tourist 2*

T1: Hello, I wonder if you can help me. I'm trying to find the Brandenburg Gate.

T2: Actually, I'm going there myself, we can walk together if you want.

T1: OK, great. Where are you from?

T2: I'm from America, but I know Berlin very well, I've visited here many times.

T1: I can't wait to see the Brandenburg Gate, it's such an important part of German history, don't you think?

T2: Yes, indeed. It was formerly a symbol of the divided city, but now it's Berlin's signature attraction.

T1: Definitely, and the architecture is very special. No other landmark is a more **potent reminder** of recent German history. Is it true that the sandstone gate was modelled on the Propylea, the gateway to the Acropolis in Athens?

T2: Yes, that's true. It is crowned by a quadriga, a bronze sculpture of the goddess of victory riding a four-horse chariot.

T1: Ah I see. My friend told me that it's a good place to visit if you have a **tight schedule** because it's a quick stop at about 15 minutes to read about the history and snap a few photos.

T2: Also, there are a few signs around the square that tell a little detail of the history. What do you know about it so far?

T1: I know that the gate was built in the late 18th century as the prominent entrance to the developing town square.

T2: We mentioned the architecture before, but my advice is to not just look from afar. Walk underneath the gate **to see up close** the artistry between the columns, it's very beautiful.

T1: OK, thanks. And the signs, are they in English? Unfortunately I can't read German.

T2: Some of the signs are in English. Luckily for me I can read German, so **if you need a hand** translating just ask.

T1: Great! Here we are! Look over there, if you walk just a bit further to the road, you can see the zigzag path of where the Berlin Wall used to be.

T2: It used **to run through** the current street, it's strange to think that less than 20 years ago this whole area was divided into two.

T1: 游客 1   **T2**: 游客 2

T1: 你好，我不知道你能否帮我个忙？我想去勃兰登堡门＊。

T2: 正好我也要去那里。愿意的话，我们可以一起走过去。

T1: 好的，太好了。你是哪里人？

T2: 我是美国人，但我对柏林很熟悉，我来过这里很多次。

T1: 我非常想去看看勃兰登堡门，它在德国历史上非常重要。你不这么认为吗？

T2: 是的，的确如此。以前它是一个城市分离的象征，但现在却成了柏林的标志性景点。

T1: 一点不错，而且这个建筑很特别，它是德国近代史最有力的见证物。听说这个沙石门是依照希腊雅典卫城的山门修建的，是吗？

T2: 是的，确实是这样。勃兰登堡门顶上有一辆四马双轮的战车，这是一座青铜雕像，雕的是胜利女神在驾驶战车疾行。

T1: 哦，我知道了。我朋友告诉我说如果行程安排紧的话，勃兰登堡门是一个参观的好去处，因为只需在那里短暂停留一刻钟就能了解相关的历史，还能抢拍一些照片。

T2: 此外，广场周围还有一些标牌也讲述了一些历史细节。现在你都知道些什么？

T1: 我知道这个大门是 18 世纪末修建的，作为通往建设中的市中心广场的主要入口。

T2: 我们以前提到过这个建筑，但我建议不要只从远处看，要从大门下面走过去向上近看柱廊间的艺术效果，真的很漂亮。

T1: 好的，谢谢。对了，这些标牌都是用英语写的吗？很遗憾，我不懂德语。

T2: 有些标牌用的是英语。所幸的是我懂德语，所以你需要帮忙翻译的话就尽管问吧。

T1: 太好了！我们到了。看那边，只要往前再走一点儿，就可以看见过去柏林墙所在的那条弯弯曲曲的道路了。

T2: 过去柏林墙就是从现在的这条街道穿过去的，很难想象十几年前这整个地区是一分为二的。

■ potent reminder　能很好地唤起记忆的某事物或情境　　■ tight schedule　计划安排很紧
■ if you need a hand　你是否需要帮忙　　　　　　　　　　■ see up close　走近看
■ run through　穿过

37. Cars（Volkswagen，BMW，Mercedes-Benz）

汽车（大众,宝马,奔驰）

S：Salesman　　**B**：Buyer

S：How can I help you?

B：I'm looking for a German car preferably, but I'm not sure which brand to choose.

S：Here we stock used Volkswagens, BMWs and Mercedes-Benz.

B：OK, great. Can you tell me something about them? I know the word "Volkswagen" means "people's car", right?

S：Yes, before the 1930s, there had been many efforts to create simple cars that everyone could afford, but none **met with profound success**.

B：So who was the first person to succeed with the "people's car"?

S：A man named Ferdinand Porsche, I'm sure you've heard that name before, set up business and made a simple car that everyone could afford.

B：Oh, you must mean the Volkswagen Beetle. Didn't Adolf Hitler have something to do with that?

S：Yes, Porsche **pushed** his idea of a small car **forward** and helped Hitler get a real people's car for the citizens of Germany.

B：I don't really like any Volkswagen models. How about BMWs?

S：BMW began almost 90 years ago, making aircraft engines, motorcycles and then cars.

B：When did they start building cars?

S：In 1927 an Austin Seven produced under licence, began production. BMW bought the company the following year, and this became the company's first car, the BMW 3/15.

B：So BMW's first car wasn't really their's at all! I know that since 2003, BMWs have been produced in Shenyang, China in a joint venture with Chinese manufacturer Brilliance.

S：Have you considered a Mercedes-Benz? Just like BMW, they are excellent quality.

B：In the past I owned an E230, but I don't know too much about the company.

S：Mercedes-Benz was established in the 1880s by two men: Gottlieb Daimler and Karl Benz. Their partnership is long and complicated.

B: Yes, I've read a little about it. Mercedes-Benz was named after Karl Benz's daughter, wasn't it?

S: Actually they were named after the daughter of an Austrian dealer who bought and successfully raced the cars. He went on to help decide some design modifications.

B: Well, if you have any SLK models **in stock**, I'd love to take one for a **test drive**.

S: 销售员　　B: 买家

S: 你想买点什么？

B: 我特别想买辆德国车，但不知道应该选什么品牌。

S: 我们这里库存有二手的大众、宝马和奔驰。

B: 哦，太好了。给我介绍一下好吗？我知道 Volkswagen 一词指的是"人民大众的汽车"，是吧？

S: 是的，1930 年以前，人们曾经多次努力想要生产一些经济型的汽车，这样每个人都能买得起，但都不是很成功。

B: 那么谁是第一个成功地制造出"大众汽车"的人呢？

S: 是一个叫做弗迪南德·保时捷的人，我肯定你以前听过这个名字。他创办了自己的企业，并生产了第一辆人人都买得起的汽车。

B: 哦，你肯定是指大众甲壳虫车。阿道夫·希特勒是不是也跟那款车有什么关系？

S: 是的。保时捷提出了生产小车的建议，并帮助希特勒为德国人民制造了一款属于大众的汽车。

B: 大众汽车的车型我都不喜欢。宝马车怎么样？

S: 宝马公司是大约 90 年前成立的，原来生产飞机引擎和摩托车，后来又生产汽车。

B: 他们从什么时候开始生产汽车？

S: 1927 年在获得许可后，他们开始投入生产叫做奥斯汀 7 型的汽车。第二年宝马公司收购了该公司，所以那辆奥斯汀 7 型汽车也就成了宝马公司的第一辆车，即宝马 3/15。

B: 所以宝马公司的第一辆车并不是它们自己生产的。我知道自从 2003 年以来，宝马公司就和中国沈阳金杯公司合资生产宝马轿车。

S: 你有没有考虑过买奔驰呢？跟宝马一样，奔驰的质量也是一流的。

B: 以前我买过一辆 E230，但我对该公司不是很了解。

S: 奔驰公司是在 19 世纪 80 年代由戈特利，布·戴姆勒和卡尔·奔驰两个人建立的。他们的合作时间很长，关系比较复杂。

B: 是的，我也知道一些。奔驰轿车是以卡尔·奔驰女儿的名字命名的，是吧？

S: 实际上，他们是以一个奥地利商人的女儿命名的。这个商人买了这款车，并在赛车比赛中获胜。他还继续帮助公司决定一些设计修改方案。

B: 好的，如果你们的 SLK 型汽车有现货的话，我想试开一下。

■ meet with profound success　获得很大成功　　■ test drive　试开一下
■ push forward　推动，促进　　■ in stock　有现货，有库存

38. Goethe

歌德

M: *Mary*　　K: *Kate*

M: Hi Kate. Every time I see you you've **got your head stuck in a book**!

K: I'm reading about European poets, this one is about Goethe, who was German.

M: He wasn't just a poet though, was he? He was also a playwright, novelist and natural philosopher. I think his most famous work was his two-part poetic drama *Faust*, which he wrote in the 1800s.

K: It took him a long time to write that one! He began in his 20s and didn't finish until shortly before his death, sixty years later!

M: He died in 1832, didn't he?

K: Yes and he ordered *Faust* to be published after his death.

M: That's why it was his masterpiece, then. He had an inconsistent education, too. His lessons were informal, taught by his father, who was an Imperial Councillor, various tutors and his mother.

K: He must have had some special talent though because by the time he was eight he had grasped Latin, Greek, French and Italian.

M: So, he **was multi-lingual**. When he was sixteen he went to university to study law, because his father wanted him to. But, I think **in his heart** he would have rather studied something like literature.

K: Me too, that's why when he was at university he started to write Rococo poems and lyrics.

M: I think his true love influenced him too. He met Anna Kathchen Schonkopf while he was there.

K: So, that's the girl in his collection of poems called "Annette", it sounds so romantic.

M: Just after that he also wrote some poems which **were put to music**. He was very sick during that time, recovering from a lung infection, I think.

K: Do you know that he wrote about another woman? *The Sorrows of Young Werther*, a novel written in 1774, was about his unrequited love for his friend's fiancée.

M: Really? He was involved in politics too I think. He worked as the Head of Commission for War and Road Construction.

K: There was another woman too, an Italian lady who was beautiful, but uneducated. He finally married her in 1806, but it was a secret.

M: What an interesting life he must have led!

M：玛莉　　K：凯特

> *《浮士德》：歌德诗剧，根据16世纪民间传说写成。浮士德博士终生探求宇宙和人生的奥秘而不得，于是向魔鬼出卖自己的灵魂以换取帮助。在经历了学术、爱情、政治、古典理想和建功立业5个阶段后，于生命的最后时刻，领悟了人生的目的应当是为生活和自由而战。

M: 你好，凯特。每次看到你，你都在埋头看书。

K: 我在看一些有关欧洲诗人的书。这本是关于歌德的，他是个德国人。

M: 不过他不只是个诗人，对吧？他还是个剧作家、小说家和自然哲学家。我认为他最有名的作品是他在19世纪写的分为上下部的诗剧《浮士德》*。

K: 他花了好长时间来写这部戏剧。他从20多岁开始写起，直到60年后他临死之前才完成。

M: 他是1832年去世的，是吧？

K: 是的，他还要求在他死后再出版《浮士德》。

M: 那就是《浮士德》之所以成为他的代表作的原因吧。歌德所受的教育断断续续，所学课程都是非正式的，由他父亲、多位家庭教师和他母亲传授。他父亲是个皇家顾问。

K: 他一定有某种特别的天分，因为他8岁时就已经掌握了拉丁语、希腊语、法语和意大利语。

M: 所以他会说多种语言。他16岁就上了大学学法律，因为他父亲希望他学这个专业。但我认为他心里其实更希望学文学之类的专业。

K: 我也这么认为，这就是他读大学时就开始创作洛可可式诗歌和抒情诗的原因。

M: 我想他的爱情也影响了他。他上大学时遇见了安娜·卡特莎恩·舍恩科普夫。

K: 他诗集里叫"安妮特"的女孩就是指她了，听起来真的很浪漫。

M: 在那之后他又写了一些诗歌，后来这些诗歌都被谱了曲。那段时间他病得很厉害，我想他是肺部感染后正在恢复过程中。

K: 你知道他还写过另外一个女人吗？1774年他写过一部小说叫《少年维特之烦恼》，写的就是他对他朋友的未婚妻那种没有回报的爱。

M: 真的吗？我想他也曾经从过政，做过军事委员会和公路建设委员会的领导。

K: 还有另外一个女人，是个意大利女人，长得漂亮但没受过教育。最后在1806年他娶了她，但那是个秘密。

M: 他的生活一定很有意思！

■ get your head stuck in a 了 book　埋头看书　　■ be multi-lingual　会多种语言
■ in his heart　在他心里　　■ be put to music　被谱了曲

39. Beethoven

贝多芬

M: Man   **W**: Woman

M: Lisa, you're a lady, what would you think of this gift?

W: *The Complete Works of Beethoven*, I'd love it because I'm interested in classical music.

M: Which piece is your favourite?

W: His nine symphonies are probably his greatest achievement, each one an unrivaled masterpiece.

M: These CDs have some other things too. For example, one opera called *Fidelio*.

W: He also wrote 5 piano concertos, piano sonatas and string quartets. I think *Moonlight Sonata* is incredibly romantic.

M: He was deaf wasn't he? Not in the beginning obviously, but he went deaf as he got older. He never married either.

W: Beethoven's personal life was troubled, he fancied lots of women he couldn't have. Around age 28 he started to become deaf, which led him for some time to **contemplate suicide**.

M: If he had killed himself the world would have missed an unbelievable talent. He was really depressed too, which stopped him from composing.

W: Around 1812-1816 he didn't really do anything, only quarrel with his family. Some say that this was because he had **finally accepted the fact** that he would never marry.

M: Well, it seems that many geniuses are a little crazy. He also had strange personal habits such as wearing filthy clothing while washing compulsively.

W: Yes, but besides these problems he worked very well, and wrote many things. His father taught him in the beginning, but unfortunately he was an alcoholic and beat him.

M: Well, there's **no wonder** he went crazy. Luckily, Beethoven's talent was soon noticed by others. That's when his career **lifed off**.

W: We talk about his career in periods: the early, middle and late periods. In his early period he emulated Haydn and Mozart, his middle period began shortly after he found he was going deaf.

M: So this is when we start to see large-scale works expressing heroism and struggle; these include many of the most famous works of classical music.

W： Yes, then his late period is greatly admired for intellectual depth and intense, highly personal expression. He stopped composing in 1826.

M： I'm so happy that you are passionate about Beethoven, because actually the gift's for you. Happy Birthday!

M：男人　　W：女人

M： 丽莎，从女人的角度看，你觉得这份礼物怎么样？

W： 《贝多芬全集》，我会喜欢的，因为我对古典音乐很感兴趣。

M： 你最喜欢哪一首？

W： 他的 9 首交响曲应该是他最大的成就，每一部都是无与伦比的杰作。

M： 这些 CD 里面还有一些其它歌曲。比如，一部叫《费德里奥》的歌剧。

W： 他还写了 5 部钢琴协奏曲、钢琴奏鸣曲和弦乐四重奏。我觉得他的《月光奏鸣曲》相当浪漫。

M： 他是个聋子，不是吗？当然他不是天生就聋，是年纪大了之后变聋的。他一生没结过婚。

W： 贝多芬的个人生活很不平静。他爱过很多女人，但都不能拥有。大约 28 岁时他就开始变聋，为此他有段时间一直想自杀。

M： 他如果自杀了的话，世界上就会少了一个难得的天才。他的情绪也很低落，并因此而无法继续创作。

W： 大约从 1812 年到 1816 年，他真的是什么也没做，只是跟家人吵架。有人说这是因为他最终接受了他将终生不娶这样一个事实。

M： 嗯，好像很多天才都有点疯狂。他还有些个人怪癖，比如穿脏衣服，也不愿意清洗。

W： 是的，但除了这些毛病，他表现得很出色，写了很多作品。起初他父亲教他，但不幸的是后来他父亲开始酗酒还经常打他。

M： 哦，难怪他会变疯。幸运的是，贝多芬的天才很快被别人发现，他的音乐事业也就从此开始了。

W： 我们按照早、中和晚期三个阶段来谈一下他的事业。早期时，他仿效海顿和莫扎特的作品，中期是从他发现自己变聋之后不久开始的。

M： 也就是从这段时期他开始创作表现英雄主义和抗争的大型作品，这里面还包括很多最有名的古典音乐作品。

W： 是的，到了后期他的作品所表现出来的深邃的智慧，强烈、非凡的个人表现力受到人们极大的赞美。1862 年他停止了创作。

M： 我很高兴你这么喜欢贝多芬，因为实际上这个礼物就是送给你的。生日快乐！

■ contemplate suicide　打算自杀　　■ finally accept the fact　最终接受了这个事实
■ no wonder　难怪　　■ lift off　上升

40. Grimm's Fairy Tales

格林童话

G1：Girl 1　　*G2*：Girl 2

G1：Do you remember reading *Grimm's Fairy Tales* when you were little?

G2：The Brothers Grimm? Yes, of course! My favourite was *Hansel and Gretel*, about the children who are abandoned in the woods by their wicked step-mother.

G1：My favourite is *Rapunzel*, about the princess with extremely long hair who was locked in a tower.

G2：**It's funny you should mention** these stories, because I've just read a really interesting book about the history of the brothers.

G1：Me too! That's why **I brought them up**, it was a very interesting read. Jacob Ludwig Carl Grimm was born in 1785, in Hanau, Germany. Just over a year later in 1786, his little brother Wilhelm Carl Grimm was born.

G2：They had a massive family, six more brothers and one sister. Their father was a lawyer, something that Jacob wanted to do originally.

G1：Yes, in 1802, Jacob went to university to study law at the University of Marburg. As always, his little brother followed him, and entered law school in 1803.

G2：It was around that time they started to collect folk and fairy tales. Folklore are stories that have been passed down from parents to children, **by word of mouth**, but at that time many had not been published in books.

G1：The Brothers Grimm were very interested in German folklore and anything that included German culture.

G2：Jacob and Wilhelm published their first book of fairy tales *Children's and Household Tales* in 1812. There were 86 folktales.

G1：Everyone must have been so happy to finally see all of these stories together in one place. It was someone's duty to write them down, because if stories are passed along only orally they can easily be changed or forgotten altogether.

G2: In the next volume of *Grimm's Fairy Tales*, the brothers added 70 more stories. It went on growing like this for six more editions. Finally, the book contained over 200 stories!

G1: You know, I think it's probably the best known work of German literature.

G2: Yes, even if you don't know who the brothers are, you must know at least one of their stories.

G1: 女生 1   **G2**: 女生 2

G1: 还记得你小时候读过的《格林童话》吗?

G2: 是格林兄弟的童话吗? 是的, 当然记得。我最喜欢的是《汉赛尔与格莱特》, 讲的是两个孩子被恶毒的继母丢弃在森林里的故事。

G1: 我最喜欢的是《莴苣姑娘》, 讲的是一个长头发姑娘被锁在一座塔里。

G2: 你提的这些故事还真有意思, 因为我刚好看了一本非常有趣的书, 写的就是格林兄弟的经历。

G1: 这本书我也看过! 这也是我提起他们的原因, 书写得非常有意思。雅各布·路德维格·卡尔·格林 1785 年生于德国的哈瑙。一年多以后, 也就是 1786 年, 他的弟弟威廉·卡尔·格林出生了。

G2: 这是个大家庭, 他们还有 6 个兄弟和 1 个姐姐。他们的父亲是个律师, 雅各布原本也想做律师。

G1: 是的, 到了 1802 年, 雅各布到马堡大学学习法律。一直以来, 他弟弟都紧随其后, 1803 年也进了法学院。

G2: 也就是大约在那个时候他们开始收集民间童话故事。民间传说是人们一代代地通过口头传播而传承下来的故事, 但那时很多都未能结集成册出版。

G1: 格林兄弟对德国民间传说和任何有关德国文化的东西都很感兴趣。

G2: 雅各布和威廉兄弟 1812 年出版了他们的第一本童话集——《儿童与家庭故事集》, 里面有 86 个民间传说。

G1: 看到所有这些故事最终被结集出版, 每个人肯定都很开心。是应该有人把它们写出来, 因为如果这些故事只靠口头留传的话, 很容易变形或消失。

G2: 在《格林童话》第 2 卷, 格林兄弟又增加了 70 个故事。后来像这样又修订出版了另外 6 个版次。最后, 这套书共收集了 200 多个故事。

G1: 你知道, 我认为《格林童话》很可能是德国文学中最著名的作品。

G2: 是的, 即便人们不知道这两兄弟是谁, 也至少肯定知道他们写的其中某个故事。

■ It's funny you should mention . . .   你会提起……还真是有趣。
■ I bring them up.   我提起他们。   ■ by word of mouth   通过口头传播

41. Gandhi

甘地

T: *Teacher*   *S*: *Student*

T: Today I want to talk about Gandhi, or **to be exact** Mohandas Karamchand Gandhi.

S: Ah, Gandhi. Yes, I've heard of him. But I don't know much about him.

T: Don't worry, I can tell you **the basics**.

S: OK, excellent!

T: Gandhi was born in the town of Porbander in Gujurat, on 2nd October 1869. His father was the adviser to the Prime Minister. At that time India was under British rule.

S: Really? What else?

T: In 1888 he went to England to study law, but his parents didn't want him to leave. Also, at this time Gandhi was already a father, he had a daughter.

S: So he left his family to travel overseas?

T: Yes, he completed his law degree in 1891 and then worked as a lawyer for a year or so, but not very successfully. He then moved to South Africa to become an adviser to a businessman.

S: He didn't continue to be a lawyer, then. Why did he **change his path**?

T: **It seemed like a good idea at the time** because he stayed in Africa for over 20 years. He wrote a book during that time called *Satyagraha in South Africa*, but his most famous and best book is *The Story of My Experiments with Truth*. It's very well known.

S: Wow! He sounds like an amazing person. What happened to him?

T: Well, he was sent to prison for 6 years because of the killing of an Indian policeman, but because of his bad health he was released in 1925. He then worked very hard to preserve Hindu-Muslim relations because they are both parts of Indian society. He also worked hard for social reform in India, from hygiene and nutrition to education and labour.

S: He did so much during his life.

T: But, after all this, he was arrested again in 1931 when he went back to India. He really wanted India to be independent. **He spent the last months of his life** helping Hindu and

Sikh refugees who had come from Pakistan. He died as he was walking in a garden at exactly 5:12 pm.

S: Thanks so much for your talk.

T: 老师　　**S**: 学生

T: 今天我要讲讲甘地，或者确切地说是穆罕达斯·卡拉姆昌德·甘地。

S: 哦，甘地。是的，我听说过他的事，但了解得并不多。

T: 别担心，我来告诉你一些基本情况。

S: 好的，太棒了！

T: 甘地 1869 年 10 月 2 日生于古加拉邦的帕班达镇。他父亲是印度总理的顾问，当时印度还在英国的统治之下。

S: 真的吗？还有什么信息？

T: 1888 年甘地去英国学法律，可是他父母不想让他离开。而且那个时候他已经身为人父，有了一个女儿。

S: 那他还是离开家人去海外旅行了？

T: 是的，1891 年他取得了法律学位，然后做了 1 年左右的律师，但不是很成功。随后他去了南非做了一个商人的顾问。

S: 那他就不再当律师了。他为什么要改换职业？

T: 在当时这想法似乎不错，因为他在非洲待了 20 多年。他在那段时间写了一本书，叫《南非的非暴力抵抗运动史》*，但他最有名、写得最好的书是《我体验真理的故事》。这本书人人皆知。

S: 哇，听起来他这个人很了不起。后来又发生什么事了？

T: 后来由于杀了一个印度警察，他被关进监狱呆了 6 年。由于健康欠佳，他在 1925 年获释。此后他努力维护印度教徒和穆斯林的关系，因为它们是印度社会的两大支柱。此外，他还在印度积极推进社会改革，包括卫生、营养、教育和劳动等各个方面。

S: 他一生做了不少贡献。

T: 可是在这之后，1931 年他回到印度后又遭到逮捕。在他生命的最后几个月，他还在帮助那些来自巴基斯坦的难民，包括印度教教徒和锡克教信徒。下午 5 时 12 分整他在花园散步时去世。

S: 谢谢你给我讲了那么多。

■ to be exact　确切地说　　　　■ the basics　基本情况　　　　■ change his path　改变他的职业
■ It seemed like a good idea at the time　在当时好像这主意不错
■ He spent the last months of his life ...　他把生命中的最后几个月用于……

83

India 印度

42. Hinduism

印度教

T: Teacher   *S*: Religious studies student

T: Today we are going to discuss Hinduism. Do you know where the word originated?

S: Yes. It comes from the word "Indus", which is a river in Pakistan.

T: Very good. What else do you know about Hinduism?

S: Well, the first people were the Harrapa, who lived there in around 2500 BC. They carved pictures of gods, but nowadays we can't read their writing.

T: That's true. Some of the gods they drew look like later Hindu gods, such as Shiva and Vishnu. This may have been the beginning of Hinduism.

S: But in 1500 BC the Aryans invaded India and gave them some new gods. A mixture of Indo-European.

T: And the first real evidence is the *Rig Veda*, which is a poem we believed to be written in 1000 BC. **It's written in Sanskrit**, the Hindu language.

S: In that poem they talk about many gods, who are mostly male. They also talk about a medicine they took to help them hear the gods talking to them.

T: Soma. We still don't know what it is made of. They also started to **believe in reincarnation or rebirth**, the idea that when you die, you can come back. If you were bad you came back as an insect, but if you were good you came back as a princess.

S: But later they wanted to change their view on this. That's when they stopped killing animals and offering them to their gods. Later, they gave prayers, food, music and incense as an offering.

T: That's right. Do you know what happened later? Around 500 BC? Something very important happened, which made a certain animal very special.

S: Cows! Yes, between AD 400 and 650 a new god was introduced, whom we call a Mother goddess. Cows were her favourite animal and very sacred to her, so gradually Hindus stopped eating beef. She is also known by many other names, such as Parvati and

84

Kali. She **brings blessings** to Hindus.

T: Remember, sometimes she is also seen as an evil goddess, perhaps known as Kali. Kali had dark skin, huge tusks (like an elephant) and a large red tongue that **sticks out**.

T: 老师   S: 研究宗教的学生

*《梨俱吠陀》：印度现存最古老的诗集。吠陀的本义是知识，梨俱是作品中诗节的名称。其编订年代约为公元前 1500 年，收集诗歌 1028 首。印度传统认为，书中诗歌是从上古流传下来的。诗的内容包括上古神话传说、现实社会生活以及祭祀和巫术，显示了印度最早的哲学思想。

T：今天我们要讨论一下印度教。你知道这个词的来源吗？

S：知道，它取自 Indus 这个词，这是巴基斯坦的一条河。

T：很好。那对印度教你还知道什么？

S：我知道最初生活在印度的民族是公元前 2500 年左右的哈拉帕人。他们雕刻了很多神像，但如今我们还是读不懂他们的文字。

T：没错。他们画的神有些很像后来的印度神，比如湿婆神（印度教的主神之一，作为世界的毁灭者和重建者而被崇拜）和毗湿奴（印度教主神之一，守护之神）。一直以来人们认为这可能就是印度教的起源。

S：但到了公元前 1500 年，雅利安人入侵印度，给他们带来了一些新神，它们是印度和欧洲混合的产物。

T：第一个真实的证据是《梨俱吠陀》*，我们相信这是写于公元前 1000 年的诗篇，是用印度语言——梵语写的。

S：在那首诗里，他们谈到了很多神，大多是男性神。此外，还谈到了他们带来的一种药品，能帮助他们听到神跟自己的谈话。

T：是苏麻液（能令人致醉的一种植物液汁）。目前我们还不知道这种药的成分。此外他们还开始相信轮回或再生，就是说人死了以后还能重生。如果你是坏人那就只能投胎做昆虫，但是如果你行善，那你就能投胎当公主。

S：但是后来他们改变了观点：不再屠杀动物，不再向神供奉动物。再后来，他们就开始祈祷，向神供奉食物、音乐和熏香。

T：你说得一点不错。那你知道后来又发生什么事了吗？大约公元前 500 年的时候？当时发生了非常重要的事，这使得某种动物具有了非常特殊的意义。

S：是牛！那是公元 400 年到 600 年间，引进了一个新神，我们称她母神。牛是她喜欢的动物，对她来说也是很神圣的动物，所以慢慢地印度人就不吃牛肉了。她还有很多其他的名字，如帕凡提女神和卡莉女神。她赐福给印度人民。

T：别忘了，她有时还被人们看作是邪恶的女神，也许就是大家熟知的卡莉。她皮肤黝黑，长着巨大的象牙（像只大象），还有一个伸出来的大红舌头。

■ be written in Sanskint   用梵语写作的   ■ believe in reincarnation or rebirth   相信轮回和重生
■ bring blessing to ...   赐福保佑……   ■ stick out   伸出，突出

43. The Ganges

恒河

T: Tourist　　*L*: Local

T: This is a beautiful spot and there are so many people here. Could you tell me why the Ganges is so significant?

L: Firstly, the Ganges is also known as the Ganga. The history of this river is as long as Indian history itself. Everyone loves this place, almost like a mother.

T: So, I guess it's very important. Tell me, what are those people doing over there?

L: They are bathing and washing their hair. Hindus believe that the Ganges can purify you if you wash yourself in its waters.

T: Oh, I see. Kind of like a religious **communal bath**, right?

L: Yes. The Ganges is a very long river and people from many towns visit and enjoy it, everyday. It's an important part of life for many people.

T: Do many tourists come here? I mean, when they come here, do they know its real significance or just look at its beauty?

L: Many foreigners come to see the many festivals we hold on its banks, throughout northern India. We have Kumbh Mela, which is based on a tale of a special drink, Makar Sankranti, which celebrates the journey of the sun using kites, and Magh Mela, where many people actually live in tents on the river banks in celebration. On eclipses we also have bathing festivals, that is what you are seeing today.

T: Why is today so special?

L: Today is actually a part of Kumbh Mela, so it's a very special day. Kumbh Mela is only celebrated every 12 years and this year we have a double celebration, because of the eclipse. The water may be icy, but that will not stop a **true believer** from bathing.

T: It is very cold today. Do people bathe here **whatever the weather**?

L: It is a holy festival, so yes, we must all **brave the cold**. We come here to wash away our sins, just like a Catholic when he goes to church to confess everything he has done. We believe the Ganges has incredible powers that can wash everything away.

T: It sounds like I have picked an amazing time to visit. Thank you so much for telling me all about it.

T: 游客　　L: 当地人

T: 这个景点很漂亮，可是人也不少。你能给我讲讲为什么恒河那么重要吗？

L: 首先，大家都知道恒河也叫 Ganga。这条河的历史跟印度历史一样悠久。所有的人都热爱这个地方，就像爱自己的母亲一样。

T: 所以我想这条河一定很重要。给我讲讲，那些人在那里做什么？

L: 他们在洗身体和头发。印度人相信在恒河里沐浴会洗去一切罪过。

T: 噢，我明白了。有点像宗教意义上的共浴，对吧？

L: 是的。恒河是条很长的河流，每天来自很多城镇的人们都来此参观和欣赏。对很多人来说，这是生活中的重要组成部分。

T: 是不是很多游客也来这里？我是说，他们到这儿旅游的时候知道这个地方的真正意义吗？还是只观赏一下美景？

L: 很多外国人来这里观看我们在整个印度北部河岸举行的各种庆祝活动。我们有大壶节（贡普节），这是根据一种特殊的酒的传说而得名的。还有风筝节，用风筝庆祝太阳的行程，以及印度历的"十一月节"，那时很多人实际上是住在河岸的帐篷里举行庆祝活动。在天蚀日，我们还有洗浴节，就是你今天看到的这一切。

T: 为什么今天是个特殊的日子？

L: 实际上今天还属于大壶节，所以非常特殊。大壶节每 12 年才庆祝一次，今年因为有天蚀，我们要庆祝两次。水可能很冰冷，但是那也阻止不了真正的信徒下河沐浴。

T: 今天是很冷。这里的人们是不是什么样的天气都洗浴？

L: 这是个神圣的节日，所以要洗浴，大家都必须勇敢面对冰冷的河水。我们来这里就是为了洗去我们的罪过，就像天主教徒去教堂忏悔他所做的一切一样。我们相信恒河有令人难以置信的力量，能把一切罪过洗掉。

T: 好像我来得正是时候。非常感谢你给我讲了那么多东西。

■ communal bath　共浴
■ whatever the weather　无论天气怎样
■ true believer　真正的信徒
■ brave the cold　勇敢面对冰冷的河水

44. Sacred Cows

圣牛

S: *Student*   *H*: *Hindu classmate*

S: Hey Raj. Why didn't you try the beef curry?

H: I'm glad you enjoyed it, but unfortunately, I don't eat beef.

S: You mean you don't eat meat. You're vegetarian?

H: No, no. I just don't eat beef, **for religious reasons**.

S: Oh, I'm sorry. I didn't know.

H: I'm a Hindu, you see. We never eat beef. To us, the cow is a sacred animal, we can't harm one in any way. We definitely can't eat one!

S: Oh, right. I heard some stories about cars stopping to let cows cross the road in Dehli. You must really love them. Why are they so important in your religion?

H: In Hinduism animals are respected like humans, many Hindus don't eat any meat at all.

S: But, I mean, why? Why cows? Why not chicken, or ducks?

H: Many believe it comes from the god Krishna, he is one of Hinduism's most **prominent figures**. When he first appeared 5,000 years ago, he was a **cow herder**, like a shepherd, but for cows. He became known as "the child who protects the cows". Krishna is also known by another name, Govinda. This means "one who brings satisfaction to the cows".

S: So, this Krishna is very important in your religion.

H: Yes, in all Hindu nations, such as India and Nepal. Milk has **religious significance**, especially during rituals.

S: Oh, really?

H: Well, drinking milk, which to us is the symbol of charity and generosity, is very important in family life. We use it to feed our babies and for a special type of butter called "ghee".

S: I see. So milk is more important than meat to the farmers in India.

H: Exactly. So, that's why I don't eat beef.

S: Your faith sounds very interesting, I hope one day you can tell me even more about it.

H: It would be my pleasure. Hinduism has a very long history and we have so many gods! I could talk and talk about it for days and never cover all of it.

S: 学生　　**H**: 印度同学

S: 嗨，雷伽。你为什么不尝尝咖喱牛肉？

H: 很高兴你喜欢吃这种食品，但遗憾的是我不吃牛肉。

S: 你是说你不吃肉。你是素食主义者？

H: 不，不是。我只是因为宗教的原因不吃牛肉。

S: 噢，对不起，我不知道这些。

H: 我是印度教徒你明白了吧。我们从来不吃牛肉。对我们来说，牛是神圣的动物，无论如何我们都不能伤害它们。我们也绝对不会吃它！

S: 哦，你说得没错。我听说过一些故事，说在新德里汽车都停下来让牛过马路。你们一定很爱牛。为什么在你们印度教中它们那么重要？

H: 在印度教中，动物受到跟人一样的尊重，很多印度人什么肉都不吃。

S: 可是，我是说，这是为什么？为什么是牛，而不是鸡或鸭？

H: 很多人认为这源于牧牛神克里希那，他是印度教最著名的人物之一。在 5000 年以前他首次出现时，只是个牧牛人，就像牧羊人一样，不过看管的是牛。后来他成了人人皆知的"保护牛群的孩子"。克里希那还有另外一个人人皆知的名字，即葛文达，意思是给牛带来快乐的人。

S: 所以，这个克里希那在你们印度教中非常重要。

H: 在所有的印度国家，如印度和尼泊尔，确实是这样。牛奶也有宗教意义，尤其在举行宗教仪式时。

S: 噢，真的吗？

H: 是的，对我们来说喝牛奶是慈善宽厚和慷慨大方的象征，在家庭生活中非常重要。我们用牛奶喂养孩子，并制成一种特殊的牛油，叫"酥油"。

S: 我明白了。所以对印度的农民来说，牛奶比肉更重要。

H: 一点不错，这就是我不吃牛肉的原因。

S: 你们的信仰听起来很有意思，希望有一天你能再给我多讲讲。

H: 那将是我的荣幸。印度教历史悠久，我们有那么多的神，就是说上好多天我也说不完。

■ for religions reason　宗教信仰的缘故　　■ prominent figures　著名人物
■ cow herder　牧牛人　　　　　　　　　■ religious significance　宗教意义

45. Bollywood

宝莱坞

P: *Person looking for a DVD*   *V*: *Video store assistant*

P: Hi. I hope you can **give me a hand**. I've seen all of the new Hollywood movies and now I want **to try something new**. I don't know what, just something different.

V: Why not try a Bollywood movie?

P: No, I've told you I've seen all of the new **Hollywood releases**, I want something different.

V: Not Hollywood, Bollywood. India's movie industry, well, Mumbai's movie industry to be exact. The name comes from a combination of "Bombay" (the old name for Mumbai) and "Hollywood". It's becoming very popular nowadays, not just for Indians, for everyone.

P: OK. What style are Bollywood movies?

V: They are usually musicals, based on love stories, with male and female **leading actors**. There's lots of dancing too.

P: Well, that does sound different! Can you give me some more information, please?

V: Bollywood is a massive movie industry, maybe the biggest in the world. It has been going for nearly nine decades! That's a long time, but the love story/musicals didn't become popular again until the late 1980s. The first Bollywood movies were silent. Now, the budgets for these movies are low by Hollywood standards, just like the Hong Kong movie industry. Low budget, but big success.

P: I don't think I would be too interested in the old movies. How about the newer ones? Love stories and musicals, you say?

V: Yes, and lots of fun to watch. **Over the years** there have been about 27,000 **feature film** and more being made each year.

P: It sounds like I have a massive choice. Which would you recommend?

V: Well, be prepared for a long evening of viewing. Most Bollywood movies last for around 3 hours, but have many different elements. As I mentioned before, song and dance, **love triangles**, stunts and comedy are all major parts of Bollywood movies.

P: How about this one? It looks new and pretty interesting ... yes, as you said, a love triangle. Two men love one girl, it looks funny and has lots of singing and dancing. All the ingredients for a perfect Bollywood movie, right?

V: Yes! This one is very popular, I'm sure you will like it.

P: Thanks a lot. When I've watched it I'll let you know my opinion.

P: 找 DVD 的人　　V: 音像店助手

P: 你好，我希望你能给帮我个忙。所有好莱坞的新电影我都看过了，现在我想看点别的。我不知道有什么与众不同的好影片。

V: 为什么不看看宝莱坞的电影？

P: 不行，我告诉过你，好莱坞发行的所有新电影我都看过了，我想看点别的。

V: 不是好莱坞，是宝莱坞。这是指印度的电影产业，确切地说，是孟买的电影产业。这个名字是由 Bombay（孟买的旧称）和 Hollywood 这两个词组合而成的。如今，宝莱坞越来越为大众所喜爱，不只是印度人，而是所有的人。

P: 好吧，那宝莱坞的电影风格是什么样的？

V: 这些影片一般是音乐喜剧，以爱情故事为主，配有男女主角，还有很多舞蹈。

P: 听起来确实与众不同！请你再给我多说说，好吗？

V: 宝莱坞是一个庞大的电影产业，也许是世界上最大的。它已经运营了将近上百年，历史悠久。但直到 20 世纪 80 年代末，其爱情故事片和音乐喜剧才再一次受到观众的欢迎。第一部宝莱坞影片是无声电影。现在，按照好莱坞的标准，这些电影的预算很低，就像香港电影公司一样：小成本，大成功。

P: 我想我不会对老电影感兴趣。有新一点的影片吗？你刚才说的爱情故事片和音乐喜剧？

V: 有，看这些影片很有意思。这些年来，宝莱坞生产了大约 27,000 部故事片，而且每年都呈上升趋势。

P: 听起来好像我的选择余地很大。你给我推荐什么片子？

V: 嗯，准备好熬夜吧。大多数宝莱坞电影的长度有 3 个小时左右，但有很多不同的风格。就像我刚才提到的，宝莱坞电影主要有歌舞、三角恋爱、特技和喜剧。

P: 这个怎么样？看起来很新，也很有意思……是的，正像你所说的，是个有关三角恋的片子。两个男人爱上同一个女孩，看起来很搞笑，还有很多歌舞。一个完美的宝莱坞影片应包括的所有要素都有了，是不是？

V: 没错！这部影片很受欢迎，我保证你会喜欢的。

P: 太谢谢了。看完之后，我会把我的感受告诉你。

■ give me a hand　帮我个忙
■ Hollywood releases　好莱坞发行的电影
■ over the years　多年来
■ love triangle　三角恋

■ try something else　想尝试点别的
■ leading actor　主角
■ feature film　故事片

46. Babylon

巴比伦

F1: Friend 1   **F2**: Friend 2

F1: What are you doing?

F2: Some strange **internet searches** about Babylon!

F1: Babylon? Where's that?

F2: It's actually in Babil Province, Iraq. Around fifty miles south of Baghdad, but nowadays it doesn't really exist anymore.

F1: Isn't the word Babylon Greek? In the *Bible*, in *Genesis*, it's translated from "Babel", which means "confusion".

F2: Yes, it's **a variant of** Akkadian "Babilu", which means "Gateway of the God". Iraq didn't exist then, it was called Mesopotamia.

F1: The Hanging Gardens of Babylon ... it says here that they were one of the Seven Wonders of the Ancient World!

F2: It was the holy city of Babylonia from around 2300 BC.

F1: 2300 BC! The oldest mention of Babylon is even before that, though.

F2: They found a **stone tablet**, from 2400 BC, during the reign of Sargon of Akkad, whoever he was.

F1: Ancient kings always have such interesting names. It says that after that its power and population waned. I wonder why?

F2: It seems like it was controlled by many different types of people, maybe the locals never knew where their next king would come from.

F1: They didn't mind too much, because here it says that Babylon was perhaps the biggest city in the world, from 1770-1670 BC, and again from 612 and 320 BC.

F2: Yes, its population was over 200,000 people. In those days that was a massive amount of people.

F1: The design of the city sounds pretty interesting, too. They built it on both sides of the Euphrates River, and joined the sides together to form a square. Can you still see it today?

F2: I think so, because in the 1980s Saddam Hussein started to rebuild the city.

F1: It says here that he put his name on every single brick ... why?

F2: It's because when the ancient kings built the city, they engraved on the bricks who built what.

F1: He also **installed a** huge **portrait** of himself. The local people must have stolen all of these things since Saddam's downfall.

F2: Yes, and they've stopped the reconstruction project. It's a shame that a place which was once so beautiful is now only famous for war.

F1：朋友 1　　F2：朋友 2

F1：你在干什么？

F2：搜索一些有关巴比伦的网站！

F1：巴比伦？它在哪儿？

F2：它本来在伊拉克的巴比省，巴格达以南约 55 英里的地方，但如今已经消失不存在了。

F1：巴比伦这个词是不是希腊语？在《圣经·创世纪》中，这个词是从"巴别"*翻译而来的，意思是"混乱"。

F2：是的，它是古阿卡德语 Babilu 的变体，意思是"神之门"。那时根本就没有伊拉克，叫美索不达米亚*。

F1：巴比伦的空中花园……据说这是世界七大奇迹之一。

F2：大约在公元前 2300 年，它是巴比伦尼亚的圣城。

F1：公元前 2300 年！不过，最早提到巴比伦的时间比这个还要早。

F2：他们曾发现了一座公元前 2400 年的石碑，大约在阿卡德王国萨尔贡统治时期，谁知道呢。

F1：古代国王总是用这样有趣的名字，据说在此之后，该国的势力越来越小，人口越来越少。我想知道这是为什么？

F2：好像该国后来政权频繁更迭，当地人或许永远不会知道他们的下一任国王是哪里人。

F1：他们对此并不介意，因为据说巴比伦在公元前 1770 年至公元前 1670 年，以及公元前 612 年至公元前 320 年期间，有可能是世界上最大的城市。

F2：是的，当时的人口有 20 多万。在那个时代，算是相当多了。

F1：那个城市的设计也非常有意思，建在幼发拉底河两岸，两边相连组成了一个广场。现在还能看到吗？

F2：我想还能看到，因为在 20 世纪 80 年代，萨达姆·侯赛因开始重建这座城市。

F1：网上说他把自己的名字写在每块砖上……为什么？

F2：这是因为古代国王建设该城市时，他们在砖上都刻上建设者的名字和功绩。

F1：萨达姆还给自己竖了一个巨大雕像。他倒台后，这些东西一定都被当地人偷走了。

F2：是的，而且他们已经停止了重建项目。令人遗憾的是，曾经这么美的一个地方现在竟然因为战火连绵而闻名。

■ internet searches　互联网搜索　　■ stone tablet　石碑
■ a variant of . . .　……的变体　　■ install a portrait　建立一座雕像

47. Music and Dance

音乐和舞蹈

S1: Student   *S2*: Foreign student

S2: What are you listening to? It sounds very lively.

S1: This is Irish music, the type usually played in bars for celebrations. But there are many different kinds of Irish music, you know.

S2: What instruments do they use for this kind of music?

S1: The human voice is the oldest instrument we know, so as we expect, there is a very old tradition of songs in Irish music.

S2: So, in old Irish music they always sang?

S1: The oldest Irish songs were **sung A Capella**. The voice was also used as an instrument for accompanying dancers when no instruments were available.

S2: If instruments were available, what did they use? I've heard of something called the Irish **bag pipes**. Are they like the Scottish ones?

S1: Irish bag pipes are a very different instrument from **their more famous cousin**, the Highland bagpipes played by military bands.

S2: I see, any others? The violin?

S1: Yes, the fiddle is extremely popular, that's what they are playing in this song.

S2: What about drums? I think that there is a special Irish drum, right?

S1: A "bodhran", which is pronounced "bow-ran".

S2: The Irish love a party, but what kind of dancing do they do? I've heard of something called a jig. And I saw something called "Lord of the Dance", a stage show.

S1: In Irish dancing, the stage was sometimes even a **table top**! Irish dancers wear special shoes with buckles. The expression "cover the buckle" means crossing your feet so rapidly while dancing that the shine of the buckle covered the entire area.

S2: Yes, they move their feet and legs very quickly indeed.

S1: There are four types of Irish dance music: the jig, reel, hornpipe, and the set dances. The jig is the most graceful with light hopping, sliding, skipping and pointing.

S2: So, that one is just for women. Which dances do men do? Or do mostly men and women dance together?

S1: Both men and women dance the reel, hornpipe and the set dances.

S2: I'd love to learn some, it just seems so different from other dancing, so happy and full of energy.

S1: 学生　　**S2**: 外国学生

S2: 你在听什么？好像很动听。

S1: 是爱尔兰音乐，酒吧里搞庆祝活动时通常演奏的那种。不过你知道，爱尔兰音乐有很多种。

S2: 这个乐曲是用什么乐器演奏的？

S1: 我们知道，人类的声音是最古老的乐器，所以爱尔兰音乐中唱歌具有非常古老的传统。

S2: 那么，在古老的爱尔兰音乐中，他们都是一直唱歌了？

S1: 最古老的爱尔兰歌曲是"无伴奏歌唱"。在没有乐器的时候，用声音当乐器来给舞蹈者伴奏。

S2: 有了乐器之后他们用的是什么？我听说过一种叫爱尔兰风笛的乐器，跟苏格兰的风笛一样吗？

S1: 爱尔兰风笛与比它们更有名气的同类——英格兰高地风笛差别很大，后者用于军乐队演奏。

S2: 我知道了，还有什么乐器？小提琴呢？

S1: 是的，小提琴非常受欢迎，这首曲子就是用小提琴演奏的。

S2: 那鼓呢？我记得有一种特殊的爱尔兰鼓，是吗？

S1: 是宝兰鼓，读作 bow-ran。

S2: 爱尔兰人喜欢聚会，那他们跳哪种舞？我听说过一种吉格舞。我也看过一种"舞蹈之王"的舞台表演。

S1: 在爱尔兰舞蹈中，有时甚至桌面就是个舞台！舞蹈演员穿着特殊的带扣鞋。词组"遮住扣子"的意思就是在跳舞时迅速交叉双脚，这样扣子的光泽就会遍及脚步所及之处。

S2: 是的，他们变换脚步的速度的确非常快。

S1: 爱尔兰舞曲有四种：吉格舞、里尔舞、角笛舞和方形舞。吉格舞是最优雅的一种，伴着动作轻快的单脚跳、滑行、蹦跳和脚尖着地。

S2: 所以，这种舞只适合女性跳。那男人都跳什么？或者说通常情况下男人和女人一起跳舞吗？

S1: 男女都跳里尔舞、角笛舞和方形舞。

S2: 我很想学一种，好像爱尔兰舞蹈与其他舞蹈都不一样，它是那么快乐、充满活力。

■ sung A Capella　无伴奏合唱　　　　　　　■ bag pipes　风笛
■ their more famous cousin　比它们更有名的同类　■ table top　餐桌桌面

95

48. The Pub

酒馆

M1: Man 1　　*M2*: Man 2

M1: Are you busy later? I'm going to that new Irish bar, do you fancy coming with me?

M2: Yes, OK. But I'm sure it won't be at all like the real pubs in Ireland.

M1: What's the difference?

M2: In Ireland, pubs or public houses **began very differently to how they are today**. Before, most households were self-sufficient, brewing enough of their own ale for **day to day needs**.

M1: That sounds more like a "personal house" not a "public house"! What changed?

M2: It didn't take long for people to see the benefits in brewing more beer and selling it.

M1: So they made their houses into little shops?

M2: Yes, these makeshift "beer-shops" were usually attached to simple stores that sold potatoes, butter, bread and other necessities.

M1: But in shops people buy what they want and go home. They don't stand around drinking.

M2: Customers who visited these shops would stop to sample the brews and would perhaps linger to chat a while as friends or neighbours came and went.

M1: Oh, I see. These simple beer-shops marked the birth of what has become a global institution: the Public House.

M2: Irish pubs developed from the local grocery shop, where beer was sold as one of life's staples, and from the country cottages, where villagers met and travelers had a rest.

M1: What beers do they sell? English pubs sell lager, ales and spirits.

M2: Of course, Irish pubs sell Guinness! It's a black beer with a very special flavour.

M1: Yes, I've tried that and I like it. Tonight, I'm going to have a few pints. What else?

M2: They also sell a local Irish whiskey, called "Poteen". It's very strong, so strong in fact some people believe that if you drink too much you'll go blind!

M1: I don't think I'll try any of that, then. What about entertainment? In English pubs they have **fruit machines**, where you can gamble and traditional pub games like dominoes.

M2: Irish pubs often have **live music**, called "session music". Many musicians, who play a whole range of instruments come and play together.

M1: Sounds great! Like a party. I hope they have some live music tonight.

M1: 男人1　　M2: 男人2

M1: 一会儿你有空吗？我想去新开的爱尔兰酒吧坐坐，想跟我一起去吗？

M2: 好的，没问题。不过我敢保证那根本不像真正的爱尔兰酒吧。

M1: 有什么不同？

M2: 在爱尔兰，最初的酒馆或酒吧跟现在的大不一样。从前，大多数家庭都是自给自足，自己酿造的麦芽酒足以满足日常需要。

M1: 听起来更像私人住宅而不是聚会场所！后来发生了什么变化？

M2: 没过多久，人们发现多酿些啤酒，然后再卖掉能使他们从中获利。

M1: 所以他们就把自己的房子变成了小商店？

M2: 是的，这些临时的"啤酒商店"通常跟一些卖土豆、黄油、面包和其他日用品的小商店连在一起。

M1: 不过人们在商店买完自己想要的东西就回家，他们不在那里停留喝酒。

M2: 后来，光顾这些商店的顾客会停下来尝尝酒，也许会在朋友或邻居进出时逗留一会儿跟他们聊聊天。

M1: 哦，我知道了。这些简易的啤酒店就标志着酒馆的诞生，它现在已经遍及全球。

M2: 爱尔兰酒吧由当地的杂货店和小村舍发展起来。在杂货店，啤酒被当作人们生活的基本食品来卖，而村舍则是村民们见面和游客休息的地方。

M1: 他们卖什么啤酒？英国酒吧卖贮藏啤酒、麦芽酒和白酒。

M2: 爱尔兰酒吧当然卖的是健力士酒！这是一种风味独特的黑啤酒。

M1: 是的，我以前尝过，很喜欢。今晚我想喝上几杯。那儿还卖什么酒？

M2: 他们还卖一种爱尔兰当地的威士忌酒，叫卜丁酒。这是一种烈性酒，事实上有人认为这种酒如果喝太多的话，会失明的。

M1: 那我想我还是不喝这种酒了吧。有什么娱乐活动吗？英国酒吧有水果老虎机，能赌博；还有传统的酒吧游戏，像多米诺骨牌。

M2: 爱尔兰酒吧经常有现场音乐会，叫"即兴音乐表演"。弹奏各种不同乐器的音乐人来这里相聚、演出。

M1: 听起来太棒了！像个聚会。希望他们今晚能有现场音乐表演。

■ begin very differently to how they are today　开始时与现在的大不一样
■ day to day needs　日常需要　　■ fruit machine　水果老虎机　　■ live music　现场音乐会

97

49. Literature

文学

W1: *Woman 1*   **W2**: *Woman 2*

W1: I'm starting a new course next week, all about Irish literature.

W2: I did a summer course last year. Irish literature is written in two languages, English and Gaelic.

W1: I hope the Gaelic is translated! The oldest Irish literature consists of stories and poems about ancient kings and heroes, which **were transmitted orally** in Irish.

W2: The written literature didn't begin until **Christian missionaries** arrived in the 5th century AD and introduced the Roman alphabet, which was then adapted to the Irish language.

W1: In Irish literature I think that Christianity and Irish traditions **go hand in hand**. Another influence on Irish literature, after Christianity, was colonization from England, which began in the 12th century.

W2: Yes, Anglo-Irish writers dominated Irish literature during the 17th and 18th centuries. But by the 19th century, they wanted to revive Gaelic culture and the Irish language. These movements **linked** literature **with** the cause of Irish political and cultural independence from Britain.

W1: I think we will mainly focus on modern Irish literature. Wit and humor—often in the form of satire or irony—have characterised much of Irish literature. That's why I enjoy reading it so much.

W2: Another defining feature has been an exploration of the riches of language and an enjoyment of wordplay. A love of language is definitely evident in Irish literature.

W1: Who's your favourite author? At the moment I'm reading Seamus Heaney.

W2: A fabulous writer! His poetry, especially *Digging* reflects farm work.

W1: I've read most of his work, but I particularly enjoyed his wife, Marie Heaney's book *Over Nine Waves*, published in 1994. That book is an important collection of retellings of the classic Irish myths and legends.

W2: I also like the playwright Brian Friel, he did a play called *Translations*. It's all about the mapping of Ireland by the Ordnance Survey in the 1830s and the introduction of the

English language into the Irish school system.

W1: I haven't read him, but he's very famous. I'm sure he will be covered in the course.

W2: Even if he isn't, I would recommend him.

W1: OK, I'll go to the library and see if I can find *Translations*. Thanks.

| **W1**: 女人 1 | **W2**: 女人 2 |

> * 爱尔兰现代文学：20 世纪的爱尔兰文学大师辈出，包括现代主义诗人叶芝、"意识流文学之父"詹姆斯·乔伊斯、戏剧大师萧伯纳、唯美主义文学的代表人物奥斯卡·王尔德、荒诞派戏剧大师塞缪尔·贝克特等。

W1: 下周我要上新课了，是爱尔兰文学课。

W2: 去年我参加了一个夏季课程学习。爱尔兰的文学作品一般是用英语和盖尔语两种语言写的。

W1: 我希望有人把盖尔语翻译过来！古老的爱尔兰文学包括有关古代国王和英雄的故事和诗歌，都是用爱尔兰语口头传播的。

W2: 书面文学直到公元 5 世纪才出现，当时基督教传教士来到爱尔兰，引进了罗马字母，然后被吸收进爱尔兰语。

W1: 爱尔兰文学中，我认为基督教和爱尔兰传统关系密切。除基督教之外，对爱尔兰文学产生影响的另一因素是，从 12 世纪开始的英格兰对爱尔兰的殖民统治。

W2: 是这样，在 17、18 世纪，英裔爱尔兰作家是爱尔兰文学的主流。但是到了 19 世纪，爱尔兰人想复兴盖尔文化和爱尔兰语言。这些运动把文学与爱尔兰争取独立于英国的政治和文化事业联系在了一起。

W1: 我认为我们要把重点放在爱尔兰现代文学 * 上。机智和幽默——通常以讽刺或反语的形式出现——是爱尔兰文学的主要特点。这就是我为什么那么喜欢读爱尔兰文学的原因。

W2: 另一个明显的特征是语言丰富多彩，喜欢文字游戏。爱尔兰人把他们对语言的热爱尽情挥洒在他们的文学中。

W1: 你最喜欢的作家是谁？现在我正在读谢默斯·希尼的诗歌。

W2: 他可是非常伟大的作家。他的诗，尤其是《挖掘》，反映了农场的生活。

W1: 他大部分的作品我都读过，可是我特别喜欢他妻子玛丽亚·希尼写的书《越过九重浪》，1994 年出版。这本书是一本重要的复述集，汇集了爱尔兰的经典神话和传奇。

W2: 我还喜欢剧作家布赖恩·弗莱尔，他写了一个剧本，叫《翻译》。该剧叙述了 19 世纪 30 年代陆地测量部对爱尔兰进行的测绘工作，以及英语进入爱尔兰学校教育体系的过程。

W1: 我没读过他的书，不过他非常有名。我这门课肯定会讲到他。

W2: 即使他没有被列进来，我也要推荐他。

W1: 好的，我要去图书馆，看看能不能找到《翻译》这个剧本。谢谢。

■ be transmitted orally　口头传播　　　　■ Christian missionary　基督教传教士
■ go hand in hand　关系密切　　　　　　■ link with ...　与……相联系

50. Jerusalem

耶路撒冷

G: Guide   **T**: Tourist

T: Can you tell me something of Jerusalem's history?

G: Well, it was founded by King David about 3,000 years ago.

T: So if Jerusalem was a Jewish city why is it also regarded as a Christian and Arab city too?

G: **That's a difficult question!** Christians regard Jerusalem as a Christian city because Jesus lived and died here. Arabs regard Jerusalem as an Arab city because of the Dome of the Rock which is a sacred temple for Muslims.

T: How did the Arabs come to build their temple here?

G: Many wars and crusades were fought here by Christians during the eleventh and twelfth centuries because they felt that because of the Jesus connection that Jerusalem should be a Christian city.

T: **I can understand that** but how did the Arabs make it their city **in the first place**?

G: When the Christians killed all the Jews in the city they occupied it for a while but the Arabs finally captured it and held it for many centuries until the British captured it in 1917 and then Israel was created a new nation in 1947.

T: So how do all these religions live happily together?

G: **To be honest** they don't. But Jerusalem is divided into three sections. There's the Old City, New City (West Jerusalem), and East Jerusalem. The walled Old City, in the center, contains Muslim, Jewish, Christian, and Armenian quarters.

T: I see. Can you tell me something about the Wailing Wall?

G: The Western Wall is a remnant of the supporting wall of the Second Temple and now is the most sacred place of Judaism.

T: You call it the Western Wall but it's **more commonly known as the** Wailing Wall. Why is that?

G: The second Temple was built by Herod and although not as magnificent as Solomon's temple yet it was a wonderful temple. Unfortunately it was totally destroyed by the

Romans in AD 70 and only this section remains.

T: So the Jews are wailing because of the loss of their temple, right?

G: Yes, and because they cannot rebuild it because the Dome of the Rock stands on the very site where the temple used to be.

G: 导游　　T: 游客

T: 你能给我讲讲耶路撒冷的历史吗?

G: 好的, 它是 3000 年前由大卫王兴建的。

＊ 圣殿: 古犹太人宗教和政治活动中心, 位于耶路撒冷。相传公元前 10 世纪为所罗门王所建, 称第一圣殿, 后被巴比伦人焚毁。前 6 世纪重建, 前 1 世纪末由希律王扩建, 称第二圣殿。公元 70 年又被罗马人所毁。相传所罗门圣殿中放置着犹太教圣物"约柜", 里面存放着刻有摩西十诫的石板, 即"约板", 是希伯来人一神教信仰的象征。

T: 如果耶路撒冷是犹太人的城市, 那为什么它还被认为是基督教徒和阿拉伯人的城市?

G: 这个问题太难了! 基督教认为耶路撒冷是他们的城市是因为这里是耶稣诞生和受难的地方。阿拉伯人把它当作自己的城市是因为岩石圆顶清真寺是穆斯林的神殿。

T: 那阿拉伯人是如何在这里建起自己的神殿的?

G: 在 11 至 12 世纪, 基督教徒在这个地方进行过多次战争和十字军东征, 因为他们觉得鉴于和耶稣的关系耶路撒冷应该是个基督教城市。

T: 我能理解, 那么阿拉伯人最初是如何来到这个城市的?

G: 基督教徒曾驱逐了该城里所有的犹太人, 并占据了一段时间, 但阿拉伯人却最终占领了该城市达几百年, 一直到 1917 年被英国人接管, 然后就是 1947 年以色列在此建立了一个新国家。

T: 那所有这些宗教是如何友好相处的?

G: 坦白地讲, 他们做不到友好共处。不过耶路撒冷被分成了 3 个区, 旧城区、新城区(西耶路撒冷)和东耶路撒冷。用高墙围起来的旧城在中间, 分为穆斯林居民区、犹太居民区、基督教和亚美尼亚居住区。

T: 我明白了。你给我讲讲犹太人的哭墙, 好吗?

G: 西墙是第二圣殿一段残余的主体围墙, 现在是犹太教最神圣的地方。

T: 你把它叫作西墙, 可是大家更熟悉的是叫哭墙。为什么?

G: 第二圣殿是由希律王建起来的, 尽管不像所罗门建的圣殿＊那么宏伟, 但也非常气派。不幸的是在公元 70 年被罗马人彻底毁掉了, 只剩下这部分残墙。

T: 所以犹太人因为失去自己的神殿就哭了, 对吗?

G: 是这样。而且还因为他们不能再建自己的神殿了, 因为岩石圆顶清真寺正好建在他们的寺庙遗址上。

■ That's a difficult question.　这个问题很难回答。　　■ I can understand that ...　我能理解……
■ in the first place　第一点, 首先　　　　　　　　■ To be honest　坦白地讲, 说实话
■ more commonly known as ...　作为……更为人们所知

51. Jesus

耶稣

I: *Israeli*   *C*: *Christian*

I: Welcome to Bethlehem, the birthplace of Jesus!

C: Thank you! I've always wanted to make a pilgrimage here. Can I see where he was born?

I: No one knows that. Some think he was born in a cowshed and others in a cave. In either case there is nothing remaining here now.

C: How long did he live here?

I: Just for a couple of years until his parents fled to Egypt to avoid persecution from King Herod.

C: I remember, Herod had been told that a king had been born here and so he determined to kill his **potential rival** although Jesus was only a baby.

I: Later Jesus came back to Israel after Herod died and the family lived in Nazareth.

C: There he had several brothers and sisters too.

I: That's right and then when he was thirty years old he began his public ministry around the Sea of Galilee.

C: That's why so many of his early disciples were fishermen like Peter and James and John.

I: And he **did so many miracles** like feeding the 5,000, turning water into wine and walking on water.

C: Not forgetting healing the blind, the lame and the sick. Although I think his greatest miracle was to bring Lazarus **back from the dead**.

I: He was a great teacher and many of the stories he told like the Prodigal Son and the Lost Sheep **have been enjoyed by young and old**.

C: I think the greatest tragedy was that most of his own people, the Jews, never believed that he was the Son of God.

I: The Jews were expecting the Messiah to come but they expected someone who would rid them of their Roman conquerors not one who would be crucified on a cross.

C: We Christians believe that Jesus died for all our sins and that one day he will return to put

102

an end to all wars and suffering.

I: We Jews believe that Jesus was a great prophet but that to call himself God was blasphemy.

C: I understand that. I guess the best thing to do is to understand each other's religion and agree to disagree agreeably, right?

I: Well put!

I：以色列人　　C：基督教徒

I：欢迎来到伯利恒，耶稣诞生地。

C：谢谢！我一直想来这里朝拜。我能看到他的出生地吗？

I：没有人知道具体的地方。有人认为他生在牛棚里，还有一些人认为他在山洞里出生。无论是哪种情况，现在是什么都没有留下来。

C：他在这儿生活了多久？

I：只住了几年，然后为了躲避希律王的迫害，他父母就带他逃到了埃及。

C：我记得，那个时候一直有人告诉希律王，说有个国王诞生于此。为了保住王位，希律就下决心杀死所有可能对他有威胁的人，尽管耶稣当时还只是个婴儿。

I：后来，希律王死后，耶稣又回到了以色列，一家人就住在拿撒勒。

C：就是在这个地方他又有了几个弟弟和妹妹。

I：是这样，然后他30岁时开始在加利利海周围地区传教。

C：这就是为什么他早年的很多弟子都是渔民的原因，比如彼德、詹姆士和约翰。

I：而且他还做了很多奇事，像喂饱了5000人、把水变成葡萄酒、在水上行走等。

C：别忘了他还治好了盲人、瘸子和病人。不过我认为他最伟大的奇迹是让拉撒路起死回生。

I：他还是个伟大的老师，一直以来他讲的很多故事都是老少皆宜，比如"浪子回头"和"迷途羔羊"的故事。

C：我认为最大的悲哀是他的大多数犹太同胞从来就不相信他是上帝之子。

I：犹太人一直盼望着复国救世主弥赛亚的到来，他们盼的是能帮助他们摆脱罗马征服者统治的人，而不是钉死在十字架上的人。

C：我们基督教认为耶稣是为了替我们赎罪而死的，他们相信有一天他会回来结束一切战争和苦难。

I：我们犹太人认为耶稣是个伟大的预言家，但他自称为上帝是对神明的亵渎。

C：这些我知道。我想我们最好能理解各自的宗教，求同存异，和平共处，对吗？

I：说得太好了。

■ potential rival　潜在对手　　　　　■ do so many miracles　施行大量奇迹
■ back from the dead　起死回生　　　■ be enjoyed by young and old　老少都喜欢

52. St. Peter's

圣彼得大教堂

F1: Friend 1   **F2**: Friend 2

F1: What have you got planned for the winter holidays?

F2: Actually, I'm off to Italy.

F1: Really? I went there in 2001, will you go to the Vatican?

F2: I plan to, I think it's something that **you cannot miss**. It's funny, but everyone thinks the Vatican is an ancient place, but in fact it **dates back to** 1929.

F1: Yes, when Mussolini and the Pope signed the Lateran Treaty. Also, it's the world's largest church.

F2: Isn't there a special place where the Pope appears, too?

F1: Yes, there's a balcony which he comes out on, but only **on special occasions**.

F2: What about St. Peter's? Is it as fabulous as they say?

F1: To be honest, **it doesn't look like much from the outside**, you don't appreciate its true beauty and enormity until you are inside.

F2: It really is huge, then?

F1: Oh my goodness! Not just huge, sensational! When you step inside you just cannot believe it, I was **lost for words**.

F2: It sounds like you had a real religious experience there.

F1: Oh yes, I believe that even someone without faith couldn't fail to be touched by something higher while inside St. Peter's.

F2: How big is it really? I read that the pillars inside are fifty feet across, that can't be true, can it?

F1: Honestly, just wait until you are inside. The pillars are massive, and even if there are hundreds of tourists, you never feel cramped. The atmosphere is always so light and airy.

F2: Also, I read that the baldacchino is pretty big, too.

F1: Pretty big! It's more than half the size of Niagara Falls! While you are there, you cannot forget to visit the Sistine Chapel, which is very impressive.

F2: I'm guessing nothing is as impressive as St. Peter's, I can't wait to see it.

F1：朋友1　　F2：朋友2

F1： 寒假你有什么计划呢？

F2： 说实话，我准备去意大利。

F1： 真的吗？2001年我去过那儿，你打算去梵蒂冈吗？

F2： 我打算去，我想那里还真不能错过。有趣的是，人人都以为梵蒂冈是个古老的地方，但实际上它的历史只能追溯到1929年。

F1： 是的，它是墨索里尼和罗马教皇签署了《拉特兰教堂条约》后才建立的，它有世界上最大的教堂。

F2： 那里是不是还有个教皇公开露面的特别地方？

F1： 是的，是有一个教皇出来露面的阳台，但只是在一些特殊的场合用。

F2： 那圣彼得教堂＊呢？是不是跟人们所说的一样神奇啊？

F1： 坦白地说，从外面看不出什么，直到进入里面才能欣赏到它真正的美丽和宏伟之处。

F2： 它真的很大，是吧？

F1： 哦，它不是一般地大，简直让人惊叹！你走进去时，简直没法相信，我都无法用言语表达。

F2： 听起来好像你在那儿真的对宗教有不少体验。

F1： 是的。我相信进了圣彼得教堂，没有人不会被它里面恢宏的气势所触动，哪怕是不信教的人。

F2： 它到底有多大呢？我从书上看到说里面的柱子直径有50英尺，那不可能是真的，对吧？

F1： 真的，等你走到里头再看吧。柱子相当高大，即使里面有几百个游客，你也不会觉得拥挤。里面的气氛也总是很轻松、快活。

F2： 而且我听说青铜祭台大华盖也很宏伟。

F1： 相当大，比尼亚加拉瀑布的一半还要大。你到了那儿时，别忘了去参观一下西斯廷教堂，那也会给你留下很深刻的印象。

F2： 我想没什么能比得上圣彼得大教堂给人的印像更深，我都等不及想去看了。

■ you cannot miss　你不能错过　　■ date back to　追溯到　　■ on special occasion　在特殊场合
■ It doesn't look like much from the outside.　从外面看没什么。
■ be lost for words　无法用言语表达

53. The Coliseum

古罗马竞技场

F1: Friend 1   *F2*: Friend 2

F1: While I'm in Rome, I think I'll visit the Coliseum.

F2: It's a great **tourist attraction**, but **get there early** because of the queues.

F1: Someone told me to get a guide, what do you think?

F2: They are **worth the extra money**, they also give you an insider's view. They tell you things you wouldn't know otherwise.

F1: I see, so they tell you things that weren't in the movie, *Gladiator*!

F2: Outside the gates you can have your picture taken with a real-life gladiator, it's expensive though.

F1: Hmmm ... it has another name too, doesn't it? "Amphitheatre Flavio"?

F2: Yes, and was built by Emperor Vespasian in honour of his empire.

F1: The name Coliseum probably comes from the big bronze statue known as the "Colossus", or giant, that Nero wanted built based on his image.

F2: Later, that statue was moved closer to the amphitheatre by Emperor Hadrian and afterwards modified to look like various emperors and also, with the addition of a "crown of sun rays", the Sun God.

F1: Before, you could watch amazing contests there. I mean, really disgusting things with lots of blood, fights to the death.

F2: Yes, just like in the movie. Around 80,000 spectators followed these combats that could go on **from sunrise to sunset** and sometimes **well into the night**.

F1: Some sports were to kill Christians, too. You know, **throwing Christians to the lions** and all that.

F2: The Coliseum was associated with the persecutions suffered by Christian martyrs, but **according to recent studies**, there is no documented proof to tell us that these slaughters actually happened.

F1: Anyway, in AD 313 the Emperor Constantine proclaimed Christianity the official religion of the empire, obviously forbidding the executions of Christians but also the combats between gladiators and the hunting spectacles.

F2: After that, they used it as a cemetery, then a fortress and then a place to store building materials, which **seems like a waste** of such a beautiful piece of architecture.

F1 : So, a visit to Rome is not complete without making a trip to the Coliseum. I'll go to the bookstore later and get a guidebook.

F1：朋友1　　F2：朋友2

F1：当我到了罗马，我想我会去竞技场看看。

F2：那是个很好的游览胜地，但最好早一点去，因为要排队。

F1：有人要我请一位导游，你怎么看？

F1：额外花钱请导游还是值得的，他们会从内行人的角度给你解说，告诉你一些你无法了解的东西。

F1：我知道了，他们会说一些在电影《角斗士》里看不到的东西。

F2：在门外你还可以跟真正的角斗士合影，不过费用很高。

F1：嗯……竞技场还有一个名字，叫"圆形剧场"，是吧？

F2：是的，它是韦斯帕西恩皇帝为了纪念他的帝国而建立的。

F1：竞技场的名字大概源于那个大家熟悉的大铜像 Colossus，或叫做巨人，那是尼禄*皇帝根据自己的形象竖立的。

F2：后来，铜像又被艾德里安皇帝移到离竞技场更近的地方，此后又按照各个皇帝的样子改造。另外还增加了一个太阳神像，即"阳光王冠"。

F1：以前，在那里你可以看到一些惊人的比赛。我是指非常令人厌恶的场面：流血不止，战斗到死。

F2：是的，就像电影里演的一样。大约有80,000个观众观看这些角斗，从日出到日落，有时候直到深夜。

F1：有些角斗活动还要杀死基督徒，就是把基督徒扔给狮子或其他动物吃。

F2：竞技场跟基督教的殉教者受的迫害也有关系。但根据最近的调查研究，没有文字材料证明这些屠杀真的发生过。

F1：不管怎样，到公元313年，康斯坦丁皇帝宣布基督教为国教，公开禁止残害基督徒，并禁止角斗士和猎物的决斗表演。

F2：之后，他们把那里作为墓地，后来又做了堡垒，接着又用来堆积建筑材料。对这么一个壮丽的建筑来说，好像很浪费。

F1：所以，到罗马旅游一定要去参观竞技场，否则就不完美。待会儿我要去书店买一本旅行指南。

- tourist attraction　游览胜地
- worth the extra money　值得另外付钱
- go well into the night　直到深夜
- throw Christians to the lions　把基督徒扔给狮子吃
- seem like a waste　感觉很浪费
- get there early　早一点到那里
- from sunrise to sunset　从日出到日落
- according to recent studies　根据近期研究

54. Venice

威尼斯

W1 : *Woman 1*　　*W2* : *Woman 2*

W1 : Have you decided where you are going on your honeymoon?

W2 : Steve wants to go to the Maldives, but I fancy Venice.

W1 : Ah, Venice! Everyone knows Venice with its gondolas bobbing on the Grand Canal, a picturesquely decaying city sinking slowly into the waters of the Lagoon.

W2 : But that's not all, it's a surprising place. One surprise is that you will spend most of your time walking—the pavements play as major a role in the city as the canals.

W1 : Yes, and there are no cars. Drivers have to leave their vehicles at the city gate, and that makes exploring the city very enjoyable.

W2 : I think it's better to **go off the beaten track** too, find some little alleys, churches and markets that most tourists don't know about.

W1 : Good idea, most tourists will probably **head for** the Basilica di San Marco, the most exotic of European cathedrals and the Gothic marvel, the Doge's Palace.

W2 : Isn't San Marco the patron saint?

W1 : Yes, that's why St. Mark's Church **is named after** him.

W2 : It used to be a fishing town, you know? 2,000 years ago hunters and fishermen lived on the mudflats. Also, many refugees escaped there to avoid Attila the Hun and later, from other wars.

W1 : Really? By the 1800s Venice, though a popular tourist destination, was poor and decaying. Saved by mass tourism—the Lido became a fashionable resort.

W2 : Before that it was a well-known trading city and was at war with Spain, the Pope and practically every European power.

W1 : I think it's got to be a unique place, it has 116 islands, 150 canals, and 409 bridges, this city is an **intricate maze**.

W2 : And some of the most unexpected architectural delights can be found as you wander around. Heavenly!

W1：Even though there are many tourists, you must do some of the touristy things. You can't go there and miss all of that history. Don't forget to take a trip down the Grand Canal. A ride on a gondola will give you a fascinating view of Venice.

W1：女人1　　W2：女人2

W1：你决定去哪里度蜜月了吗？

W2：史蒂夫想去马尔代夫，但我特别想去威尼斯。

W1：啊，威尼斯！人人都知道威尼斯有冈多拉（黑色平底船）在大运河上穿梭。这是一个风景如画的城市，但现在面临逐渐沉入周围礁湖水域的威胁。

W2：而且不止这些，它还是个不同寻常的地方。其中一怪是你大部分时间都要步行，人行道在城里就像运河一样扮演着重要角色。

W1：是的，而且那里没有汽车。人们得把车辆停在城门口，这样去游览这个城市感觉就会相当愉快。

W2：我认为最好也去一些偏僻的地方看看，找一些大多数游客都不知道的小巷子、教堂和市场。

W1：好主意。大多数游客可能直奔圣马可教堂，这是最富有异国情调的欧洲大教堂，还有哥特式建筑的奇迹总督宫。

W2：圣马可是个守护神吧？

W1：是的，这就是圣马可教堂以它命名的原因。

W2：你知道吗？那里过去是个渔村。2000多年前，猎人和渔夫们住在泥滩上。还有很多难民逃亡到那里以躲避匈奴王阿提拉*以及后来的其他战争。

W1：真的吗？到了19世纪，尽管威尼斯已经成了一个很受欢迎的旅游胜地，但那里还是很贫穷、很衰败。多亏了旅游业，丽都岛变成了一个时尚的度假胜地。

W2：在那之前它是一个有名的贸易城市，当时还在跟西班牙、罗马教皇，实际上是跟每一个欧洲强国做战。

W1：我认为威尼斯是个非常独特的地方，它由116个岛屿，150条运河和409座桥组成，整个城市就是一个复杂的迷宫。

W2：当你在那里漫步时，会发现一些最意想不到的建筑美景。美如天堂！

W1：尽管那里游客很多，你也得游览一些地方。不能到了那里却没机会了解它全部的历史。别忘了在大运河上游览一番。坐上冈多拉会让你将威尼斯的迷人美景尽收眼底。

> * 阿提拉（约406-453）：匈奴帝国国王。在位时一再攻打东罗马帝国，迫其纳贡求和。公元451年在卡塔隆尼之战中被西罗马帝国击败，退至莱茵河以东。第二年再次侵入，经教皇斡旋撤军。453年，阿提拉在婚礼后暴亡，匈奴帝国迅即瓦解。传说阿提拉本人面目可怖，铁骑过处令罗马人心颤、日耳曼人胆寒，在欧洲史中人称"上帝之鞭"。

- go off the beaten track 离开繁忙的街道
- be named after ... 以……命名
- head for 前往，奔往
- intricate maze 错综复杂的迷宫

55. Leonardo Da Vinci

莱昂纳多·达·芬奇

J: James　　**S**: Sophia

J: I've just finished reading a great book, *The Da Vinci Code*, by Dan Brown.

S: I've read it, too. It got me really interested in Leonardo Da Vinci, so I started doing some research.

J: Me too! What did you discover?

S: Well, it sounds like he was a strange, but very gifted man. He was a painter, inventor, architect, engineer, mathematician and philosopher.

J: Yes, a genius **the world has never seen the like of** again so far. He was born in 1452, in Anchiaro, probably in a farmhouse.

S: But his father didn't marry his mother, because she was the daughter of a farmer and not from a wealthy family.

J: Today, all we know about her is her name, Catarina. When he was five years old he moved to a nearby town called "Vinci".

S: It sounds like he was a **precocious child**, his teachers despaired about all the questions he asked and doubts about the world.

J: It seems that many geniuses asked too many questions during childhood! When he was fourteen he moved to Florence where he **began an apprenticeship** in the workshop of Verrocchio.

S: At that time Verrocchio was the most gifted artist in Florence. There's no doubt that Verrocchio had a great influence on Leonardo.

J: He worked with lots of other famous artists, too. Such as Botticelli, Perugino and Lorenzo di Credi.

S: Really? So he was definitely in the company of some great people, their talents must have **rubbed off on him**.

J: In 1472 Leonardo became a member of the Painters Guild of Florence, so he ended his apprenticeship. But he continued to work in Verrocchio's workshop.

S: I read that his first known work was a pen and ink drawing of a valley next to the river Arno. It's drawn from an aerial perspective, this style would later become known as "the perspective of disappearance".

J: After that he created many famous works, *The Baptism of Christ*, *The Annunciation* and of course *The Mona Lisa*.

S: With all of his paintings and inventions, like the first flying machine, it will take us a long time to research everything!

J：詹姆斯   S：苏菲娅

J：我刚看完《达·芬奇密码》，这本书不错，是丹·布朗写的。

S：我也看了。它真的使我对莱昂纳多·达·芬奇产生了兴趣，所以我就开始在这方面做些研究。

J：我也是！你有什么发现？

> ＊达·芬奇：是世界上少有的全面发展的学者，被称为"文艺复兴时代最完美的代表人物"。他不仅是绘画大师，在数学、天文学、物理学、解剖学和生理学上也取得了超越时代的成就，被认为是近代生理解剖学的始祖。达·芬奇的研究和发明还涉及到军事和机械方面，他发明了飞行机械、直升飞机、降落伞、机关枪、手榴弹、坦克车、潜水艇、双层船壳战舰、起重机等等。可以说，达·芬奇的思想和才能深入到人类知识的各个领域。

S：是这样，他看上去很奇怪，但很有天赋。他既是画家，又是发明家、建筑师、工程师、数学家和哲学家＊。

J：是的，一个迄今为止世界上再也找不出来的天才。他 1452 年生于安基亚诺村，可能是在一个农舍里出生的。

S：但他父亲并没有娶他母亲，因为他母亲是个农夫的女儿，不是富家小姐。

J：今天我们只知道他妈妈的名字叫凯特里安。达·芬奇 5 岁时，他搬到了附近一个叫"芬奇"的小镇。

S：听起来他好像是个早熟的孩子，他的老师们都被他提出的问题难住了，也无法向他解释他对周围世界的疑惑。

J：好像很多天才童年时都喜欢问很多的问题！达·芬奇 14 岁时，搬到了佛罗伦萨，在那里他开始在韦罗基奥的画室当学徒。

S：那时韦罗基奥是佛罗伦萨最有天份的艺术家。毫无疑问他对达·芬奇产生了巨大影响。

J：达·芬奇还跟许多其他有名的艺术家工作过，如波提切利、佩鲁贾和洛伦佐·迪·克勒迪。

S：真的吗？那就是说他一定经常接触一些伟人，他们的天才肯定也影响了他。

J：1472 年，莱昂纳多成为了佛罗伦萨画家协会的一员，也因此结束了他的学徒生涯。但他仍然留在韦罗基奥的画室工作。

S：我知道他的第一幅名画是关于亚诺河附近一个山谷的钢笔画。这幅画是用空间透视法画的，这种风格就是后来人人皆知的"明暗渐进法"。

J：此后，他又创造了很多有名的作品，如《基督受洗图》、《天使报喜》，当然还有《蒙娜·丽莎》。

S：他所有的绘画作品和发明创造，就像第一架飞行器一样，要想每样都研究得花我们很长时间。

■ the world has never seen the like of ...   至今世人还没有看到相同的或相似的……
■ precocious child 早熟的孩子   ■ begin an apprenticeship 开始学徒生涯
■ rub off on him 因接触而对他产生了影响

56. Opera

歌剧

M: Man　　**W**: Woman

M: You've been listening to that music **for ages**, what is it?

W: It's an opera, **composed by** Monteverdi.

M: Oh, it's by Monteverdi. It's too old for me! Who invented it anyway?

W: Opera was invented by a group of wealthy people in Florence, who wanted to reproduce ancient Greek dramas.

M: Wasn't the first real opera *Daphne*, by Jacopo Peri, written over 400 years ago?

W: Yes, it was. I'm surprised you know that. Peri's opera is lost, because there were no music publishers then, but we know it existed because so many people wrote comments about the performance of *Daphne*.

M: So, Monteverdi started after this, changing the form into the modern style we know today. He added arias allowing the singers to express the emotions of their characters, and **to show off** their singing abilities.

W: Right, and later on other composers added many other things. For example, chorus parts, dances and instrumental parts. After this, opera grew and changed in many ways.

M: It comes from Italy, right? I mean, all of these composers were Italian, but Mozart was Austrian.

W: That's because it was so popular and **spread to** Germany, France, England, Russia, Spain, Portugal and other countries. But yes, it originated in Italy.

M: Were all of the first operas written in Italian?

W: Yes, even foreigners like Mozart wrote in Italian, but later as it expanded, they started to write in their own languages.

M: OK, so I know it started in Italy and became widespread across Europe pretty quickly, but that doesn't explain how it came to America.

W: European immigrants brought opera to the United States in the 18th and 19th centuries. That's why we have "The Met", or Metropolitan Opera House. It opened in 1883.

M: I see, but why is it still so popular nowadays? Opera fans still love to attend operas at "The

Met."

W: Most operas on at "The Met" nowadays are 18th and 19th century ones, written by Mozart, Puccini, Wagner, and so on. I guess people just find them incredibly beautiful, I know I do!

M: It is an interesting topic, but I think I'll stick to my pop music.

M: 男人   W: 女人

M: 这首乐曲你听很久了，是什么音乐？

W: 是蒙泰威尔第创作的一部歌剧。

M: 噢，是蒙泰威尔第的。对我来说太古老了。歌剧到底是谁发明的？

W: 歌剧是由佛罗伦萨的一群富人创作发明的，他们想重现古希腊戏剧。

M: 第一部真正的歌剧《达芙妮》是不是400多年前由雅各布·佩里写的？

W: 是的。这个你也知道，真让我大吃一惊。佩里的歌剧已经遗失了，因为那时没有音乐出版。不过，我们知道有这部歌剧是因为很多人就《达芙妮》的演出写了不少评论。

M: 之后，蒙泰威尔第开始改变写作形式，就变成了我们今天所了解的现代风格。他增加了咏叹调部分，允许歌手们表达他们所扮演角色的情感，表现自己的歌唱才能。

W: 没错，后来其他的作家又增加了很多其他成分。比如，合唱部分、舞蹈和乐器演奏部分。这之后，歌剧在很多方面又进行了发展和改进。

M: 歌剧起源于意大利，是吧？我是说除了莫扎特是奥地利人以外，所有的作曲家都是意大利人。

W: 那是因为歌剧非常受欢迎，被传到了德国、法国、英国、俄罗斯、西班牙、葡萄牙和其他国家。不过歌剧的确是起源于意大利。

M: 是不是最初所有的歌剧都是用意大利语写的？

W: 是的，即使像莫扎特这样的外国人也用意大利语进行创作，但后来随着歌剧的广泛传播，他们开始用自己的语言创作。

M: 好了，我知道歌剧起源于意大利，很快遍及欧洲各地，但这并不能解释它是怎么传到美国的。

W: 18、19世纪欧洲移民把歌剧带到了美国。这就是为什么我们有了"大都会歌剧院"的原因，该剧院1883年开始对外开放。

M: 我明白了，可是为什么歌剧至今还这么流行呢？歌剧迷们仍然喜欢到"大都会歌剧院"去听歌剧。

W: 大多数在"大都会歌剧院"上演的歌剧都是18、19世纪由莫扎特、普契尼、瓦格纳等创作的。我想人们只是觉得这些歌剧真的非常动听罢了，我自己也这么认为！

M: 这个话题真有意思，不过我想我还是坚持听我的流行音乐。

■ for ages 很长时间   ■ be composed by ... 由……创作
■ to show off 显示，炫耀   ■ spread to 传播到

57. Pizza

比萨饼

R：*Reporter*　　*C*：*Chef*

R：Today, I'm speaking with Chef Marco.

C：Hello Judy.

R：Marco, what can you tell me about pizza?

C：Well, pizza was originally a peasant food, but nowadays pizza can be very expensive.

R：I see. It's a kind of meal with a bread plate, I guess. So it would have been easy for farmers to eat during their **lunch breaks**.

C：Exactly, Judy. Modern Pizza is believed to have been invented by Raffaele Esposito, a baker in Napoli.

R：Some say that pizza was actually invented by the Greeks, who ate flat round bread with an assortment of toppings.

C：Some say that, yes. But I'm an Italian! I believe Italy invented the pizza.

R：Pizza is patriotic because it looks like the Italian flag, with its colours of green, from the basil, white, from the mozzarella, and the red of the tomatoes. It was a favourite dish of the Queen.

C：Yes, that's how we get the name "Margherita", or mozzarella and tomato pizza. The queen's name was Queen Margherita.

R：Nowadays, people **go crazy with** toppings, even using chocolate and other sweet things, but what toppings would we find on a traditional, Neapolitan pizza?

C：Pizza Napoletana is made with fresh mozzarella, home-made sauce from fresh vine ripened tomatoes and fresh herbs, and the artistry of the pizzaioli, the pizza makers.

R：So, how did pizza migrate to America? We have many pizza **chain restaurants** which serve American style pizza, or "deep pan" which are much thicker than the original Italian ones.

C：Pizza came to America with Italian immigrants in the latter half of the 19th century. **By the turn of the century**, Italians had begun to open their own bakeries and were selling groceries as well as pizza.

R: The first pizza restaurant, or "Pizzeria" opened in 1905, in New York. But it wasn't until after World War II when the soldiers came home, that pizza became so popular.

C: Yes, the soldiers based in Italy had eaten lots of pizza and wanted to continue eating it when they came home.

R: Today, pizza is one of the top 3 foods eaten by Americans and a staple of the American diet.

R: 记者　　C: 厨师

> * "玛格丽特"：19世纪末，意大利皇后玛格丽特到那不勒斯度假。因为喜食比萨，她就请了当地最有名的师傅制作了三款匹萨，其中以当地西红柿、莫扎雷拉奶酪和罗勒制成的比萨最得皇后欢心，于是被赐名"玛格丽特比萨"。而红色的西红柿、白色的奶酪、绿色的罗勒草也正符合意大利国旗的颜色。

R: 今天我要和厨师马克聊聊。

C: 你好，朱迪。

R: 马克，你能跟我说说比萨吗？

C: 哦，比萨饼原先是一种乡下人吃的食物，但现在却相当贵。

R: 我知道。我猜这是一种盘状面包食品，因此对农夫们来说午休时吃很方便。

C: 一点不错，朱迪。人们认为现代比萨是那不勒斯的一个面包师拉菲勒·埃斯波西发明的。

R: 有人说比萨实际上是希腊人发明的，他们常吃一种扁平的圆面包，上面带有多种馅料。

C: 是有人那么说。但我是意大利人！我认为比萨是意大利人发明的。

R: 比萨是爱国的象征，它看起来像意大利国旗，有绿、白和红三种颜色：绿色的是香料罗勒，白色的是奶酪，红色的是西红柿。它也是王后最喜欢吃的食物。

C: 是的，这就是我们给比萨取名"玛格丽特"*或者奶酪比萨和西红柿比萨的由来，因为王后的名字就是玛格丽特。

R: 如今，人们放在比萨上的馅料越来越杂乱，甚至使用巧克力和其他的甜食，但传统的那不勒斯比萨的馅料是些什么呢？

C: 那不勒斯比萨选用新鲜的奶酪，新鲜的自制西红柿酱和新鲜的香草由比萨师精心制成。

R: 那比萨又是怎么传到美国的？我们有很多比萨连锁店卖美式比萨，或者说是"深盘比萨"，它们比原来的意大利比萨要厚很多。

C: 比萨是19世纪后半期随着意大利的移民传到美国的。19世纪末20世纪初，意大利人开始经营他们自己的面包房，卖杂货还有比萨。

R: 第一个比萨店，或"意式比萨店"是1905年在纽约开业的。但直到二战以后美国士兵们回到家乡，比萨才开始变得流行起来。

C: 是这样的，当时驻扎在意大利的美国士兵吃了很多比萨，他们回到家乡后还想继续吃。

R: 现在，比萨是美国人的三大食品之一，也是他们常吃的一种主食。

■ lunch break　午休时间
■ chain restaurant　连锁餐厅
■ go crazy with ...　对……发疯，着迷
■ by the turn of the century　世纪之交

58. Geisha

艺伎

T: *Tourist*　　*G*: *Museum guide*

T: Excuse me, **could you tell me something about** this exhibition.

G: Yes, certainly. You are interested in Geisha then?

T: Oh, yes, very interested. I have just finished reading an amazing book, *Memoirs of a Geisha*, and I felt I must come to Japan to discover more. It's such a wonderful, but hidden profession. Well, it's hidden to us in the West anyway. Most people believe Geisha are just prostitutes. That isn't true though, is it?

G: The word "Geisha" actually means "person of the arts" and a Geisha's training is extensive and lasts throughout their life. A Geisha never stops training in the arts, such as dancing, singing and playing certain musical instruments. You see this one here? That's a shamisen, it's a little like a guitar. Many Geisha excel in shamisen.

T: So, Geisha are musicians too?

G: Yes, they must have **a wide range of skills** including intellectual conversation and wit. They must have the gift of entertaining, using the arts, conversation and **the ability to** tell a funny joke!

T: Wow! So Geisha must be multi-skilled, then. I've heard some stories about young girls being **sold into slavery** and then forced to become Geisha.

G: It's true, being a Geisha is sometimes a cruel profession. Some Geisha were born into it, their mothers and grandmothers were Geisha, so they started their training at the traditional age of 3. But some girls, who worked as servants wanted a new life, so if they had something special, maybe about their appearance and were lucky enough to be chosen, they too could train.

T: I see. In the book I mentioned, the girl who became a Geisha was sold to a Geisha house, worked as a maid and later became a Geisha. She had something very special, blue eyes.

Quite different here in Japan!

G: Yes, have you seen the movie of the book? It was very popular in Western countries.

T: It starred Zhang Zi Yi. It's a wonderful movie, although I enjoyed the book much more.

G: I agree. The original book is always better than the movie. Let's continue walking, we can take a look at some kimonos next . . .

T: 游客　　G: 博物馆导游

> *《艺伎回忆录》：作者阿瑟·高顿（Arthur Golden），生于美国田纳西州，本科毕业于哈佛大学艺术史系，专攻日本艺术。1980 年，获哥伦比亚大学日本史硕士学位，兼修中文。在北京大学进修一个夏季之后，他到东京工作。回到美国后，他在波士顿大学获英文硕士学位。《艺伎回忆录》是他的第一部长篇小说。

T: 请问，你能给我讲讲这次展览会吗？

G: 好的，没问题。那么说你对艺妓很感兴趣了？

T: 噢，是的，很感兴趣。我刚刚看完一本很有意思的书，叫《艺伎回忆录》*，我觉得一定得去日本多了解一些情况。这种职业太奇妙了，就是不太为人所知。不管怎么说在西方我们对此是不了解的。大多数人认为艺伎就是妓女，这是不对的，是吧？

G: 艺伎这个词实际意思是"从事艺术的人"，艺伎的训练内容很广，一辈子不间断。她们要一直进行艺术训练，比如舞蹈、唱歌和乐器弹奏。你看到这个了吗？那是三味线，有点像吉他。很多艺伎都擅长这种乐器。

T: 那艺伎也是音乐人了？

G: 是的，她们必须有广博的技能，包括高水平的谈话技能，语言要风趣。她们一定要有应酬天赋，懂艺术、会交流、能讲笑话。

T: 哇！所以艺伎一定要多才多艺。我听说过一些故事，说年轻的女孩被卖为奴隶，然后被迫成为艺伎。

G: 确实是这样，有时艺伎是个很残忍的职业。一些艺伎生来就注定当艺伎，因为她们的妈妈、祖母都是艺伎，所以她们一般 3 岁就开始训练。但是还有一些女孩，她们身为仆人，但想过一种新的生活，所以如果她们有什么特别的本钱，或许是长相好或者是运气好，她们也能被选中接受训练。

T: 我明白了。在我提到的那本书里，就有一个女孩被卖进艺伎馆，先做女仆，后来就成了艺伎。她与众不同的是那双蓝眼睛。在日本这样的眼睛很少见！

G: 是的，你看过根据这本书改编的电影吗？在西方国家非常受欢迎。

T: 影片由章子怡主演。电影很精彩，不过我还是更喜欢看这本书。

G: 我同意你的看法。原著总是要比电影好。我们接着往前走走，可以看看后面的一些和服。

■ Could you tell me something about . . . ?　你能给我讲讲……？　　■ the ability to ……的能力
■ a wide range of skills 广博的技能　　　　　　　　　　　　■ be sold into slavery 卖为奴隶

59. Kimono

和服

G: *Museum guide*   T: *Tourist*

G: This is the Kimono House. Look, there are many different designs and colours. In Japan, **men, women and children** all wear different types of kimono. It also depends **on the time of year**, for example in the spring, women can wear a kimono depicting scenes of blossoms or birds, but this design could never be worn during the winter.

T: So, was this a strict rule? I mean, for everyone?

G: For Geisha especially. There was a Geisha Registry that controlled what kimono was worn at what time.

T: How about this? It's very beautiful, but the shape isn't like a kimono. What is it?

G: That is an obi. An obi is tied around the waist, on top of the kimono. Obi are often very heavy and can come from the hips all the way up to the shoulder blades. They are often more beautiful than the kimono itself.

T: Everything looks so big! But I always think of Japanese people, especially women, as being small. How do they get dressed?

G: People often employed dressers, who helped to fit the kimono and obi. The kimono is the same size, no matter how small the lady is. It's a difficult process and almost impossible to do alone. As you can see, the obi **is tied at the back**, so someone must assist the kimono wearer while they are dressing.

T: This kimono is different. The sleeves are so long! It looks like they would **drag on the ground**. Who would wear a kimono like this?

G: This is one of the most elaborate kimono designs, which is only worn by an apprentice Geisha. As you can see, the colours are brighter, the flower design is much more detailed, the sleeves are longer and the obi is made of a heavier fabric.

T： Yes, I can see. It must be difficult to stand with so much extra weight wrapped around your body.

G： The kimono and obi of an apprentice is very difficult to wear. Very heavy, which makes it difficult to walk in. But it does look really beautiful.

G：博物馆导游　　T：游客

G： 这里是日本和服馆。你看，有很多不同的图案和颜色。在日本，男女老少穿的和服*都各不相同。这也要看是什么季节，例如在春天，妇女可以穿绘有花鸟图案的和服，但这样的和服在冬天是从来不穿的。

> ＊和服：和服是在中国唐代服装的基础上，经过一千多年演变而形成的。男式和服色彩比较单调，偏重黑色，款式较少，腰带细，附属品简单；女式和服色彩丰富，腰带很宽，款式多样，还有许多附属品。依据场合与时间的不同，人们会穿不同的和服。穿和服时讲究穿木屐、布袜，还要根据和服的种类，梳理不同的发型。深红色和深紫色和服为皇室专用。非隆重仪式，一般不选用白色和红色，因为白色代表神圣、纯洁；红色象征魔力。

T： 那这个规定严格吗？我的意思是，大家都得遵守吗？

G： 尤其对艺伎是如此。有个艺伎登记处负责她们在什么时候穿什么样的和服。

T： 这件呢？很漂亮，但样子不像是和服。这是什么衣服？

G： 这是宽腰带，系在腰间，用来系和服的。宽腰带通常很重，可以从臀部一直围到肩胛骨。它们通常要比和服本身要漂亮。

T： 和服和腰带看起来都那么大！但我一直认为日本人，尤其是女子，身材应该很矮小。她们怎么穿得了这样的衣服？

G： 她们常常雇用一些穿衣员，帮助她们穿和服、系腰带。无论女士有多瘦小，和服都是同一号码的。穿和服的过程很复杂，所以一个人基本上是穿不了的。你也可以看到，腰带系在后面，所以必须要有人帮忙穿。

T： 这件和服就不一样。袖子那么长！看起来能拖到地上。谁会穿这样的和服？

G： 这件是图案最精致的和服之一，只有艺伎学徒才能穿。你看颜色比较鲜艳，花的图案也较细致，袖子很长，而且腰带是用比较厚的织物做成的。

T： 是的，我能看出来。那么重的衣服裹在身上一定很难受。

G： 学徒的和服和腰带是很不好穿的。非常重，所以走起路来也很困难。但是看起来真的很漂亮。

- men, women and children　男女老少
- be tied at the back　系在背后
- on the time of year　根据季节
- drag on the ground　拖到地上

60. Cartoons

卡通画

C: *Comic book store owner*   *S*: *Shopper*

C: Hi! Do you need some help?

S: Yes, thanks. It's my friend's birthday next week and he loves Japanese cartoon and comic books. But, to be honest I know very little about it! Could you help me to choose something he would like?

C: **No problem**. I'm an expert in this area, which we call "Anime".

S: "Anime?" Yes, I've heard my friend talk about this. **I had no idea** he meant cartoons!

C: Anime began a long time ago, the first short pieces were made in 1917, but these were mainly folk tales. Nothing like the anime we get today. It then developed into western-style humour during the 1930s and then on to giants, robots and outer space adventures.

S: Yes, my friend watches a cartoon about robots and strange cars and things like that.

C: These types of anime are very popular nowadays, with both children and adults. He probably enjoys the ones which started in the 1980s and were made by Miyazaki and Takahata, these are the most popular ones. Have you heard of the movie *Akira*? That was made in 1988, and is still very popular today.

S: Yes! My friend loves that movie.

C: But, **before you decide** I have many other things to show you. Over here, we have some "Manga" items. Manga was first created in 1815 by a woodblock artist called Hokusai and means "unintentional drawings". Manga is much more graphic than usual anime, but there are different styles for different ages and sexes. It can be very violent. We've got videos, DVDs, VCDs and comics.

C: OK, great. What would you suggest?

S: Today's manga has many different genres. Such as joke-books, melodrama and science

120

fiction. I think your friend would love some sci-fi!

C: Yes, sci-fi seems like a good idea. Which one do you suggest?

S: This one. *Basilisk*: *The Kouga Ninja Scrolls*. It follows the war between two ninja clans, which have **had a truce** for 400 years. But suddenly, they begin fighting again. It's very popular.

C: Excellent! I'll take it. Thanks very much for all of your help.

C: 连环漫画店主　　　S: 购物者

> * 宫崎骏：日本动画电影大师，生于1941年，代表作有《天空之城》、《龙猫》、《魔女宅急便》、《红猪》、《心之谷》、以及《幽灵公主》等。

C: 你好！需要帮忙吗？

S: 是的，谢谢。下周是我朋友的生日，他喜欢日本卡通画和连环漫画册。可是，说实话，我对这些了解很少！你能帮我选些他喜欢的东西吗？

C: 没问题。我是这方面的专家，我们把这些叫"动画片"。

S: "动画片"？对，我听我朋友说起过。我不知道他指的是"卡通片"！

C: 动画片在很早以前就有了，第一个短片完成于1917年，但这些主要是民间传说，和我们今天看到的动画片一点也不一样。后来20世纪30年代发展成西方的幽默风格，接着又发展成巨人、机器人和太空探险片。

S: 是的，我朋友就看这些关于机器人和奇怪的汽车之类的片子。

C: 这类动画片现在很流行，孩子和大人都爱看。他大概是喜欢那些20世纪80年代开始出现的片子，由宫崎峻*和高松信司制作的，这些都卖得最火。你听说过电影《亚基拉》吗？那是1988年制作的影片，如今还是很受欢迎。

S: 没错！我朋友喜欢那部影片。

C: 不过我还有很多东西给你看，看了以后你再决定。在那边，我们还有一些漫画。一开始，漫画是由一个叫葛饰北斋的木版画艺术家发明的，意思是"无意识画"。它比一般的动画要生动细致，但风格因读者群的年龄和性别的不同而有所区别。有些漫画内容可能会很暴力。我们这儿还有录像带、DVD、VCD和连环画。

S: 那太好了。你有什么建议？

C: 如今的漫画种类很多，有笑话集、剧情片和科幻片。我觉得你朋友喜欢一些科幻片。

S: 是这样，买科幻片这个主意好像不错。你建议买哪一个？

C: 买这个：《甲贺忍法贴》。故事描述的是日本两个忍者派系之间的斗争。他们休战了400年，但突然又开始打了起来。这部影片卖得非常好。

S: 太棒了！我买了。非常感谢你的帮助。

■ No problem.　没问题。　　　　　■ I have no idea.　我不知道。
■ before you decide　在你决定之前　　■ have a truce　休战

61. Sake

清酒

S: *Shopper* *E*: *Sake expert*

S: Hi, I wonder if you can help me. I have a friend from Japan, who has just been promoted, so we are holding a big party for him. I would like to get some good quality sake, but I have no idea where to start.

E: Well, **you've come to the right place**. You know, to Japanese, sake is not just a drink. It's much more important than that.

S: Oh, really? **In what way**?

E: Sake is often associated with festivals and rituals, it's been an important part of Japanese life from the ancient period **right up to the present**. Production was started in 300 BC, but the first written record **dates back from** AD 300. Originally, it was drunk by the Imperial Court and in some very large temples.

S: So, it wasn't for ordinary people then? I mean **the general public**.

E: No, sake is very special indeed.

S: What exactly is sake made from?

E: It's basically made from rice and water with microbes called "koji", and sake yeast. We always use very good quality rice, because the better the rice, the better the sake. This special rice is called "Sakamai".

S: I see. Is there a special way to drink sake?

E: Yes, you can drink sake **hot or cold**. It changes its flavour with different temperatures, so one type of sake will taste very different when served hot and when served cold.

S: Well, it's summer so maybe cold would be better for the party.

E: If you want to drink cold sake, the best type is this one, "high flavour sake", or "light and smooth sake". They taste much better when **served chilled**.

S: OK, thank you. Now, I'm not in charge of the food, but **what would you recommend to eat** with the sake? Sushi or some other type of fish?

E: Well, actually sake enhances the flavour of ingredients and at the same time softens the strong smell of meat and seafood. So, honestly, you could eat anything with it.

S: Thank you for your time. It's been really interesting to learn all about sake, hopefully the party will be a success now I know which type to buy.

S: 顾客　　E: 米酒专家

S: 你好，我不知道你能否帮我一个忙。我有个日本朋友，他刚刚升职，所以我们要为他举办一个大型聚会庆祝一下。我想买些质量较好的清酒，可是我不知道怎么挑。

E: 哎，你算是来对地方了。你知道，对日本人来说，清酒不只是一种饮品，它要比这个重要得多。

S: 哦，真的吗？怎么重要？

E: 清酒常常和节日、庆典有关，从古至今一直是日本人生活中的重要组成部分。清酒的生产开始于公元前300年，但是第一份文字记载的资料要追溯到公元300年。原来只是向皇宫和一些大型寺庙供应。

S: 那就是说，当时清酒不是普通人所能享用的？我是指普通老百姓。

E: 没错，清酒的确很特殊。

S: 清酒到底是用什么制成的？

E: 主要由大米、水以及一种叫清酒曲的微生物和清酒酵母加工而成。我们一直用质量上乘的大米，因为用的米越好，制出来的酒就越香。这种特殊的米叫"酒米"。

S: 我知道了。喝清酒有没有特别的讲究？

E: 有的，可以加热也可以冰镇饮用。温度不同，味道也会有变化，所以同一种清酒冰镇和加热饮用的味道是大不一样的。

S: 好的，现在是夏天，所以聚会上冰镇饮用可能会不错。

E: 如果你想喝凉清酒，最好要这种"醇香型（大吟酿）"或"淡丽型"。冷藏后，米酒的味道会更好。

S: 好的，谢谢你。虽然我不负责食品采购，不过你能否推荐一下跟清酒搭配的食品？寿司或其它什么鱼类？

E: 是这样，实际上清酒可以改善食料的味道，同时也使很浓重的肉味、海腥味变得淡些。所以，说实话，喝清酒你吃什么都可以。

S: 谢谢，占用你那么多时间。全面了解一下清酒真的很有意思。现在我知道要买哪一种了，希望我们的聚会办得成功。

- You've come to the right place.　你来对地方了。
- right up to the present　直到现在
- the general public　广大民众
- be served chilled　冷藏饮用
- What would you recommend to eat?　你建议吃什么？
- in what way　在哪个方面
- date back from　追溯到
- hot or cold　加热或冰镇

62. Maya Culture

玛雅文明

K: *Katie*   **S**: *Saskia*

K: Saskia, I'm **doing some research** about ancient cultures in South America. Which one do you think I should choose?

S: I think the Maya are **your best bet**, there's so much information available about them.

K: Maya ... OK. There's certainly a lot of them! They lived all over Mexico, in Tabasco, Chiapas, Guatemala, Belize and Western Honduras.

S: They were believed to be the most intelligent of the ancient cultures. The culture's beginnings have been traced back to 1500 BC, entering the Classic period about AD 300 and flourishing between AD 600 and AD 900.

K: They seemed to be excellent farmers, too. They cultivated maize, beans, squash, and chili peppers, and also "**cash crops**" of cotton and cacao.

S: This can't have been easy, **the climate was inhospitable**. They also built their settlements next to "cenotes", natural **watering holes**.

K: The Maya devised a complex style of **hieroglyphic writing** that has yet to be fully deciphered and they knew lots about science, maths and astrology.

S: They used maths and astronomy to predict eclipses and other heavenly events with great precision and formulated a unique calendar system more exact than the one we use today.

K: That's amazing! It says here that they were very religious too, but they accepted science and religion together. That's interesting, because nowadays we think of science and religion as being totally different things.

S: Their architecture was very interesting too, like all cultures in Mesoamerica. They built tall pyramidal temples, warren-like single story palaces and courts around a broad central plaza.

K: Hmm ... they painted many **exotic murals** too, usually containing the human form.

S: They were also very talented in working with ceramics and **stoneware**.

K: But why did such a wonderful, gifted civilization fall? Why did they disappear?

S: Now that, my friend, is an interesting story. I've heard some people say that aliens took them away because they were much too advanced to be human.

K: That can't be true! Maybe it was because of insufficient food supply, earthquakes, pestilence, invasion by outsiders, internal rebellion or a combination of these factors.

S: Well, whatever it was, by AD 900 the Maya's numerous ceremonial centers had been abandoned.

K: 卡蒂　　**S:** 萨斯珂雅

K: 萨斯珂雅，我正在对南美的古代文化*做些研究。你认为我应该选什么？

> ＊美洲古代文明主要包括墨西哥的阿兹特克文明、中美洲北部的玛雅文明、秘鲁的印加文明和更古老的奥尔梅克文明。玛雅文明是当中的杰出代表，16世纪为西班牙殖民者摧毁，此后长期湮没在热带丛林中。1839年，美国探险家约翰·斯蒂芬斯在洪都拉斯的热带丛林中发现了玛雅古文明遗址。

S: 我觉得玛雅人应该是最好的选择，这方面的资料很丰富。

K: 玛雅人……好的。的确，有关他们的信息太多了！他们遍布墨西哥各地，在塔巴斯科、恰帕斯、危地马拉、伯利兹城和西洪都拉斯。

S: 玛雅人被认为是古代文明中最聪明的人。玛雅文明的开始可以追溯到公元前1500年，公元300年进入古典期，公元600至公元900年走向繁荣期。

K: 玛雅人好像也是非常出色的农民。他们种植玉米、豆类、南瓜和辣椒，还有"经济作物"棉花和可可豆。

S: 这些可不是容易种植的，因为那里的气候不太适宜。他们还在靠近"竖井"（天然水井）的地方建起了自己的居住地。

K: 玛雅人发明了一种复杂的象形文字，到现在还没有被完全破译。他们懂得很多科学、数学和占星术知识。

S: 他们用数学和天文学来预测日食和其他天文事件，非常精确。此外，还设计出独一无二的历法体系，比我们今天用的还要准确。

K: 真了不起！据说他们也比较信奉宗教，但对科学和宗教一并接受。如今我们把科学和宗教当作完全不同的两种东西，所以这种观点很有意思。

S: 他们的建筑也很特别，就像中美洲所有文明一样。他们在宽阔的中央广场周围建起高高的金字塔形寺庙，迷宫般的单层宫殿和庭院。

K: 嗯……他们还画了很多异国情调的壁画，通常少不了人体绘画。

S: 他们还在陶器和瓷器制作方面很有天赋。

K: 可为什么这样一个神奇伟大的文明会衰落呢？他们为什么会消失？

S: 我的朋友，这事说起来非常有意思。我听有些人说是外星人把他们带走了，因为他们太高级了，不能再做人类。

K: 这不可能是真的！也许是因为食物不足、地震、瘟疫、外族入侵、内部叛乱或这些因素综合在一起造成的。

S: 好了，不管是什么原因，到公元900年的时候，玛雅人无数的仪式中心都废弃了。

■ do some research　做些研究　　　　　　■ cash crop　经济作物
■ The climate is inhospitable.　那里气候不是很适宜。　■ hieroglyphic writing　象形文字
■ exotic mural　异国情调的壁画　　　　　■ stoneware　瓷器

63. Tulips

郁金香

M: *Man*　　**W**: *Woman*

M: I want to get some flowers for my girlfriend's birthday but she absolutely hates roses.

W: Have you thought about tulips?

M: They're from Holland, aren't they?

W: They are grown in Holland, yes. But originally they came from Central Asia where they **grew wild**.

M: Really?

W: The flower was introduced in Western Europe and the Netherlands in the 17th century by Carolus Clusius, a famous biologist from Vienna.

M: Oh, I see. Sounds like a good choice, they were very different to roses.

W: Very different, some people believed they had **medicinal powers**.

M: Well, I just need them to look pretty. They were very popular as a trading product, especially in Holland. Are your tulips very expensive?

W: That was years ago. Nowadays they are very reasonably priced. We have many different kinds, because botanists in the 1500s found ways to make the tulip even more decorative and tempting. **Hybrids and mutations** of the flower were seen as rarities and **a sign of high status**.

M: OK, so that must have marked the beginning of "Tulipmania", I think they are probably still as popular today. My parents love to go to Holland to see all of the different types growing there. I had never really considered buying them before, though.

W: In those days tulips looked very different from the ones we can see today. The tulip became so popular because of its bright colours, dramatic flames and frilly petals.

M: Frilly petals? But these are totally smooth, I thought all tulips had smooth petals.

W: In the 20th century it was discovered that the frilly petals and dramatic flames that gave the flower its stunning look were, in fact, the symptoms of an infection by the mosaic virus.

M: A virus? So that's why today we think tulips should be solid, smooth and monotone.

Where did the virus come from?

W: The virus came to the tulip from a louse living on peaches and potatoes. We can still find some varieties with frilly petals today, but they are hybrids. The diseased varieties are no longer sold.

M: Good, because I don't think my girlfriend would be too happy with sick flowers!

M：男人　　W：女人

M： 我想买些花为我女朋友庆祝生日，可是她一点也不喜欢玫瑰。

W： 你有没有想过买郁金香呢？

M： 郁金香产自荷兰，是吧？

W： 是的，它们是长在荷兰。但它们原本是长在中亚地区的野生植物。

M： 真的吗？

W： 17 世纪时，一位著名的维也纳生物学家卡罗拉斯·克鲁休斯把郁金香引入西欧和荷兰。

M： 哦，我知道了。这样听起来买郁金香是个不错的选择，毕竟跟玫瑰很不一样。

W： 区别是很大，有些人认为郁金香还有药效。

M： 哦，我只要它们看起来漂亮就行。郁金香以前作为一种商品还是很受欢迎的，尤其在荷兰。你这儿的这种花很贵吗？

W： 几年前是很贵。现在价格相当合理了。我们的郁金香有很多品种。16 世纪时植物学家们发现了使郁金香变得更漂亮动人的方法。杂交和变异的郁金香被认为是稀有品种，也是高贵身份的标志。

M： 所以，那肯定标志着"郁金香狂潮*"的开端。我想这样的郁金香现在仍然很受欢迎。我父母喜欢去荷兰欣赏那里种植的所有种类的郁金香。不过我以前真的从来没想过买它。

W： 那时候的郁金香跟我们现在所看到的大不一样。人们那么喜欢它是因为它亮丽的色彩、惊人的光芒和褶皱的花瓣。

M： 褶皱的花瓣？但这些郁金香的花瓣都很平滑啊，我一直以为所有郁金香的花瓣都是平滑的。

W： 20 世纪时人们发现褶皱花瓣和惊人的光芒使郁金香看起来更加漂亮动人，但实际上这是它们感染了花叶病毒而引起的一种病症。

M： 一种病毒？这就是为什么我们今天认为郁金香应该是花瓣厚实、平滑和单色的原因。这些病毒都是哪儿来的？

W： 这些病毒来自于桃子和土豆上的一种寄生虫。今天我们仍然可以看到很多带褶皱花瓣的郁金香变种，但它们都是杂交的。那些带病的郁金香变种不再出售了。

M： 很好，我想我女朋友也不会太喜欢带病的花儿。

> ＊郁金香狂潮：郁金香在 16 世纪晚期从土耳其传入荷兰，起初只有富人才买得起。从 17 世纪 30 年代起，人们对郁金香的狂热开始蔓延。郁金香球茎成为投资保值的对象，人人都对其趋之若鹜。在法国，一个新娘的所有嫁妆就是一株稀有的郁金香球茎。1637 年初，郁金香的价格几乎每天都在翻番。据说一个郁金香种植者因为牛吃光了他所有的存货而自杀。

- grow wild　野生
- hybrid and mutation　杂交和变异
- medicinal power　有药效
- a sign of high status　有身份的象征

127

64. Windmills

风车

M1: Man 1   *M2*: Man 2

M1: What a great picture, I'm guessing it's Holland, right?

M2: Yes, of course! The windmills **must have given it away**.

M1: There are lots in Holland and some are very old, but they have been preserved perfectly. I saw them when I was travelling around Europe last summer.

M2: There are lots of different types, too. This one here is a drainage mill, but there are also corn mills and industrial mills for all kinds of purposes.

M1: I just think they **brighten up** the landscape, especially in a country as flat as Holland, standing tall against the horizon with their sails whirling in the air.

M2: I agree. Did you know Cervantes wrote about Don Quixote's famous attack on the windmills?

M1: Yes, not just that though. There are many paintings of the East Anglian countryside in England by John Constable, whose family owned mills.

M2: The windmill has played a part in the historic and artistic, as well as economic, development of Western civilization.

M1: Holland **comes to mind first** as the windmill capital of the world, but England's windmills were equally plentiful and important to the economy of the country.

M2: Yes, that's why there are so many paintings of them. They were first used in Europe in the 12th century.

M1: That's certainly a long time ago. The first one was built in Yorkshire in England, not Holland.

M2: Oh, really? I thought the oldest ones must have been in Holland. I wonder why people started using them? I mean, I know they were used to grind grain, but why?

M1: I think it was to save on man power. Imagine how tiring it must have been to grind grain **by hand**, the windmill was definitely an inspired addition to energy sources.

M2: In Holland the drainage windmills are the most important, because lots of Holland is actually lower than the sea level.

M1: Nowadays the remaining ones are just for tourists, they don't use them for keeping the canal and sea levels down anymore.

M2: The sea defences have been greatly improved, they don't really need them. I'm glad they kept them though, even if they are just for tourists.

M1：男人1　　M2：男人2

M1：照片太漂亮了！我猜拍的是荷兰吧？

M2：是的，当然是荷兰。一定是这些风车泄的密。

M1：在荷兰有很多风车，有些还很古老，但都被保存得很好。去年夏天我去欧洲旅游时还曾亲眼见过风车。

M2：风车还有很多不同种类。照片上的这种是排水用的，还有一些碾磨谷物的风车以及各种用途的工业生产用风车。

M1：我只是觉得，尤其是在荷兰这样一个地势平坦的国家，风车真是为这里的风景增色不少：它们高耸在地平线上，翼板在风中旋转着。

M2：我也这样认为。塞万提斯写过堂吉诃德攻击风车的故事，非常有名，这些你知道吗？

M1：知道，不过还不只这些。还有约翰·康斯特伯尔创作了很多画都是关于英格兰乡下的东安格利亚风景的，他家里就有很多风车。

M2：风车曾经在西方文明发展过程中，以及艺术和经济领域都发挥过重要作用。

M1：荷兰首先是以世界风车之都而出名的，但英格兰的风车同样也很多，对国家的经济发展也很重要。

M2：是的，这就是为什么有这么多画都跟风车有关的原因。风车最初是在12世纪的欧洲使用的。

M1：那的确是很久以前的事了。第一个风车是在英格兰的约克郡组建的，而不是在荷兰。

M2：哦，是吗？我以为最古老的风车一定是在荷兰。不知道人们为什么开始使用风车？我是说风车以前是用来碾磨谷物的，但是什么原因呢？

M1：我猜大概是为了节省人力。想想要是手工碾磨谷物的话该多累啊。所以从节能、省力的角度看，风车的确是一个很有灵感的发明。

M2：在荷兰，排水的风车是最重要的，因为那里很多地区实际海拔都低于海平面。

M1：现在遗留下来的风车都只是观光用的，人们不再用风车来维持运河和海水的水位了。

M2：海面的防卫设备也得到了很大的改善，他们不再需要风车。不过，我还是很高兴看到人们把风车保存下来，即使只是用来观光也好。

■ must have given it away 一定泄了密
■ come to mind first 首先想到
■ brighten up 使增色，发亮
■ by hand 手工

65. Amsterdam

阿姆斯特丹

D: Danny **J**: Jamie

D: You look relaxed! How was your holiday?

J: It was wonderful, we went to Amsterdam. Have you ever been there?

D: Yes, a couple of years ago, I had an amazing time. It's such an interesting city, don't you think?

J: Absolutely. There are so many things to do. We explored everywhere, the canals, the galleries and museums, the coffee houses ... **the list goes on and on**.

D: When I was there I stayed in a houseboat on one of the canals. Now that was something special, although I couldn't sleep for the first couple of nights. It felt strange being so close to the water.

J: Lucky you! We just stayed in a hotel, the Hotel Falcon Plaza, it was pretty nice, though.

D: What do you think is the most interesting thing in Amsterdam? I mean, I know there are so many to choose from, but try and pick one.

J: Maybe the Rijksmuseum. It's huge! There are around 250 rooms filled with some wonderful paintings. I really enjoyed that.

D: I think my favourite thing was **wandering up and down** the Damrak, the main street. You can see so many different types of people there, shopping, sitting around lazily or rushing off somewhere.

J: Yes, the Damrak is an interesting place, I spent quite a lot of time there. I also visited the Anne Frank museum, which was chilling because there were so many photos of Nazi soldiers killing Jews.

D: The strangest thing about Amsterdam is the legal drugs. I can't believe that marijuana can be legal anywhere, but it seems that everyone smokes it there.

J: The coffee shops sell marijuana cigarettes with coffee, when they asked me if I wanted my coffee "with or without", I thought they meant sugar, not drugs!

D: The only unfortunate thing about Amsterdam is that it's **full of** graffiti, I saw lots. Not good graffiti, mindless writing.

J: Graffiti can be art if it's done well, but **I know what you mean**. I saw some too, even on old beautiful buildings. It was a shame, really.

D: I plan to go again as soon as I can. I think it's perhaps the best city in the world.

D：丹尼   J：詹米

D： 你看上去很悠闲，假期过得怎么样？

J： 好极了，我们去了阿姆斯特丹。你去过吗？

D： 几年前去过，我在那里玩得很开心。那个城市很有意思，是吧？

J： 没错，可以做很多事。我们什么地方都去了，有运河、美术馆、博物馆，还有咖啡屋等等一长串地方。

D： 我在那里时，就住在运河上的一条船屋里。尽管前几个晚上都睡不着觉，但还是觉得很新奇。在离水这么近的地方感觉就是不一样。

J： 你太幸运了！我们只是住在一家旅店里，就是猎鹰广场大酒店，不过那个酒店也很不错。

D： 你认为阿姆斯特丹最有意思的东西是什么？我知道，有太多东西可供选择，但你尽量只选择一种。

J： 应该是荷兰国立博物馆＊吧。它特别大，大约有250个房间，里面都摆满了绘画精品。我真的很喜欢。

D： 我想我最喜欢的就是在水坝大道上来回漫步。在那里可以看到很多不同的人，有购物的，有懒洋洋坐着无所事事的，还有匆忙赶着离开去别处的。

J： 是的，水坝大道是个有趣的地方，我在那里也呆了很长时间。我还参观过安妮·弗兰克博物馆，那里有点可怕，因为有很多纳粹士兵残杀犹太人的照片。

D： 阿姆斯特丹最奇怪的事情是吸毒合法。我不敢相信吸食大麻在那里会是合法的，但那里的人好像个个都在吸。

J： 咖啡屋卖咖啡，还卖大麻香烟。我要咖啡时他们就问我"加不加"，我原以为他们指的是加糖而不是加毒品。

D： 阿姆斯特丹唯一令人遗憾的是那里到处都是街头涂鸦，我看到过不少。涂写的都是一些乱七八糟的东西。

J： 街头涂鸦弄得好可以成为艺术，但我知道你指的是什么样的。我也看到一些，甚至一些古老的漂亮建筑上都有，真是令人遗憾。

D： 我计划尽快再去那里一次。我认为阿姆斯特丹可能是世界上最好的城市。

■ the list goes on and on 等等一长串地方　　■ wander up and down 来回漫步，徘徊
■ be full of 充满了　　　　　　　　　　　　■ I know what you mean. 我知道你指的是什么。

66. Anne Frank

安妮·弗兰克

W1: *Woman 1*　　*W2*: *Woman 2*

W1: That looks like a heavy book! It'll take ages to read.

W2: Actually, I've almost finished. It's the diary of Anne Frank.

W1: The Jewish girl who was taken away by the Nazi's in Holland?

W2: That's right. I think it has been perhaps **the most moving book I've ever read**.

W1: The diary was a birthday gift, right? I think she called it "Kitty".

W2: It was a gift for her 13th birthday, and while they were hiding in the tiny apartment above her father's spice shop, "Kitty" was her only friend, so she told her everything.

W1: Also, she dreamed of becoming a writer, so she took to writing a diary **with ease**. Her diary is now one of the most published books ever, and in over 60 different languages.

W2: What a life she must have led! Locked away in that tiny space with her whole family, **day after day, year after year**.

W1: Well, before they went into hiding Jews weren't allowed to do many things, for example, they had to wear a special yellow star, so everyone could see who they were.

W2: They weren't allowed to do much of anything that they used to be able to. They even had a curfew.

W1: They were lucky to have some wonderful friends Victor Kugler, Johannes Kleiman, Miep Gies, and Bep Voskuijl who managed to find them food everyday.

W2: That couldn't have been easy because Holland was under strict rationing during this time. They didn't want anyone to find them, so they had to keep extra quiet during the day time because of the shop downstairs.

W1: They had to keep the windows blacked out; their only sunlight was a skylight that Anne would spend hours looking out of. She hated being trapped in that small space.

W2: Anne didn't survive, did she? She and her whole family were discovered and taken to a concentration camp.

W1: Unfortunately Anne died of typhus just one month before the Jews were freed. Everyone in her family died, except her father.

W2: But her **spirit lives on** today in her own words because of her wonderful friend "Kitty".

W1: 女人 1　　　**W2**: 女人 2

W1: 那本书看起来很厚。要看完得花不少时间。

W2: 实际上，我差不多快看完了，是安妮·弗兰克的日记。

W1: 是在荷兰被纳粹抓走的那个犹太女孩吗？

W2: 是的。我想这可能是我曾经读过的最感人的书了。

W1: 这日记本是一份生日礼物，对吧？我记得安妮·弗兰克叫它"基蒂"。

W2: 这是她 13 岁的生日礼物。他们躲在她父亲调味品商店上面的小房间时，"基蒂"是她唯一的朋友，所以她什么都对它倾诉。

W1: 此外，她还曾经梦想成为一个作家，所以写起日记来驾轻就熟。她的日记是至今出版得最多的书籍之一，而且用 60 多种语言出版过。

W2: 她过的是一种什么样的生活啊！日复一日，年复一年地和全家人一起藏在那样一个小房间里。

W1: 在他们躲藏起来之前，有很多事都是犹太人不许做的，比如他们必须佩带一枚特殊的黄色星章，那样每个人都能知道他们是犹太人。

W2: 很多以前允许做的事，后来都不准做了，纳粹甚至对他们实行宵禁。

W1: 幸运的是他们还有一些很好的朋友，如维克多·库格勒，约翰尼斯·柯雷曼，米普·吉斯和佩普·沃斯库基尔，这些朋友每天都设法给他们送些食物。

W2: 那可不是件容易的事，因为当时荷兰正处于严格的食物定量配给时期。安妮一家不想让任何人找到他们，所以白天必须格外保持安静，因为楼下就是商店。

W1: 他们不得不把窗户关严。唯一能看到阳光的地方是一扇天窗，安妮常常几小时地望着窗外。她不喜欢被囚禁在那么一个小天地里。

W2: 安妮最后没能幸免于难，是吧？她和她的家人被发现了，并被押送到了集中营。

W1: 不幸的是，安妮在犹太人获得自由的前一个月得了斑疹伤寒症。除了她父亲以外，她的家人都死了。

W2: 但是多亏了她的好朋友"基蒂"，她的精神通过自己的文字至今还保留着。

- the most moving book I've ever read 我曾经读过的最感人的书
- day after day, year after year 日复一日，年复一年
- with ease 轻松容易地
- spirit lives on 精神长存

67. Rembrandt

伦勃朗

S1: Student 1   *S2*: Student 2

S1: Who was that painting done by? The colours are so rich!

S2: That's a Rembrandt, a self-portrait. Many of his paintings were of himself, but he used different painting techniques to show different feelings.

S1: He was from Holland, right? Born in the 17th century? He was the greatest artist of the Dutch school.

S2: Yes, he was a master of light and shadow whose paintings, drawings, and etchings made him a giant in the history of art.

S1: I read that he wasn't meant to be an artist, though. His father wanted him to **follow in his footsteps** and become a miller, but Rembrandt **dropped out of university to** study painting.

S2: Yes, I think the Italian painter Caravaggio inspired him to become a painter. He was fascinated by the works of many other Italian artists, perhaps because of their use of colour.

S1: Rembrandt's early works show that he was devoted to showing the lines, light and shade, and colour of the people he saw about him.

S2: So, it wasn't just colour that was important to him. But he did start to use these darker, richer colours we see here during the 1640s. His life was full of tragedy during that period.

S1: Yes, most of his children **died in infancy** and then a couple of years later his beloved wife died too. When she modeled for him, his works were characterized by strong lighting effects.

S2: It was around that time he painted his most famous work *The Night Watch*. It depicts a group of city guardsmen awaiting the command to **fall in line**.

S1: I've seen it, each man is painted with the same care that Rembrandt gave to single portraits. It is brilliant with colour, movement and light! Especially the little girl dressed in yellow who is in the centre of the painting.

S2: During his life he produced many works of art, not only paintings. Approximately 600 paintings, 300 etchings, and 1,400 drawings.

S1: I read that his etchings are incredible, some say he **ranks among** the foremost of all time. I believe his works showed human life, in great colour and detail. What an amazing artist he was.

S1: 学生1   **S2**: 学生2

> *《夜巡》：画面的场景原本是在白天，但画作最初被存放在一个烧泥炭的大厅里，被蒙上了厚厚一层煤灰，以至于被后人认为画的是晚上，从而被称为《夜巡》。当时，伦勃朗没有按照流行式样把民兵们画成呆板的一排，而是有明有暗、错落有致。但民兵们不愿被分出主次，要求重画。伦勃朗出于一个画家的艺术主张，坚持不重画。打这以后，再也没有人找伦勃朗画集体肖像了，画家因此失去了主要的生活来源。

S1: 这是谁画的？色彩这么丰富。

S2: 那是伦勃朗的自画像。他画的很多画都是他自己，但采用了不同的绘画技巧来表达不同的感情。

S1: 他是荷兰人，对吧？生于17世纪？是荷兰画派最有名的画家。

S2: 是的，他善于运用光线和阴影。他的油画、素描和铜版画作品使他成为了艺术史上一位巨匠。

S1: 我从书上看到过，其实他本来并不想做一位艺术家。他父亲希望他继承家业做一个磨坊主，但伦勃朗大学辍学去学了绘画。

S2: 是的，我想是意大利画家卡拉瓦乔的作品激发了他当画家的信念。他还对其他很多意大利画家的作品着迷，也许是对他们运用的颜色感兴趣吧。

S1: 伦勃朗的早期作品显示出他致力于表现线条、光和影，以及他所看到的周围人们的颜色。

S2: 所以不仅仅是颜色对他很重要。他还开始采用一些较暗、较饱满的色彩，这是我们现在看到的属于17世纪40年代的色彩。那段时期他的生活中发生了很多不幸的事。

S1: 是的，他的很多孩子都夭折了，几年后他深爱的妻子也去世了。他画他妻子时，他的作品表现出来的都是强烈的光线效果。

S2: 大约就是在那段时期，他画出了他最有名的作品《夜巡》*，描绘的是一群城市守卫等待命令的集合场面。

S1: 我曾经见过那幅画，每一个守卫都被描绘得很精致，就像伦勃朗描画单个人时一样细致。这幅画因为它的颜色、人物的动作和光线而大放异彩。尤其画正中穿黄色衣服的小女孩，其形象逼真得无与伦比。

S2: 伦勃朗一生画了很多作品，不只是油画。大约有600多幅油画，300幅铜版画，1400幅素描。

S1: 我听说他的铜版画很了不起，有人说他是有史以来最伟大的画家之一。我认为他的作品通过精妙的色彩和细节反映了人类的生活。他是多么伟大的艺术家啊！

- follow in his footsteps 跟随某人的步伐，指继承
- die in infancy 夭折，早逝
- rank among 名列
- drop out of university 大学辍学
- fall in line 集合，列队

68. Van Gogh
梵·高

D: *Darren*   **C**: *Craig*

D: Craig, look at this. I'm looking at this website all about famous people who committed suicide. It's really interesting and **a little gross**.

C: **Check out** Van Gogh, I need to do some research about him.

D: Van Gogh ... here we are. Vincent Van Gogh, born 1853 in Holland, died 1890 in France of a self-inflicted gunshot. He cut his ear off before that, didn't he?

C: Yes, he was a troubled genius. His brief, turbulent, and tragic life epitomizes the mad genius legend. What else does it say?

D: Only one of his paintings was sold while he was alive, and his most famous ones were painted during a period of 29 months where he worked and worked, and then became suicidal.

C: Actually, one reason he became suicidal was because he was **suffering from** epilepsy. In his grim struggle Vincent had one constant ally and support, his younger brother Theo.

D: He wrote Theo many letters talking of his dreams and aspirations, I think Theo tried to keep him from going insane.

C: He didn't succeed, though. Before he became a painter he worked for an art dealer, didn't he?

D: Yes, but I don't think he enjoyed his job. He **antagonised customers** until he was dismissed. He then tried preaching, as he was a strong Humanitarian, about the oppression of mining families.

C: No one took him seriously, people just laughed at him. He couldn't get a girlfriend because of the conflicts in his personality and he couldn't keep a friend. Most of his friendships ended in bitter arguments.

D: He must have been a lonely man. It says here that he didn't become a painter until 10 years before his death? I didn't know that.

C: Yes, his early paintings during the 1880s showed a use of greens and browns, like in this picture *The Potato Eaters*. That's an early one.

D: After that his style changed, maybe because he left Paris and moved to Arles. That's where he painted *Sunflowers* and when he cut off his ear.

C: He was sent to a mental hospital after that, where he painted the swirling *Starry Nights*, and just a few months later . . .

D: Bang! He shot himself.

D：达伦　　C：克雷格

D： 克雷格，看这个。我正上网查看所有自杀而死的名人。真的很有意思，倒真有几个。

C： 查查梵・高吧，我想对他做些调查研究。

D： 梵・高……找到了。文森特・梵・高，1853 年生于荷兰，1890 年在法国用一把自制手枪自杀。此前他曾割下自己的耳朵，是吧？

C： 是的，他是个麻烦缠身的天才。他那短暂、狂躁而又富有悲剧性的生活就是这位疯狂天才传奇般的缩影。网上还说什么了？

D： 说他活着的时候只卖出去过一幅画，他最有名的画大多是在 29 个月里不停地画出来的，之后就自杀了。

C： 他自杀的一个真正原因是他身患癫痫症。在他挣扎着与疾病抗争时，文森特只有一个永恒的支持者，就是他的小弟弟提奥。

D： 他给提奥写过很多信，谈到他的梦想和抱负，我想为了防止他变疯，提奥曾经做出过努力。

C： 不过，他并没有成功。梵・高在成为画家之前，曾为一个艺术品商人工作过，是吧？

D： 是的，但我认为他并不喜欢那份工作。他对顾客充满敌意，后来就被解雇了。之后他曾尝试过为那些受压迫的矿工家庭讲道，因为他是个人道主义者。

C： 但没人把他当回事，人们只是嘲笑他。因为他自身矛盾的性格，他找不到女朋友，也不能维持友谊。他大部分的友谊最终都以激烈的争吵而宣告结束。

D： 他一定很孤独。这儿说他在生命的最后十年才开始成为画家，是吗？我还不知道呢。

C： 是的，19 世纪 80 年代他早期的绘画作品里采用的是绿色和棕色，如《吃土豆的人》。那是他早期的一幅作品。

D： 之后，他的风格发生了变化，可能是由于他离开巴黎，搬到了阿尔。在那里他画了《向日葵》，也是在那时他割掉了自己的一只耳朵。

C： 后来，他被送进一家精神病院，在那里完成了那幅漩涡状的《星月夜》，几个月之后……

D： 砰的一声，他用枪结束了自己的生命。

■ a little gross　有几个	■ check out　查查
■ suffer from . . .　患……病	■ antagonise customer　对顾客有敌意

69. Red Square and the Kremlin

红场和克里姆林宫

P: *Professor*　　**VP**: *Visiting professor*

P: Dr Prince, how are you enjoying it **so far**?

VP: Well, **I must say** it's very exciting to be in Russia.

P: I'm glad you are enjoying yourself. Today, Red Square and the Kremlin.

VP: Wonderful! I can see the Kremlin over there, on the left. And across there is the historic **merchant quarter**, known as "kitai Gorod".

P: The square separates the Kremlin, the former **royal citadel** and currently the official residence of the President of Russia, from kitai Gorod.

VP: I think the reason that most people say this is the centre of Moscow, even Russia, is because all the major streets go from here out to the highways.

P: Yes, that's true. Do you know the history of the square, its name for example?

VP: The name *Red Square* derives from the Russian word "krasnaya" which means "red".

P: **Spot on!** Also, it was first known as the centre many years ago, in the 1400s. The land that the Red Square is situated on was originally covered with wooden buildings, which were dangerously susceptible to fires.

VP: I see. So, it gradually came to serve as Moscow's primary marketplace. I know that it had other functions too, such as being used for various public ceremonies and occasionally as the coronation site for Russia's tsars.

P: As you can see, it's a very special and important place. On to the Kremlin!

VP: The Kremlin is a national sanctuary and a unique creation of world culture. It stands on the left bank of the Moscow River, where it joins the Neglinnaya River.

P: Yes, over there as you said. It used to be built of wood, but again suffered from many fires. They began reconstructing it in 1485, when they built the Tainitsky Tower.

VP: So, from then on they used it in the defense of the state. And now, of course it too is made of red brick.

P: Today, **as in the old days**, the square is always full of people. Numerous groups of tourists from different cities in Russia and overseas come to admire the beauty of these architectural masterpieces.

VP: Yes, and me too!

P: 教授　　**VP:** 客座教授

P: 普林斯博士，到目前为止，你玩得开心吗？

VP: 哦，我得说俄罗斯真令人兴奋。

P: 很高兴你能喜欢。今天我们去红场和克里姆林宫看看。

VP: 太好了！我能看到那边的克里姆林宫，在左侧。穿过去是历史上著名的商业区，就是大家熟知的"中国城"。

P: 红场把克里姆林宫和"中国城"分隔开。前者是以前王室的城堡，现在是俄罗斯总统的官邸。

VP: 我想大多数人说这里是莫斯科乃至俄罗斯的中心，其原因是所有的主要街道都是在此交汇，通向高速公路。

P: 是的，就是这样。你知道这个广场的历史吗？比如说它的名字？

VP: 红场的名字源于俄语单词 krasnaya，意思是"红色"。

P: 完全正确！此外，很多年以前，大约在 15 世纪，最早出名是因为它是市中心。它所在的地方原来到处是木结构楼房，非常危险，容易引起火灾。

VP: 我明白了。所以，这个地方就逐渐变成了莫斯科的主要集贸市场。我知道它还有其他的用处，例如用来举行各种公共仪式，偶尔也作为俄罗斯沙皇举行加冕礼的地方。

P: 你看，这个地方非常特殊、非常重要。接下来我们了解一下克里姆林宫。

VP: 克里姆林宫是国家神圣的场所，是世界文化中独一无二的建筑艺术品。它位于莫斯科河的左岸，与涅格林纳河交汇的地方。

P: 是的，就像你刚才说的，它就在那边。过去是木头结构，也多次发生火灾。于 1485 年重建，当时还建了泰尼斯卡亚塔。

VP: 所以，从那时开始，他们就用这些建筑物来保卫国家。当然它是用红砖建成的。

P: 和过去一样，今天的广场上到处都是人。来自俄罗斯和国外不同城市的无数旅游团都来此欣赏这些美丽的建筑杰作。

VP: 是的，我就是其中一个。

- so far　到目前为止
- merchant quarter　商业区
- spot on　非常准确
- I must say ...　我要说……
- royal citadel　皇室城堡
- as in the old days　同过去一样

70. Ballet

芭蕾舞

FW: *Female writer* **MW**: *Male writer*

FW: I've been asked to write a piece about Russian Ballet, and I don't know where to start! You're interested in dance, **any ideas**?

MW: Well, actually Russian Ballet isn't Russian at all. It was introduced by foreigners in the 17th century by the second Romanov ruler Tsar Alexis Mikhailovich.

FW: OK, for what reason?

MW: He wanted to watch it during his wedding celebrations. Then, Peter the Great took a personal interest in dancing at his court by bringing in western dances and taking part in them himself.

FW: But was that really the formal beginning? I thought it began in a letter written in 1737 to the Empress Anne by the teacher of gymnastics at the Imperial Cadet School. The letter said: "I humbly ask Your Majesty that I shall be given twelve children—six males and six females—to create ballets and theatre dances".

MW: That's right, and in 1738 the first Russian Ballet School was **set up**. It was a small school, with just two rooms in the Old Winter Palace.

FW: Didn't that school go on to become the St. Petersburg Ballet School? Very famous, I think.

MW: Yes, it did. But the first great period of ballet didn't begin until the 1800s. A Frenchman, Charles-Louis Didelot is considered to be the "father of the Russian ballet." He put on productions there.

FW: After that there were many famous ballerinas! I always dreamed of being a ballerina when I was a child, but I think it was really quite **a hard life**. I know many died **at a young age**.

MW: Nowadays it's a bit different though. Take Rudolf Nureyev for example, he died when he was in his 50s, much older than some of the early teenage dancers.

FW: I think he must be the most famous Russian ballet dancer. He danced with Margot Fonteyn, they were known as "Rudi and Margot".

MW: Russian influence on ballet continues today, both through visits from Russian companies and the activities of defecting Soviet dancers such as Rudolf Nureyev, Natalia Makarova, and Mikhail Barishnikov.

FW: Yes, Russian ballet is still definitely popular, that's why I'm writing this piece. I think we should go to the ballet and see what it's really about.

FW: 女作家　　MW: 男作家

FW: 有人请我写一篇关于俄罗斯芭蕾舞的文章，可是我不知道从哪儿入手。你对舞蹈感兴趣，有什么好建议吗？

MW: 是这样，实际上俄罗斯芭蕾舞根本不是俄罗斯的。它是 17 世纪罗曼诺夫王朝第二个统治者亚历克西斯·米哈伊尔沙皇在位时由外国人介绍进来的。

FW: 噢，他为什么要引进芭蕾舞？

MW: 因为他想在自己的结婚庆典上观看芭蕾舞演出。当时，彼得大帝个人对舞蹈很感兴趣，把一些西方的舞蹈引进宫廷，自己还亲自参与。

FW: 这真是俄罗斯芭蕾舞的正式由来吗？我还以为它源于 1737 年皇家军官学校的体操教师写给安妮皇后的一封信，信上说："我向陛下恳求，我想要 12 个孩子，6 个男孩和 6 个女孩，来表演芭蕾剧和和戏剧舞蹈"。

MW: 你说得没错，俄罗斯第一所芭蕾舞学校于 1738 年成立。这是一所小学校，在旧冬宫只有 2 间教室。

FW: 是不是那所学校后来成了圣彼得堡芭蕾舞学院？我想，那是一所非常有名的学校。

MW: 确实是这样。但是，直到 1800 年，芭蕾舞的第一次辉煌时期才到来。一个名叫查尔斯-路易斯·狄德罗的法国人被认为是"俄罗斯芭蕾舞之父"。他在俄国演出了一系列芭蕾舞作品。

FW: 此后，出现了很多著名的芭蕾舞女演员。我小时候一直梦想当个芭蕾舞演员，但我觉得这种生活一定很艰苦。我知道很多舞蹈演员在很年轻的时候就死了。

MW: 不过，现在情况有些不一样了。拿鲁道夫·尤里耶夫为例，他是 50 多岁去世的，比那些青少年时就去世的舞蹈演员年纪大多了。

FW: 我想他一定是最著名的俄罗斯芭蕾舞演员了。他和玛戈·芳廷配合得很好，以"鲁迪和玛戈＊"而闻名。

MW: 通过一些俄罗斯芭蕾舞团的访问和从前苏联叛逃的舞蹈演员的一些活动，俄罗斯对芭蕾舞的影响延续至今，这些演员有鲁道夫·尤里耶夫、纳塔莉亚·玛卡洛娃和麦克黑尔·巴瑞辛尼可夫。

FW: 是的，俄罗斯芭蕾舞的确很受欢迎，这就是我为什么要写这篇文章的原因。我觉得我们应该去看看芭蕾舞，真正地去了解一下。

■ Any ideas?　有什么好建议？　　　■ set up　建立，成立
■ a hard life　生活艰苦　　　　　　■ at a young age　在年轻时

71. Tolstoy

托尔斯泰

M：Mary   *E*：Edward

M： So, Ed. What do you know about this? Tolstoy's history, what do you know about him?

E： Tolstoy wasn't just one person, you know. They were a whole family of Russian nobility. The Tolstoy's have left **a lasting legacy** in Russian politics, military history, literature, and fine arts.

M： They got around a bit then! Sounds like they did everything, but let's start with the politics ... it says here that Peter Andreevich Tolstoy was a member of Peter the Great's party.

E： Yes, he gradually gained Peter's confidence serving first as the Russian ambassador to Constantinople, then as the head of the secret police.

M： OK, so what about the military Tolstoy's? I've heard of one called Alexander Ivanovich Tolstoy. He was in the Battle of Charnova in 1807 where his regiment **held out** for 15 hours against the whole army commanded by Napoleon.

E： It sounds like you know plenty about him already. Let's go on to the literary Tolstoy's, shall we?

M： Leo Tolstoy is one of the greatest Russian novelists of the 19th century. He wrote *War and Peace* and *Anna Karenina*.

E： I think those books are the two most famous in the whole world! I wonder why he started writing.

M： He started his career in the military, he was first drawn to writing books when he served in Chechenya, and already his first novel, *Kazaky*, was something quite unlike anything written before him.

E： Oh, I see. OK, on to fine arts. It says here that there were many Tolstoy's in high society.

M： Yes, Count Feodor Petrovich Tolstoy was one of the most fashionable Russian drawers and painters of the 1820s. Although he prepared fine illustrations, his true vocation was wax modeling and the design of medals.

E: And also, Count Feodor Ivanovich Tolstoy who was a **notorious drunkard**, gastronome, and duellist. It is said that he killed 11 people in duels.

M: He was involved in a different kind of art though. In 1803 he participated in the first Russian **circumnavigation of the Earth** and after he had his body tattooed!

E: Well, it certainly seems that the Tolstoy's were interesting people, that's for sure.

M：玛莉   E：爱德华

M: 爱德华，这方面你了解吗？有关托尔斯泰的生平，你知道多少？

E: 你知道，不只有一个托尔斯泰，他们家是一个俄罗斯名

> * 列夫·托尔斯泰（1828-1910）：他不仅是一名伟大的作家，还是一名人道主义者，被称为"俄罗斯的良心"。他为自己的贵族身份感到羞愧，同情贫苦的农民，尽可能给予他们各种帮助。他在一封信中写道："生活中我唯一喜欢的就是做我力所能及的事情，也就是根据基督的教义爱上帝和亲人。爱上帝——意思是：爱善行和尽可能地接近它。爱亲人——意思是：像爱自己的兄妹一样，爱所有的人。我致力于做到的正是这一点，也仅仅是这一点。"

门望族。托尔斯泰家族在俄罗斯的政治、军事、文学和美术方面都留下了不朽的遗产。

M: 那时他们有些影响力。好像他们无所不能，不过我们先从政治方面开始……据说彼得·安德烈耶维奇·托尔斯泰是彼得大帝的宠臣。

E: 是的，他逐渐赢得彼得的信任，先做了驻君士坦丁堡的俄罗斯大使，后来又担任了秘密警察机构的领导。

M: 噢，那托尔斯泰家族在军事方面呢？我曾经听说过一个叫亚历山大·伊凡诺维奇·托尔斯泰的人，他1807年参加了查诺瓦战役，他的军团与拿破仑领导的军队对抗达15个小时。

E: 听起来你对他已经了解不少了。那我们接着看看文学界的托尔斯泰，好吗？

M: 列夫·托尔斯泰是19世纪俄罗斯最伟大的小说家之一，著有《战争与和平》和《安娜·卡列尼娜》。

E: 我认为这是全世界最著名的两本书。我想知道他为什么要开始写作。

M: 他一开始的职业是军人，在车臣服役时第一次对写书产生了兴趣，写出了第一部小说《哥萨克》，与他之前的人写的那些书大不一样。

E: 哦，我知道了，接下来看看美术方面。据说在上流社会也有很多托尔斯泰家族的人。

M: 是的，费奥多尔·彼德罗维奇·托尔斯泰伯爵是19世纪20年代俄罗斯最受欢迎的制图员和画家之一。尽管他的插图细致精美，但他真正的职业是做蜡铸模，设计奖章。

E: 此外，费奥多尔·彼德罗维奇·托尔斯泰伯爵还是个声名狼藉的酒鬼、美食家和决斗专家。据说他在决斗中杀死了11个人。

M: 不过他还参与各种不同的艺术创作。1803年他参加了俄罗斯第一届周游地球活动，后来他给自己纹了身。

E: 好了，看起来托尔斯泰家族的人的确很有意思，这一点是肯定无疑了。

■ a lasting legacy　不朽的遗产　　　　　■ hold out　坚持
■ notorious drunkard　声名狼藉的酒鬼　　■ circumnavigation of the Earth　环游地球

72. Vodka

伏特加酒

M: *Man*   *W*: *Woman*

M: Linda, **what do you fancy to** drink? A beer or a glass of wine?

W: To be honest, I'm **sick of both**. I want to try something different.

M: This bar is famous for its vodka, you know. They've got many different flavours, even chocolate, which should be suitable for a chocoholic like you.

W: I'm not sure if I like the taste of vodka, and it's very strong too. It's from Russia, isn't it?

M: Yes, but they make it in other countries too, such as Finland and Sweden.

W: It says here that they sell Russian, flavoured vodka. Oh, they make it from grain. I thought they made it from potatoes!

M: I think in the past they made it from lots of different things. Look here, there's a pamphlet with a brief history.

W: "As early as the beginning of the 16th century 'burning wine' was brought not to Russia, but from it. It was the first experience of the Russian export of vodka that later would take over the whole world".

M: Yes, you can buy it everywhere now!

W: It also says here that they distill it four times. That seems like a lot. And even in the 1700s they were making many **weird and wonderful** flavours. Every landowner had his own special one.

M: What's this flavour? Bird cherry and sage? I don't think you can buy that one nowadays. I wonder which rich landowner decided on that flavour.

W: Look at this, before 1885 vodka was sold only in buckets measuring 12.3 litres. Who could drink that much vodka?

M: Don't worry, here we can just buy it in **a shot**, a single measure of about 25 millilitres.

W: That sounds better. In 1953 the Moscow Special was awarded a gold medal at an international exhibition in Switzerland. That's the one they have here, now we call it

Stolichnaya.

M: So, Linda which flavour are you going to try? They've got various fruits, like strawberry, peach, pear ... and this one ...

W: Chili flavour!? That sounds a bit hot for me! I think I'll start with the chocolate after all, then I might try another one.

M: 男人   **W:** 女人

M: 琳达，你想喝点什么？啤酒还是葡萄酒？

W: 说实话，这两种酒我都喝够了。我想换换口味。

M: 这个酒吧以卖伏特加酒出名。这种酒有很多不同的口味，甚至还有巧克力味的。你那么喜欢吃巧克力，这个应该适合你。

W: 我不敢说是否喜欢伏特加酒的味道，它毕竟也是一种烈性酒。这酒是俄罗斯产的，对不对？

M: 对，不过其他国家也生产，如芬兰和瑞典。

W: 据说他们卖给俄罗斯人那种加香味的伏特加酒。哦，还有，他们是用粮食加工酒的。我过去以为是用土豆加工而成的。

M: 我想在过去它们是用很多不同的原料加工的。看，这儿有一本小册子，里面有简史介绍。

W: "早在16世纪初，'烧酒'还没有被引进俄罗斯，但伏特加酒就已经出口了。这是俄罗斯第一次出口伏特加酒，后来就传到世界各地。"

M: 是这样，现在哪儿都能买到伏特加酒。

W: 小册子上还说这些酒要经过4次蒸馏。似乎次数不少。18世纪他们甚至还生产了很多味道怪异奇妙的伏特加酒。每个贵族地主都有自己独特的伏特加酒。

M: 这个是什么味的？稠李和鼠尾草？我想现在你买不着这一种了。我不知道这种味道的伏特加酒是哪个富有的贵族地主生产的。

W: 看这里，1885年以前，伏特加酒只按桶卖，每桶装12.3升。谁能喝那么多伏特加酒？

M: 别担心。在这里我们可以只买一杯，只有25毫升。

W: 这样听起来还不错。1953年在瑞士国际展览会上，这一莫斯科特产获得了金奖。这是他们在那次展览会获得的唯一奖项，现在我们叫它红牌伏特加。

M: 琳达，你想尝哪种味道？有各种水果味的，像草莓、桃子、梨……这个是……

W: 辣椒味!？对我来说，这个好像有点太辣了！我想我还是喝巧克力味的吧，然后我再试试其他味道的。

■ What do you fancy to ...? 你想……?   ■ be sick of both 两个都不喜欢
■ weird and wonderful 怪异和奇妙   ■ a shot 一杯

73. Mandela

曼德拉

D: *Director*   **S**: *Scriptwriter*

D: I've had a great idea for a movie, Nelson Mandela.

S: Well, that would certainly be an interesting topic.

D: I thought that we could start in his childhood, his life in prison and then his achievements later in life.

S: Sounds good. Mandela was educated at a local **mission school**. He entered the University College of Fort Hare and quickly became active in student politics.

D: Is that why he **was kicked out of** university?

S: That's right. I think he was a little too outspoken for his time.

D: So then he moved to Johannesburg and finished his university education. He then entered into the study and subsequently the practice of law.

S: I think law was a good choice of major for him.

D: After that, he formed the ANC (African National Congress) Youth League, to transform the ANC from an elitist political union into a more **broadly-based** political movement.

S: As the apartheid policy began to reach deeper into South African life, Mandela found himself constantly in opposition to the official political line of the Afrikaner-dominated government. He was banned, then arrested during the late 1950s.

D: I guess that was the beginning of why he was sent to prison in 1962 for 27 years. Can you imagine, 27 years in **solitary confinement**!?

S: And most of that time was spent doing **hard labour**. That just shows his **strength of character**. Many men would have gone insane, I'm sure.

D: During his imprisonment, Mandela became a symbol of the anti-apartheid movement among South Africa's black population and among the international community that opposed apartheid.

S: Yes, and he also rejected government offers for him to leave prison, as long as he renounced violence.

D: Mandela shared the Nobel Peace Prize in 1993 with F. W. deKlerk, South Africa's last white president. Their combined efforts ended apartheid in South Africa.

S: What an amazing man! Three years after his release, South Africans of all races were allowed to vote for the first time in a national election. They selected Mandela as their president, giving him 62% of the vote.

D: I think that this **bio-pic** could be our best project ever.

D: 导演   **S:** 编剧

D: 我有个好主意，拍一部有关纳尔逊·曼德拉的电影。

S: 这个话题肯定有意思。

D: 我想我们可以从他的童年开始讲起，接着是狱中生活，再下来是他晚年所取得的成就。

S: 听起来不错。曼德拉是在当地一所教会学校上的学，后来上了海尔堡大学，很快就成了学生政治运动的积极分子。

D: 他是不是因为这个被大学开除了？

S: 是这样。我认为在当时那个时代，他讲话太大胆了。

D: 所以后来他搬到了约翰内斯堡，在那里上完了大学。接着又开始钻研法律，随后就开业当律师。

S: 我想，对他而言法律专业是最佳选择。

D: 此后，他组建了非洲人国民大会（非国大）青年联盟，把非国大从一个由少数精英参与的政治联盟变成了广大群众参与的政治运动。

S: 由于种族隔离政策开始越来越深地影响了南非人民的生活，曼德拉经常发现自己与南非白人领导的政府立场相反。20 世纪 50 年代末他被禁止参加公众集会，随后遭到逮捕。

D: 我想这就是为什么他在 1962 年入狱后被关了 27 年的原因。你能想象吗，27 年单独监禁！？

S: 27 年间，他大部分时间都是在做苦役。这正好突显了他坚强的性格。我肯定，在同样情况下，很多人都会发疯的。

D: 监禁期间，曼德拉成了南非黑人以及国际社会反对种族隔离运动的象征。

S: 是的，他还拒绝了政府提出的要他正式宣布放弃暴力的释放他的条件。

D: 1993 年曼德拉和南非最后一任白人总统弗雷·威廉姆·德克勒克一起获得了诺贝尔和平奖。他们共同努力结束了南非的种族隔离制度。

S: 多么了不起的人！他获释之后 3 年，南非人民首次不分种族全部获准参加全国的大选投票。他们推选曼德拉做他们的总统，62% 的选票都投向了他。

D: 我想这个传记片可能会成为我们有史以来最好的一个计划。

■ mission school 教会学校
■ broadly-based 广大群众为基础的
■ hard labour 苦役
■ bio-pic 传记片

■ be kicked out of 开除出
■ solitary confinement 单独监禁
■ strength of character 坚强的性格

74. Diamonds

钻石

P: *Paris*   **N**: *Nicole*

P: Nicole, look at this!

N: Is that your **engagement ring**?

P: Yes, it's a South African diamond.

N: I think those are the best in the world, it must have cost your boyfriend **an arm and a leg**.

P: You're right! It all started when in 1867 a pretty pebble found near the Orange River, in the wilds of South Africa, was identified as a 21-carat diamond.

N: That's bigger than yours, but not the biggest. Placer diamonds were found between the Vaal and Orange Rivers later in the year, and in March 1869 an 83-carat diamond turned up.

P: So that must have been the start of the **diamond rush**. By the end of 1871 two well-defined areas were recognized as the source areas, or "pipes", for the diamonds. Four pipes were discovered all together at the town of Kimberley.

N: So many people worked there. In 1872 the pipes were giant open quarries worked by 2500 miners and 10,000 hired laborers.

P: That's huge! But, as they went deeper, the more difficult it got. The number of **claim owners** in the Kimberley pit **dropped dramatically** as people **bought out** their neighbours.

N: Yes, but then the Diamond Trade Act allowed the companies to set up "searching-houses" in a system of routine surveillance, searching, and stripping by company police.

P: The companies were forced by strikes to be more lenient to their white workers than to blacks. So, I guess this was the first apartheid.

N: Unfortunately, yes. The methods were successful, however. After De Beers set up its "searching-houses" in March 1883, its diamond production rose significantly, showing that there had been a hemorrhage of diamonds from the workings.

P: The De Beers? I think my 21st birthday present was by De Beers.

N: It probably was. You know who headed De Beers? Lord Rothschild, probably one of the most famous rich men in the world.

P: Oh, so that's why my dad always says, "Who do you think I am, Rothschild?"

N: I'm going to have their pale pinkish yellow diamond, called "Champagne" for my engagement ring.

P: Good choice. After all, a diamond is for ever!

P: 帕里斯　　N: 尼科尔

P: 尼科尔，看看这个！

N: 是你的订婚戒指吗？

P: 对，是南非钻戒。

N: 我认为这是世界上最好的钻石，一定花了你男朋友很多钱。

> ＊世界上最大的宝石金刚石名叫"库利南"，1905 年发现于南非。它纯净透明，带有淡蓝色调，是最佳品级的宝石金刚石。1907 年库利南被赠送给英国王室，1908 年由荷兰的阿斯查尔公司加工成 9 粒大钻石和 96 粒小钻石。最大的一粒名叫"非洲之星一号"，镶在英国国王的权杖上；次大的一粒镶在英帝国王冠上。
> ＊罗斯柴尔德家族：犹太商人最会赚钱的代表，19 世纪崛起于法国，控制世界黄金市场和欧洲经济命脉长达 200 年，成为欧洲金融市场呼风唤雨和左右政局的最大力量。

P: 你说得没错！1867 年，一颗漂亮的小石头在南非奥兰治河附近的荒野中被发现，后来被鉴定为 21 克拉的钻石。

N: 那比你的这颗要大，但不是最大的＊。1867 年下半年，在瓦尔河和奥兰治河交界的地方找到了钻石砂矿，1869 年 3 月发现了一颗 83 克拉的钻石。

P: 所以这一定是引起钻石潮的原因。到 1871 年末，有两个地区被明确认定为钻石区或管状矿脉。在金伯利城共发现了 4 个管状矿脉。

N: 所以很多人都到那里工作。1872 年各矿脉都成为巨大的露天采掘场，有 2500 名矿工，还有 1 万名雇佣工人。

P: 真够大的！可是后来这工作越来越难做了。而且，随着有些人买下他们邻居的土地所有权，金伯利矿坑产权拥有者人数也急剧下降。

N: 是这样，而且当时出台的《钻石贸易法案》允许各公司在例行的日常监督体制下设立"搜身室"，由公司警察对工人进行搜查和脱衣服检查。

P: 由于罢工，公司不得不对他们的白人工人比对待黑人工人更宽大些。因此，我想这就是第一次种族隔离的出现。

N: 非常遗憾，确实是这样。不过，这种方法的确奏效。1883 年 3 月，德·比尔斯公司设立自己的"搜身室"之后，该公司的钻石产量大大增加，这表明工作过程中一直存在钻石大量流失现象。

P: 德·比尔斯公司？我记得我 21 岁的生日礼物就是这家公司出产的。

N: 可能是吧。你知道德·比尔斯公司的领导是谁？是罗思柴尔德＊勋爵，他可能是世界上最富有的人之一。

P: 噢，所以这就是为什么我爸爸经常说："你以为我是谁，罗思柴尔德吗？"

N: 我想买个订婚戒指，就是他们生产的浅粉红色又带点黄色的钻石，叫做"香槟色"。

P: 眼光不错。毕竟钻石是恒久不变的嘛。

■ engagement ring 订婚戒指　　　　■ an arm and a leg 非常高的价格
■ diamond rush 钻石潮　　　　　　　■ claim owner 产权拥有者
■ drop dramatically 急剧下降　　　　■ buy out 买下所有权

75. Rain

雨

S: *Shopper*   *M*: *Music shop owner*

S: Hi, would it be possible for you **to give me a hand**? I'm looking for South Korean pop.

M: Yes, no problem. The section is over here, we have material by BoA, Se7en and Rain.

S: Rain! That's what I'm looking for, my friend bought me a CD of his and now I can't stop listening to it!

M: He's really popular, we call him "The South Korean King of Pop". **He's huge** in Japan, Hong Kong, China, Thailand and across much of Asia.

S: Really? I had no idea. Why do you think he's so popular?

M: Well, it's a combination of his **angelic face**, great body and Justin Timberlake style dance moves. He stars in **soap operas** as well as being a singer.

S: I see. Do you know more about him?

M: Actually, yes. I'm **a big fan**, you see. He's 23, his real name is Ji Hoon Jung and he used to be poor. He lived in Seoul in a one room apartment, but dreamed of being famous. He must have **pushed himself** very hard to get where he is today.

S: Yes, many famous people come from humble beginnings.

M: Did you know he was listed on *Time* magazines "World's Most Influential People" list?

S: Really? I guess he must have a lot of influence in South Korea, maybe throughout Asia. Through his music, soaps and so on.

M: He plans to star in a movie next year but he says he has no desire to be in a big budget film. Maybe that's because he was a soap actor.

S: Probably. Do you think he will ever be famous in the West?

M: I hope so. At the moment he's studying English **day and night** because he wants to become famous in America. Before he visited the U. S. , Rain already had **a fan base**, thanks to Internet music sites, **satellite TV** and DVDs of his soap operas. He's also had two **sell out concerts** in the small venue at Madison Square Garden.

S: Oh, so he's pretty popular over there already then?

M: Yes. And he's releasing an English language album later this year.

S: Great! Now I will be able to understand his songs!

M: That's true.

S: 顾客　　**M**: 唱片店主

S: 你好，能帮我个忙吗？我想买韩国流行歌曲。

M: 好的，没问题。流行歌曲在那边，我们有宝儿、Se7en 和雨的唱片。

S: 雨！我就是要找他的唱片，我朋友给我买了一张他的 CD，现在我听得爱不释手。

M: 他非常受欢迎，我们叫他"韩国流行歌王"。他在日本、香港、中国、泰国和亚洲很多国家都很有名。

S: 真的吗？我不知道。你觉得他为什么那么受欢迎？

M: 是这样，他长得纯真可爱，身材健美，会跳贾斯汀·汀布莱克式的舞蹈。还在很多电视剧中担任主角和歌手。

S: 我知道。那你还了解什么更多的信息吗？

M: 当然了解。你知道，我是他的大粉丝。他 23 岁，真名叫郑智薰，过去很穷。他住在首尔的一套一居室公寓里，但梦想成为名人。他肯定是不断鞭策自己才取得今天这样的成就。

S: 是的，很多名人都出身贫寒。

M: 他被列入《时代周刊》"世界上最有影响力的人物"排行榜，你知道这个吗？

S: 真的吗？我想他在韩国的影响一定很大，也许遍及整个亚洲。包括他的唱片、电视剧等等。

M: 他计划明年在一部电影中担任主角，但他说不想演预算投入太大的电影。这也许是因为他是个电视剧演员的缘故吧。

S: 有这种可能。你认为他在西方国家也会成名吗？

M: 我希望如此。他正在日夜学习英语，因为他想在美国成名。凭借互联网音乐网站、卫星电视和他拍的电视剧的 DVD，他在去美国之前已经拥有了自己的粉丝团。此外，他还在麦迪逊广场花园的小球馆举办了两场音乐会，全部爆满。

S: 噢，那他现在是不是在那边已经很红了？

M: 是的，而且他今年下半年就要发行英文专辑。

S: 太好了！那样我就能听懂他的歌曲了。

M: 没错。

■ give me a hand　帮我个忙		■ He's huge.　他非常有名。
■ angelic face　可爱的外形		■ soap opera　肥皂剧
■ a big fan　大粉丝		■ push oneself　不断鞭策自己
■ day and night　日日夜夜		■ a fan base　粉丝团
■ satellite TV　卫星电视		■ sell out concerts　满座音乐会

151

76. Kimchi

韩式泡菜

R：*Reporter*   *C*：*Chef*

R：Hi there. I'm doing a story about Asian cuisine and wondered if you could give me some details about Korean food? I'm particularly interested in "kimchi".

C：Of course! Well, kimchi is basically a salted, pickled vegetable dish, often a basic **side dish** in any Korean meal. The fermentation of different vegetables, complemented by salted fish and other seasonings, give it a unique flavor. It is also a nutritious dish, providing vitamins, lactic acid, and minerals. Kimchi can also **be preserved for a long time**.

R：OK, so pickles. Is there more than one type of kimchi?

C：Yes, there are many, many types of kimchi. Here are some basic ones, whole cabbage kimchi, the cabbage isn't actually whole though, it's cut in half lengthways. Next is wrapped kimchi, where seafood, fruit and many other ingredients are wrapped inside cabbage leaves.

R：Mmmm ... that one sounds lovely. It smells good too.

C：It's delicious, we can try some later. On to white cabbage kimchi, this is less watery than the other types. It uses more pickled fish and red pepper, too. Then, stuffed cucumber kimchi, which can be done using baby cucumbers. Followed by hot radish kimchi, where the white radishes are **cut into small cubes**.

R：OK, I see. There are so many! Are there any others?

C：Yes, over here we have whole radish kimchi, made using whole small, salted radishes. Next we have radish water kimchi, which is made without red pepper powder. And finally, water kimchi, made of thinly sliced radish and cabbage, watercress and spring onions.

R：Wow! And this is just a selection? Which is your favourite?

C: I have to say I enjoy the stuffed cucumber kimchi. It is suitable for the spring and summer months, when most people **lose their appetites**. Cucumbers are fermented after being stuffed with different seasonings. The crunchiness and fragrance of well-fermented cucumbers make them a true delicacy. Only the desired amount can be prepared at one time as it easily turns sour. Which would you like to try?

R: All of them! But, I think I'll try the wrapped kimchi. That one sounds the most interesting to me.

R：记者　　C：厨师

R: 你好，我在写亚洲菜肴方面的报道，不知道你能否给我讲讲韩国食品？我对韩式泡菜尤其感兴趣。

C: 当然可以！韩式泡菜＊就是用盐腌制的蔬菜，是韩国人餐桌上的佐餐小菜。各种蔬菜发酵后，佐以咸鱼和其他调味品，味道的确与众不同。泡菜也很有营养，为人体提供维生素、乳酸和矿物质。此外，它还能保存很长时间。

> ＊ 韩式泡菜：过去，韩国家庭都将一排排泡菜缸摆放在庭院里、地窖中。这在当今高楼林立的大都市已无法做到，取而代之的是现代化的泡菜工厂。尽管如此，韩国家庭主妇仍喜欢自制风味独特的泡菜，用小罐腌制好后储存在冰箱里。招待客人时拿出自家的泡菜也是一种待客之道。

R: 没错，泡菜就是这样。泡菜不只一种吧？

C: 是的，泡菜有很多种。我给你介绍几种最普通的：整白菜泡菜，当然白菜不是整个泡的，要从中间一分为二切开。另一种是包心泡菜，白菜叶子里包着海鲜、水果和其他东西。

R: 嗯……这种泡菜好像很好看，闻起来也挺香的。

C: 味道很好，我们一会儿可以尝尝。接下来是元白菜泡菜，它比其他的泡菜水分要少，里面的咸鱼和辣椒也多。还有一种全部用黄瓜做的泡菜，用的都是嫩黄瓜。再有就是辣萝卜泡菜，把白萝卜切成小丁做的。

R: 噢，我知道了。种类真多！还有其它的吗？

C: 有，我们这里还有整萝卜泡菜，是用盐腌的整棵小萝卜。还有一种萝卜水泡菜，不用辣椒粉。最后一种是水泡菜，用切得很薄的萝卜条、卷心菜和葱做成。

R: 哇，这只是其中的一部分吧？你最喜欢哪一种？

C: 要我说，我喜欢黄瓜泡菜。它适合春秋两季食用，那时大多数人食欲不振。黄瓜里面填满各种不同的调味品，发酵后就变成了泡菜。发酵好的黄瓜又脆又香，真是美味佳肴。但这种泡菜容易变酸，所以比较理想的做法是一次只做一定的量。你想尝哪一种？

R: 都想尝！不过，我想我还是尝尝包心泡菜吧，这个我最感兴趣。

- side dish 佐餐小菜
- cut into small cubes 切成小丁
- be preserved for a long time 保存很长时间
- lose one's appetites 食欲不振

77. Bullfighting

斗牛

L: *Local*   *T*: *Tourist*

T: Hi. I wonder if you can help me. One of my friends recommended going to see the bullfighting. Could you tell me where I should go?

L: I'm happy to help. In Andalusia it's the only thing to do, but I hope you have **some time on your hands**. A "corrida" can **take the whole afternoon**.

T: Really? Why does it take so long?

L: There are six bulls, which are to be killed by three matadors.

T: Matador ... that's the man who fights the bull?

L: Absolutely! You can only find the finest ones in Andalusia.

T: How do they fight them? I mean, I saw on TV that they wave capes around at them.

L: They do not just wave the cape, it's an art. They also use a sword, called an "estoque" and a smaller cape, called a "muleta" which is used at the end of the fight.

T: I see. And how long does each fight last?

L: Usually, around fifteen minutes, **give or take**.

T: And the matadors wear such beautiful clothes! What can you tell me about them?

L: The matadors wear a **distinctive costume**, consisting of a silk jacket heavily embroidered in gold, **skintight trousers**, and a "montera", which is a special hat.

T: I bet the costumes are expensive.

L: Very expensive. A "traje de luces", which means "suit of lights", can cost several thousand pounds; a **top matador** must have at least six of them a season.

T: They must spend more on clothes than most women do!

L: But not only are their costumes expensive, the bulls are too.

T: Really? Why do they use expensive bulls if they are just going to kill them?

L: **Only the best** can be used. Most bulls weigh more than 460 kilos, the fully experienced matador uses bulls which are only older than four years. It costs a lot of money to keep a bull for four years.

T: It sounds so interesting. Where is the arena?

L: **You are in luck**, because there is one at the end of this street. That's where I'm going, come along if you'd like.

T: Oh, yes please.

L: 当地人　　**T**: 游客

T: 你好。能帮我个忙吗？我有个朋友建议我去看斗牛*表演，你能告诉我应该去哪儿看吗？

L: 很高兴我能帮上忙。在安达路西亚这个地方，只有斗牛值得一看，不过我希望你多准备些时间，因为看一次斗牛要用整整一下午。

T: 真的吗？为什么要那么长时间？

L: 因为3个斗牛士要杀掉6头牛。

T: 斗牛士……是斗牛的那个人吗？

L: 没错！只有在安达路西亚才能看到最棒的斗牛士。

T: 他们怎么跟牛斗？我是说，我在电视上看过，他们围着牛晃动披风。

L: 他们不只是晃动披风，这是一门艺术。他们还用一种剑，叫 estoque，还用一种比较小的布，叫斗牛红布，在斗牛结束时才用。

T: 我明白了。那斗一场牛需要多长时间？

L: 15分钟左右，一般没有太大变化。

T: 斗牛士穿的衣服非常漂亮！你能给我讲讲吗？

L: 斗牛士的装束是与众不同，有一件丝质夹克，上面有密密麻麻的金色刺绣，还有紧身裤和布帽———一种特殊的帽子。

T: 我敢说这套装束一定很贵。

L: 非常贵。一件 traje de luce，意思是"光明之衣"，要花几千英镑，一个出色的斗牛士一个季节必须至少准备6套这样的衣服。

T: 他们花在衣服上的钱一定比大多数女人要多！

L: 不但衣服很贵，牛的价钱也不低。

T: 真的吗？既然他们要杀死这些牛，那为什么还要用这么贵的牛？

L: 他们只用最好的牛。大多数的牛重达460多公斤，经验较丰富的斗牛士只用4岁以上的公牛，而把这些牛养4年要花好多钱。

T: 听起来很有意思。竞技场在哪儿？

L: 你的运气真好，这条街走到头就有一个。我也要去那里，如果你愿意，我们一起去吧。

T: 噢，好的，请。

> *斗牛：西班牙斗牛起源于祈求农牧业丰收的仪式，最早出现于11世纪。现在，西班牙共有大小斗牛场400多个，最大的斗牛场可容纳2万人，每年斗牛次数达5000场以上。斗牛的魅力，在于这是一种冒险的艺术，一种被美化的生死之争。斗牛士被视为独特的人群，具备了勇敢、高雅、技巧、体力、敏锐、浪漫及疯狂。有很多艺术家从斗牛中获得了创作灵感，像毕加索、哥雅、海明威、比才等。海明威说过："斗牛最大的乐趣之一，就是感受到在死亡的控制下产生的对死亡的反抗。"

- some time on your hands　由你支配的一些时间
- take the whole afternoon　需要整个一下午
- give or take　无大变化；允许有小的误差
- skintight trousers　紧身裤
- distinctive costume　与众不同的装束
- top matador　出色的斗牛士
- You are in luck.　你的运气好。
- only the best　只有最好的

155

78. Flamenco Dancing

弗拉明戈舞

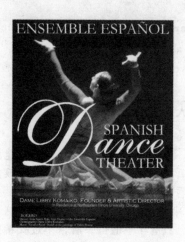

T: Dance teacher   *S*: Student

T: OK, today we are going to look at something new, something **very close to my heart** ...
Flamenco!

S: Flamenco ... that comes from Spain, doesn't it?

T: Yes, and so do I. So, today we are going to concentrate on a new dance, but first you
must know all about Flamenco.

S: I know it's a very old dance. It can be **traced back** for centuries, **right back to** the
1400s.

T: Yes, that's right. King Ferdinand V and Queen Isabella disliked anyone who was different,
so the minorities came together to help each other, and so, Flamenco was born.

S: I read that Flamenco, in general, consists of three artistic elements: the singing, known as
"cante", the dance, called "baile" and the guitar, or "guitarra".

T: Yes, we must mix these three elements together for true Flamenco. In addition, there are
often members of a Flamenco group playing "palmas" or hand-clapping.

S: I see. So, I suppose the relationship between the artists is similar to that of Jazz—there is a
basic structure that one must follow, but **at its heart**, it is an improvised form.

T: Right. But the singing is the centre, the dancer physically interprets the words and emotion
of the singer through his or her movements, which include percussive footwork and
intricate hand, arm and body movements.

S: What about the guitarists? What role do they play?

T: The guitarist provides the accompaniment to the singer and dancer, accentuating his or her
vocal lines or melodies.

S: So, where did Flamenco start? I know when it started, but where?

T: Most scholars will agree that the birthplace of Flamenco is Jerez de la Frontera, a small city
in Southern Spain.

S: Just in one place? But I thought Flamenco was from a mix of cultures?

T：However, because many people moved from town to town, Flamenco quickly **gained roots** in several Andalucian towns, including Sevilla and Granada.

S：But nowadays it is so popular, **nothing short of** an international phenomenon!

T：Yes, and we can go to the annual Flamenco Festival in Jerez.

S：I hope the class has the opportunity to visit next year, that would be fantastic.

T：舞蹈老师　　S：学生

T：好了，我们今天要看一些新舞蹈，我最喜欢的……弗拉明戈舞。

S：弗拉明戈舞……是西班牙的舞蹈吗？

T：是的，我也是西班牙人。好，今天我们要集中精力练习新舞蹈，但首先你们一定要全面了解一下弗拉明戈舞。

S：我知道这是一种非常古老的舞蹈，可以追溯到几百年前，直到 15 世纪。

T：是的，就是这样。斐迪南国王五世和伊莎贝拉王后不喜欢跟他们不一样的人，所以各少数民族就聚在一起互相帮助，弗拉明戈舞就这样诞生了。

S：我了解过弗拉明戈舞，它一般包括 3 个艺术要素：唱歌，就是大家熟悉的 cante；舞蹈，叫做 baile；还有吉他，叫做 guitarra。

T：是这样，我们必须把这 3 种要素综合在一起，才能懂得真正的弗拉明戈舞。此外，弗拉明戈舞表演队的演员还经常打拍子或击掌。

S：我知道。所以我认为各演员之间的关系有点像爵士乐中各要素的关系——有一个大家必须遵循的基本框架，但实质上却是一种即兴表演。

T：你说得对。但唱歌是最主要的，舞蹈者用身体动作来传递信息和情感，这包括敲击的步伐，以及手、胳膊和身体的复杂动作。

S：那吉他手呢？他们起什么作用？

T：吉他手为演唱者和舞蹈者伴奏，突出他们的歌词或旋律。

S：那弗拉明戈舞是从哪儿兴起的？我知道了它兴起的时间，那发源地呢？

T：多数学者认为弗拉明戈舞的发源地是赫雷斯，西班牙南部的一个小城市。

S：只有这一个地方吗？可是我认为弗拉明戈舞是多种文化的组合，不是吗？

T：事实上，由于很多人从这个城镇搬到另外一个城镇，弗拉明戈舞很快在安达卢西亚的一些城镇扎根，包括塞维利亚和格拉纳达。

S：但是，如今弗拉明戈舞非常受欢迎，简直可以说是风靡世界！

T：是的，而且我们还可以参加每年在赫雷斯举行的弗拉明戈节。

S：我希望全班同学明年都有机会去参观一下，那一定会棒极了。

- very close to my heart　我最喜欢的
- right back to　一直到
- vocal lines　歌词
- nothing short of　完全是，简直可以说
- be traced back　追溯到
- at its heart　实质上
- gain roots　扎根，立足

79. Don Quixote

堂吉诃德

S1: *Student*   *S2*: *Foreign student* (*from Spain*)

S1: I just found a book in the library, a Spanish one. Is it famous? I don't know the name, but I'm sure I've heard of the author.

S2: Let's see. Hmm ... Cervantes? He's a very famous author. This book is *Don Quixote*. But nowadays, we spell it "Quijote" in Spanish.

S1: Oh, so "Quixote" is **old fashioned**. Yes, I knew I'd heard of Cervantes, but I've never read this book.

S2: Well, I guess it's pretty **heavy going**, but if you can finish it, it's really worth it. It's a masterpiece!

S1: Really? It says here that the first part was published in 1605 and the second in 1615. That's a long time ago.

S2: But, it's one of the earliest written novels in a modern European language and is one of the most influential works of Spanish literature.

S1: I see. So he must have been an excellent writer, perhaps **well ahead of his time**.

S2: His full name was Miguel de Cervantes Saavedra, and most people believe him to be brilliant. I've read the book before, but as I say, it can be challenging.

S1: What's it about? I mean, Don Quixote was a bit crazy, wasn't he?

S2: The book tells the story of Alonso Quixano, a man who has read so many stories about brave knights that, he goes mad and, renames himself Don Quixote de la Mancha.

S1: So, he thinks he really is a knight? OK, and what does he do? Where does he go?

S2: Well, he **sets out** to fight injustice in the name of his beloved maiden Aldonsa, or as he knows her in his mind, Dulcinea del Toboso.

S1: So, it's a love story, then. But, I think nowadays we have words in English based on him. For example, the adjective "quixotic", which means "idealistic and impractical", derives from his name.

S2: Oh, really? You use his name in English? I never knew that.

S1: Yes, we do. So, I think he wasn't just famous in Spain, he's famous throughout the whole English speaking world.

S2: If I were you, I'd read it. You may even find some more words or phrases we use in English.

S1: 学生　　S2: 西班牙学生

S1: 我刚从图书馆找到一本关于西班牙的书。它有名吗？书名我不熟悉，但我确实听说过这本书的作者。

S2: 我看看。嗯……塞万提斯？他可是一位非常著名的作家，这本书叫《堂吉诃德》*。不过现在，在我们西班牙语中拼成 Quijote。

> *《堂吉诃德》：西班牙作家塞万提斯（1547－1616）创作的长篇小说，共两部。穷贵族堂吉诃德阅读骑士小说入迷，带领侍从桑丘·潘沙出门行侠，企图用理想化的骑士精神改造社会。他痛恨专横残暴，主持正义，但耽于幻想，脱离实际，在现实面前四处碰壁，最后终于醒悟。小说不仅讽刺骑士文学和骑士制度，而且嘲讽封建贵族的腐朽没落，同时也反映了作者的人文主义理想，是欧洲早期的优秀现实主义小说。

S1: 噢，那么说吉诃德是一个过时的名字了。是的，我听说过塞万提斯，可是从来没读过这本书。

S2: 不过，我认为这本书很不好读，但是如果你能读完，应该还是很值的。这是一部杰作。

S1: 真的吗？书上说第一部分在 1605 年出版，第二部分在 1615 年出版。时间距我们很遥远。

S2: 但是这本书是最早用欧洲现代语言写出的小说之一，是西班牙文学中最有影响的作品之一。

S1: 我知道。那他一定是个优秀的作家，也许远远走在了他那个时代的前面。

S2: 他的全名叫米盖尔·德·塞万提斯·萨阿维德拉，多数人认为他非常出色。我以前读过这本书，但就像我刚才说的，这本书很不好读。

S1: 这本书是讲什么的？我是说，堂吉诃德有点疯疯癫癫的，对不对？

S2: 这本书讲述的是阿伦索·吉哈诺的故事，他读了很多有关勇敢骑士的故事，然后变得疯疯癫癫，给自己起了个新名字叫堂吉诃德·德·拉·曼恰。

S1: 那样，他就认为自己成了真正的骑士了？好了，那他都做些什么事？去了哪些地方？

S2: 他爱着一个叫阿尔东萨的姑娘，或者说他在心里叫她达西妮亚·托博索，他就是为了她出发去与所有的不平之事做斗争。

S1: 那么说这是个爱情故事了。不过，现在根据他的故事出现了很多英语词汇。例如，形容词"堂吉诃德式的"，意思是"理想主义的，不切实际的"，这来源于他的名字。

S2: 哦，真的吗？你们英语中也用他的名字？我怎么就从来不知道这些。

S1: 没错，我们在用。所以我想他不只是著名的西班牙人物，在所有讲英语的国家中也是个名人。

S2: 我要是你的话，就好好读读这本小说。在我们英语中你还会找到很多这样的词或词组。

- old fashioned　过时的
- well ahead of his time　远远走在了他那个时代的前面
- heavy going　进展艰难/缓慢
- set out　出发，动身

80. Picasso

毕加索

E: *Eleanor*   *J*: *Jules*

E: Jules, just look at this amazing painting.

J: It is amazing, but what is it exactly?

E: It's a Picasso! The style you are looking at is called "Cubism", it does look kind of strange, I must admit.

J: Yes, strange but beautiful. What's it called?

E: Let me see ... this one is *Les Demoiselles de Avignon*, painted in 1907.

J: 1907? That's one hundred years ago, but his work looks so modern!

E: Well, he was born in 1881, so I guess all of his pieces are old. Did you know he created over 20,000 paintings, prints, drawings, sculptures, ceramics, theatre sets and costumes?

J: He must have lived to be a very old man to do all of that during his life.

E: He died when he was 92, so he had a long life, yes.

J: I heard he was **a bit of a womaniser**, he had many girlfriends, who he often painted and had many children.

E: Yes, that's true. But I think he only married twice. His true love was a lady called Jacqueline, who he married in 1961. By then he was already 79 years old!

J: Oh, yes, I have heard of her, he painted something for her. I remember reading that in a magazine.

E: In the painting he was a faun, calmly and coolly gazing with mature confidence and wisdom at a nymph who **blows** her **instrument** to the stars.

J: So, the picture embraces his spellbound love for Jacqueline. How romantic!

E: That one was called *Faun and Starry Night*, he painted it in 1955 before they got married. Look, it's here in the book.

J: Yes, that's the one! I know that one, but what's this one? It says it was painted in 1929.

E: This one is called *Nude Standing by the Sea*, this one is very strange!

J: Look at her body, all the shapes are wrong. It's **very striking** though.

E: This is called "Surrealist Imagery", where he **distorted figures** and morphed them together. He started it during the 1920s.

J: Well, it may be strange, but I like it. I think that Picasso must have been a real genius.

E: 埃莉诺   J: 朱尔斯

E: 朱尔斯，过来看看这幅画，真令人叫绝。

J: 真的太让人惊讶了，不过这究竟画的是什么？

E: 是毕加索*的画！你看到的这种风格叫立体派，我得承认确实看起来有点古怪。

J: 是的，有点怪但很漂亮。这幅画叫什么名字？

E: 我看看……叫《亚威农的少女》，画于1907年。

J: 1907年？那是100年前了，可是他的作品看起来那么现代！

> * 毕加索（1881－1973）：他的创作历程大致分为几个时期：蓝色时期、粉红时期、非洲时期、分析立体主义、综合立体主义、新古典时期、超现实主义。无论风格如何变化，他的作品都保持着粗犷刚劲的个性，都能达到内部的统一与和谐。在漫长的93年人生中，他创作了约6万件作品，除绘画、素描之外，还包括雕刻、陶器、版画、舞台服装等。在20世纪，没有一位艺术家能像他那样，以惊人的坦诚和创造力任意地塑造画布上的世界。

E: 的确是。毕加索生于1881年，所以我想他所有的作品都是年代很久远的。他创作了20,000多幅油画，还有版画、素描、雕刻、陶艺、舞台设计和服装，你知道这些吗？

J: 他一定是毕生都在创作，而且很长寿。

E: 他去世时是92岁，寿命是很长。

J: 我听说他很风流，有很多女朋友，经常为她们作画，还有很多孩子。

E: 是的，确实如此。但是我认为他只结过两次婚。他真正爱的是一个叫杰奎琳的女子。他们在1961年结婚，那时他已经79岁了。

J: 哦，没错。我听说过她。他为她画过一些画。我记得在一本杂志上读过相关报道。

E: 在这幅画中他是半人半羊状的农牧神，带着成熟的自信和智慧，平静、沉着地凝视着宁芙女神，她正对着星星吹奏乐器。

J: 所以，从这幅画就可看出他对杰奎琳执着的爱。多么浪漫啊！

E: 这幅画叫做《农牧神和星夜》，是1955年在他们结婚前画的。看，就在这本书里。

J: 是的，就是这个，我知道这画。那这幅是什么？上面说画于1929年。

E: 这幅画叫《在海滨的女人》，非常与众不同！

J: 看，她的身体曲线全画错了。不过很引人注意。

E: 这叫做超现实主义肖像，他扭曲了人的外形，然后再把它们组合在一起。他是从20世纪20年代开始创作这种作品的。

J: 也许是有点怪，不过我喜欢这种作品。我认为毕加索一定是个真正的天才。

- a bit of a womaniser　风流
- very striking　非常显眼，醒目
- blow instrument　吹奏乐曲
- distort figure　扭曲外形

81. St. George

圣乔治

E：*Englishman*　　*T*：*Tourist*

E：Hi. You've **chosen a good day** for visiting England.

T：Oh. Why is that?

E：Today is St. George's Day.

T：I've never heard of that. What's special about it?

E：Well, **for a start**, it's England's National Day. And St. George is our patron saint.

T：What's a patron saint?

E：A patron saint is a real or mythical character who in times of national trouble comes to the rescue of that country.

T：Tell me something about St. George. He must have been a famous Englishman, right?

E：Wrong. Actually he was a Roman soldier in about the 2nd or 3rd century AD. George held the rank of tribune in the Roman army and was beheaded by Diocletian at Nicomedia on 23 April, 303, for protesting against the Emperor's persecution of Christians. George rapidly became venerated throughout Christendom as **an example of** bravery in defence of the poor and the defenceless and of the Christian faith.

T：But what has a Roman soldier to do with England?

E：You remember what I told you about a patron saint?

T：Erm, yes.

E：Well, during the crusades a vision of St. George was seen just before an important battle and the result was that this helped our knights to win.

T：I see. Can you tell me anything else about him?

E：The most famous story about him involves a dragon which was threatening a city of Libya, called Selena. The people had to give the monster a human victim every day to satisfy its hunger, and **lots were drawn to determine** the victim. On one occasion the lot fell to the king's little daughter. Then St. George chanced to ride by, and when the dragon appeared, St. George, making the sign of the cross, bravely attacked it and killed it with his lance. Then he rode away.

T：So how do you celebrate this day?

E：Well, actually we don't. For most English people St. George's Day is just another ordinary day.

T：That's a pity. You should be proud of him and do something special on this day.

E：You are right. Perhaps we will someday.

E：英国人   T：游客

E：你好！你可挑了个好日子来英国。

T：噢，为什么这么说？

E：今天是圣乔治节。

T：我从来没听说过这个节日。有什么特殊的意义吗？

E：哦，首先这是英国的国庆节。其次，圣乔治还是我们的守护神。

T：什么是守护神？

E：守护神就是一个真实的或神话中的人物，他在国家危难时刻挺身而出拯救国家。

T：那给我说说圣乔治吧。他一定是个英国名人，对吗？

E：你说错了。实际上，乔治是大约公元2世纪或公元3世纪的一个罗马士兵。他是罗马军队的护民官，因为抗议罗马皇帝戴克里先对基督教徒的迫害*，于公元303年4月23日在尼克米迪亚被斩首。很快，乔治就受到广大基督徒的崇敬，成了勇敢者的代表，以捍卫穷人和无防御能力者的利益，维护基督教信仰。

> * 对基督徒的迫害：303年，罗马帝国在皇帝戴克里先统治期间开展了最后且最大的一次对基督徒的逼害。基督徒要么放弃信仰，要么被处死。迫害行动持续至313年信奉基督教的皇帝君士坦丁一世颁布《米兰敕令》为止。在此后不到100年的时间里，基督教成为罗马帝国里居支配地位的法定宗教。

T：可是一个罗马士兵和英格兰有什么关系？

E：你还记得我跟你讲过的守护神吧？

T：哦，记得。

E：那是在十字军东征时，就在一场重要的战斗之前，有人看见了圣乔治，接下来战斗的结果是我们的骑士打了胜仗。

T：我明白了。你能再说点他别的事情吗？

E：他最有名的故事与一条威胁着利比亚塞雷那城的恶龙有关。那里的人们必须每天都把人当祭品送给这个怪物充饥，他们通过抽签决定牺牲者。有一次，国王的小女儿被抽中了。圣乔治正好骑马路过那里，当恶龙出现时，他手划十字，勇敢地向恶龙发起进攻，用长矛杀死了它。然后他就骑马走了。

T：那你们如何庆祝这一天呢？

E：唉，说实话我们没有什么庆祝活动。对大多数英国人来说，圣乔治节只是另一个普通的日子而已。

T：那太遗憾了。你们应该为他感到骄傲，在这一天举行点特别的活动。

E：你说得对。也许以后我们会这么做的。

■ choose a good day 选对日子了	■ for a start 一开始，首先
■ an example of 代表	■ Lots were draw to determine the victim. 抽签决定牺牲者。

82. The Bible

《圣经》

C：*Chinese student*　　*F*：*Foreigner*

C：I have heard a lot about the Bible but never read it.

F：Well, someone once said that it's the world's **best-selling book** but also the world's least read book!

C：Why is that?

F：Some people think that the *Bible* is difficult to read because they are used to the *King James Version* where some of the English is difficult but there are many modern translations available now.

C：You said that the *Bible* is the world's best-selling book. Why is that?

F：Several reasons. There are many great stories in it such as David and Goliath, Jonah and the Whale and the Good Samaritan.

C：Wasn't he the one who helped someone in distress when nobody else would?

F：That's right. Jesus told that story to emphasise that everyone is our neighbour and we have a responsibility towards them.

C：So Jesus was a great teacher as well as a good man.

F：He was actually more than that. He was **fully man** and God too.

C：I find that hard to believe. Isn't the *Bible* just a collection of myths and fables?

F：Some people think so but most Christians take it literally as God's word which is another reason for its popularity.

C：But God didn't write it.

F：About 40 different people wrote it over a period of 1500 years on 3 different continents and in 3 different languages but all the writers claimed to have been inspired by God.

C：I see. Can you tell me another reason?

F：Many people see it as the finest literature produced in English, even better than Shakespeare. There are some incredibly poetic passages in it that have **stood the test of time**.

C：Can you give me an example?

F：There's I Corinthians chapter 13 which is called *The Gift of Love*. Prime Minister Tony Blair read it at Lady Diana's funeral. **Among other things** it says, "Love is patient; Love is kind; Love is not envious or boastful or arrogant or rude."

C: So the *Bible* is full of exciting stories, great literature and a book of faith for Christians?

F: That's right. But remember too that the *Old Testament* is also known as the *Hebrew Bible* which is the faith book for Jews. That's another reason for its popularity.

C: 中国学生   F: 外国人

C: 我常听人说起圣经,但还从来没读过。

F: 哦,有人说《圣经》*是世界上最畅销的书,但也是看的人最少的书。

C: 为什么这么说?

F: 有人认为《圣经》不好理解,因为他们读的是《詹姆士国王钦定本》,那时的英语很难懂。但现在已经有了很多现代文译本。

C: 你刚说到《圣经》是世界上最畅销的书,为什么?

F: 有几个原因。《圣经》里有很多伟大的故事,比如"大卫王和歌利亚"、"约拿和鲸鱼",以及"好撒马利亚人"。

C: 耶稣是个在人们危难时唯一能提供帮助的人吗?

F: 没错。耶稣讲这些故事是要强调每个人都是我们的邻居,我们对他们都负有责任。

C: 所以耶稣既是伟大的导师,又是一个好人。

F: 不仅如此。他还是个完善的人,是上帝。

C: 我觉得很难让人相信。《圣经》不就是一本神话和寓言集吗?

F: 有些人是这样认为的,但大多数基督徒真的把《圣经》当成是上帝的语录,这也是《圣经》如此受欢迎的另外一个原因。

C: 但上帝并没有写《圣经》。

F: 《圣经》是由大约40个人在前后长达1500年里用3种不同的语言写成的,他们来自3个不同的大陆,但所有的作者都声称是受了上帝的启发。

C: 我懂了。那另外一个原因呢?

F: 很多人认为《圣经》是英国最优秀的文学作品,甚至比莎士比亚的作品还要好。书里面一些令人难以置信的好诗篇都经受住了时间的考验。

C: 举个例子?

F: 哥林多前书第13章"爱的颂歌",首相托尼·布莱尔就曾在戴安娜王妃的葬礼上朗诵过。其中提到"爱是恒久忍耐,又有恩慈;爱是不嫉妒,爱是不自夸,不张狂。"

C: 这么说《圣经》里到处都是激动人心的故事,它是部伟大的文学作品,也是基督教的教义,对吗?

F: 是这样。但是也要记住《旧约》也叫做《希伯来圣经》,是犹太人的教义。这也是《圣经》受欢迎的另一个原因。

> *《圣经》:犹太教的圣经是《旧约全书》,主要内容为关于世界和人类起源的故事传说,犹太民族古代历史的宗教叙述和犹太法典、先知书、诗歌、格言等,原文为希伯来文,公元前3世纪至公元前2世纪译成希腊文。基督教圣经包括《新约全书》和《旧约全书》,《新约全书》主要记载耶稣及其使徒的言行和故事,原文为希腊文,公元4—5世纪译成拉丁文。16世纪宗教改革运动前后,《圣经》被译成欧洲各国文字。英国国王詹姆士一世委托47名学者一起翻译并出版的"钦定版"是标准的英文版《圣经》。

- best-selling book   最畅销的书
- stand the test of time   经得住时间的考验
- fully man   完善的人,完人
- among other things   在其它同类事物中

165

83. The Royal Family

皇室

TG：*Tour guide*　　*T*：*Tourist*

TG： And this is Buckingham Palace, home of the Queen of England.

T： How long has England had a monarchy?

TG： For well over a thousand years.

T： Who was the most famous king of England?

TG： Perhaps it was Henry VIII who had six wives.

T： Why did he have so many wives?

TG： He wanted a son and when none of his wives gave him one he would either divorce them or have them beheaded.

T： Who was the most famous Queen of England?

TG： I think there are two contenders for that title. Queen Elizabeth I who never married and was known as the Virgin Queen and Queen Victoria. Both lived for a long time and expanded Britain's trade and colonies overseas.

T： Is the monarchy popular in England?

TG： Yes, I think so. Queen Elizabeth II has ruled for over 50 years and is very popular with her subjects just like her mother who lived to be 101 years old.

T： Who will succeed her?

TG： Her eldest son, Prince Charles, who recently married Camilla. His eldest son, Prince William will then succeed him.

T： So it's always the eldest son who succeeds?

TG： Yes, but if there are no sons then it passes to the eldest daughter which is what happened in Queen Elizabeth's case.

T： Can you tell me something about Princess Diana.

TG： Well she was certainly the most popular of the royal family in recent years.

T： I know she did a lot of charitable work but it was really tragic that she **died so young**.

TG： Yes. I remember that day and the national **outpouring of grief** that followed. I think everyone in the UK was **glued to their seats** watching the funeral on TV and there wasn't **a dry eye** in the whole of the country.

T: I think that Prince William is very handsome and I would love him to be king one day. I think he would make a better king than his father.

TG: I think most people think that but he will have to wait until his father dies just as Charles has to wait until his mother dies.

TG: 导游　　T: 游客

TG: 这里是白金汉宫，英国女王的家。

T: 英国君主立宪制的历史有多长？

TG: 有一千多年了。

T: 英国最有名的国王是谁？

TG: 也许是那位有 6 个妻子的亨利八世*。

T: 他怎么有这么多妻子呢？

TG: 他想要个儿子，当没有一个妻子能给他生儿子时，他要么离婚要么就把她们杀头。

T: 英国最有名的女王是谁？

TG: 对于这个名号，我想有两位女王不相上下。一个是终生未婚被称为"童贞女王"的伊丽莎白一世*，另一个是维多利亚女王*。她们两个都活了很长时间，而且还向海外扩大了英国的贸易和殖民地。

T: 君主立宪制在英国受欢迎吗？

TG: 我认为是受欢迎的。伊丽莎白二世统治了 50 多年，和她那位活了 101 岁的母亲一样，受到臣民们的拥戴。

T: 将来谁会继承她的王位？

TG: 她的大儿子查尔斯王子，最近娶了卡米拉的那个。查尔斯王子的大儿子，威廉王子以后也会继承他的王位。

T: 也就是说，一直都是长子继承王位了？

TG: 是的。但如果没有儿子，就会传位给长女，伊丽莎白女王就是这样继承王位的。

T: 你可以跟我讲讲有关戴安娜王妃的事吗？

TG: 哦，她的确是近几年来王室成员中最受欢迎的人。

T: 我知道她做了很多慈善工作，但她那么年轻就去世的确是个悲剧。

TG: 是的。我记得，那天全国上下都沉浸在悲痛之中。我想所有的英国人都端坐在椅子上一刻不离地观看电视上直播的葬礼，没有一个不落泪的。

T: 我认为威廉王子长得很英俊，我希望他将来某一天能够做国王。我想他会成为一个比他父亲更好的国王。

TG: 我想大多数人也是这样认为的。不过他得等到他的父亲去世后才能继承王位，就像他父亲也得等到他的母亲去世后一样。

> * 亨利八世（1491-1547）：英国国王。大力加强王权，抗拒罗马教廷干预其婚事。1533 年与教皇决裂，次年宣布为英国教会首领，并将英格兰圣公会立为国教。
>
> * 伊丽莎白一世（1533-1603）：英国女王，亨利八世的女儿。在位时依靠新贵族和资产阶级，厉行专制统治。确立英国国教制度。击溃西班牙"无敌舰队"，奠定英国海上霸权。鼓励海外殖民，成立英国东印度公司。
>
> * 维多利亚（1819-1901）：英国女王。在位期间，英国工商业快速发展，扩大对殖民的掠夺，号称"日不落帝国"，几乎垄断世界贸易和工业，被称为英国历史上的"黄金时期"。

■ died so young 英年早逝　　　　　　■ outpouring of grief 沉浸在悲痛中
■ be glued to their seats 粘在座位上（指坐着不动）　　■ a dry eye 不哭的人

167

84. Tea

茶

O: Tea shop owner   *T*: Tourist

O: Welcome to Ye Olde Tea Shoppe.

T: Thanks. It's my first time to visit England and I've heard so much about English tea. Which would you recommend?

O: We have quite **a large selection**. How about Darjeeling or Earl Grey? They're very popular.

T: Darjeeling? Whereabouts is that in England?

O: It's not in England at all. It's a district in West Bengal, in India. Darjeeling is considered to be the "champagne" of tea. In fact, we don't grow tea in England at all. Most English tea comes from India.

T: That's odd. In China, all Chinese tea comes from China.

O: Yes I know. I'll fetch you a pot of Darjeeling for you to try.

T: Is there any special English tea ceremony like we have with Chinese tea?

O: **Good heavens**, no. We just pour a little hot water into a teapot first to warm it, empty it, put some tea leaves in, add hot water and then leave it for a few minutes to brew.

T: I've heard that you Englishmen have afternoon tea everyday. Is that true?

O: Well, afternoon tea is said to have originated with one person; Anna, 7th Duchess of Bedford. In the early 1800s she launched the idea of having tea in the late afternoon to bridge the gap between luncheon and dinner, which in fashionable circles might not be served until 8 o'clock at night. Nowadays, afternoon tea has gone **out of fashion** for the majority of British people but it's very popular among tourists like yourself.

T: Yes. And I can see why. So it's ready to drink now, is it?

O: Yes. I'll pour some out for you. As you can see it's a black tea and very fragrant. Try smelling it first.

T: OK. Mmmm ... Smells nice. Can I taste it now?

O: We normally add some milk to it and maybe some sugar if you prefer.

T: OK. I'll try a little milk first.

O: What do you think?

T: It's certainly different from Chinese tea! We **would never dream of** adding milk or sugar to our tea. But it tastes quite nice.

O：茶叶店主　　　**T**：旅游者

O：欢迎光临老茶叶店。

T：谢谢。我这是第一次来英国旅游，以前听说过很多英国茶叶方面的故事。你有什么可推荐的？

O：我们这儿的茶叶品种多着呢。大吉岭茶或格雷伯爵茶怎么样？这两种茶卖得非常好。

T：大吉岭？在英国什么地方？

O：根本不在英国。这是印度西孟加拉的一个地区。大吉岭被人们当作茶叶中的"香槟酒"。事实上，我们英国根本不种茶叶。英国大多数的茶叶都是从印度进口的。

T：这倒有点奇怪。在中国，所有的茶叶都是本地产的。

O：是的，这我知道。我给你泡一壶大吉岭茶尝尝。

T：喝中国茶有特别的讲究，英国茶是不是也有？

O：谢天谢地，没什么讲究。我们只是先往茶壶里倒点热水暖暖壶，然后把水倒掉，再放进些茶叶，加些热水，然后泡上几分钟就行了。

T：我听说你们英国人每天都喝下午茶，是这样吗？

O：是的，据说下午茶与一个叫安娜的人有关，她是贝德福德第7任公爵夫人。19世纪初，她提出了傍晚喝茶的想法，以填补午餐和晚餐的空档，因为上流社会的人们要到晚上8点才吃晚餐。如今，对大多数英国人来说，下午茶已经过时了，但在你这样的游客中间却很受欢迎。

T：是这样，而且我明白这是为什么。那现在可以喝了吧？

O：可以了。我来给你倒。你看，这是红茶，味道很香。先闻闻看。

T：好的。嗯……闻起来不错。现在可以尝了吗？

O：我们一般要加些牛奶进去，你喜欢的话也许还可以加些糖。

T：好的，那我先放点牛奶试试。

O：怎么样？

T：真是跟中国茶不一样！我们从来就没有想过往茶里加牛奶或糖。不过味道还真不错。

- a large selection 品种多，选择余地大
- out of fashion 不合时尚；不流行
- Good heavens! 谢天谢地！
- would never dream of 从来就没有想过

169

85. The Weather

天气

C: *Chinese student*   F: *Foreigner*

C: I have heard that in Britain it often rains a lot. Sometimes I have heard the expression **"raining cats and dogs"** when it's raining very heavily. Is that right?

F: Yes, it does rain quite a bit in Britain and we sometimes do say it's raining cats and dogs when it's raining very heavily. But, we often just have showers, as in a small amount of rain, and then we say **"It's drizzling."**

C: Is it true that English people always carry umbrellas around with them?

F: Only when it's raining. Actually that is one of the big differences between our two cultures.

C: Oh, why is that?

F: Well, when the sun is shining we like to wear as few clothes as possible to **get the maximum benefit from** the sun but you use umbrellas to protect yourself from the sun's rays.

C: Yes, that's true. We think a pale skin is more beautiful.

F: But we think a tan makes us look more healthy.

C: Is it often sunny in England?

F: Not as much as we would like! It certainly does not get as hot as it does here in Beijing and the weather is not dry like here. I know we complain about the weather a lot but really I think we get a good mixture of sun and rain and snow.

C: What about fog? I hear that there's a lot in London.

F: Well, that used to be true up to 50 years ago but now London is **fog free**.

C: Why is that?

F: Ever since the Clean Air Act of the early 50s we have moved away from coal to smokeless fuel and so the air has got a lot cleaner.

C: Which is your favourite season?

F: I would have to say autumn because all the trees change colour as the leaves go from green to red, orange and brown and it really makes for a wonderful sight.

C: What is winter like?

F: Really cold! We would get quite a bit of snow from December to March. Children love it but older people don't like it as much.

C: 中国学生   F: 外国人

* 伦敦雾：伦敦是世界著名的"雾都"，这里5天中就有一天是雾天。泰晤士河两岸的建筑在雾中若隐若现，宛如空中楼阁。大雾常给市民带来麻烦。1952年12月5日的一场大雾持续4天，市区交通停顿，居民感到胸闷、呼吸困难，白厅街的大理石建筑遭到腐蚀。80年代以来，由于英国政府采取了一系列措施加强环境保护，伦敦上空的可见度已比过去有了提高。

C: 听说英国经常下雨。我还听过 raining cats and dogs 这样的说法，指倾盆大雨。是这样吗？

F: 是的，英国经常下雨。下大雨时我们有时的确会用 raining cats and dogs 这样的说法。但是，我们一般下的只是小雨，雨量很少，这时我们就说 It's drizzling.。

C: 英国人是不是总随身带着雨伞啊？

F: 只在下雨的时候带。实际上这是我们两种文化间一个很大的区别。

C: 哦，怎么回事？

F: 是这样，阳光普照时我们都尽量少穿衣服多晒晒太阳，但你们却用伞来遮挡阳光。

C: 的确如此。我们认为皮肤白一点更漂亮。

F: 但我们却认为皮肤晒黑了看上去更健康。

C: 英国晴天多吗？

F: 并不像我们希望的那样多。那里的确不像北京这么热，也没有这么干燥。我知道我们英国人常抱怨天气，但实际上我认为我们充分享受了阳光和雨雪。

C: 那雾呢？我听说伦敦雾* 多。

F: 哦，那至少是50年前的事了，现在伦敦都没有雾了。

C: 怎么回事？

F: 自从50年代初颁布了《空气清洁法》以来，我们就一直用无烟燃料取代煤，所以空气已经变得干净多了。

C: 你最喜欢哪个季节呢？

F: 我最喜欢的是秋季，因为所有的树叶都由绿色变成红色、桔黄色和褐色，那景色真的漂亮极了。

C: 冬天是什么样的？

F: 非常冷！我们从12月起一直到次年3月份都会有很多雪天。孩子们非常喜欢下雪天，但年纪大一点的人就不是很喜欢了。

■ raining cats and dogs 下倾盆大雨   ■It's drizzling. 在下毛毛雨。
■ get the maximum benefit from ... 尽量从……获取好处   ■ fog free 没有雾

86. Big Ben

大本钟

C: *Chinese student*   *G*: *Guide*

C: Big Ben is a lot bigger and more impressive than I thought.

G: Yes a lot of people say that when they see it for the first time.

C: So how tall is it?

G: 316 feet. It's one of London's most visible landmarks, especially at night when the clock faces are illuminated.

C: Tell me some more about the famous clock faces.

G: The four dials of the clock are 23 square feet, the minute hand is 14 feet long and each of the twelve Roman numerals is 2 feet high.

C: I can see a light on above the clock. What does that mean?

G: It means that parliament is in session.

C: So Big Ben is closely associated with the Houses of Parliament?

G: Yes. There are even prison cells within the clock tower where Members of Parliament can be imprisoned for a breach of parliamentary privilege, though this is rare; **the last recorded case** was in 1880.

C: How did Big Ben get its name?

G: Most people think that Big Ben is the name of the clock but the name Big Ben actually refers not to the Clock Tower itself, but to the 13 ton bell hung within which was cast in 1858 at the Whitechapel Bell Foundry in East London. **To this day** one of the largest bells they have ever cast. The bell was named after the first commissioner of works, Sir Benjamin Hall.

C: Has the clock ever stopped?

G: No. Not even the destruction of the Commons chamber during World War II could stop it but once a workman was cleaning one of the faces and hung his bucket on one of the hands and so it was slowed by about 10 minutes.

C: How did Big Ben become **much loved** by the British public?

G: I think it started on 31st December 1923 when the BBC first broadcast the chimes of Big Ben over the radio and everybody heard the chimes **ring in the New Year**.

C: I would love to be here on New Year's eve to hear them.

G: You would be very welcome.

C: 中国学生　　G: 导游

C: 大本钟真的比我原来想的更大，更令人难忘。

G: 是的，很多人第一次见到的时候都这么说。

C: 那它有多高呢？

G: 316 英尺。它是伦敦最明显的地面标志之一，尤其是在晚上，钟面亮着的时候。

C: 给我多说说这个有名的钟面吧。

G: 大本钟的 4 个钟盘有 23 平方英尺，分针有 14 英尺长，而 12 个罗马数字都有 2 英尺高。

C: 我可以看到钟上方亮着灯。那是什么意思？

G: 那代表着正在召开议会。

C: 所以大本钟跟英国议会*的上下两院密切相关了？

> * 英国议会：英国的国会由上议院和下议院组成。上议院是英国最高司法机关，有权审查下议院通过的法案，并通过必要的修正案；议员不由选举产生，部分是世袭贵族。下议院的主要职权是立法、监督财政和政府，其议员由直接选举产生。通常情况下，下议院总有一个拥有绝对多数席位的政党，该党领袖被国王任命为首相，第二大党的领袖则成为反对党领袖。

G: 是的。钟楼里甚至还有一些囚室，用来关押那些违背了议会特权的议会成员。不过这样的情况很少发生，最后一次记录的案例发生在 1880 年。

C: 大本钟这个名字是怎么来的呢？

G: 大多数人都以为"大本"是这个时钟的名字，但实际上它并不是指钟楼本身，而是指里面挂着的 13 吨重的大钟。它于 1858 年铸造于伦敦东部的怀特铸钟厂，是迄今为止他们所铸造的最大的钟。该钟以第一个负责此项工程的本杰明·霍尔爵士的名字命名。

C: 这个钟有没有停过？

G: 没停过。即使在第二次世界大战期间下议院被炸毁时它都没停。但曾经有一次，一个清洁工在清洁钟面时把水桶挂在了一根指针上，导致它慢了 10 分钟。

C: 英国老百姓怎么那么喜欢大本钟呢？

G: 我想事情起因于 1923 年 12 月 31 号 BBC 电台首次通过广播播放了大本钟的钟声，每个人都听到了新年的钟声。

C: 我也想在除夕到这里听听钟声。

G: 非常欢迎。

■ the last recorded case　最后一次记录的案例　　■ to this day　迄今为止
■ become much loved　很受喜欢　　■ ring in the New Year　新年的钟声

173

87. The British Museum

大英博物馆

C：Chinese tourist   *B*：British Museum director

C：It's kind of you to show me round the British Museum. Can you tell me something about its history?

B：Well, it was founded in 1753 on the principle that people should be able to see in one place art and antiquities from all the world's civilisations.

C：So who founded it?

B：It was started by Sir Hans Sloane who had a collection of over 71,000 objects and not wishing them to be split up or sold on his death. He **bequeathed them to the nation** in return for 20,000 pounds.

C：So do you know how many objects you have now?

B：**At the latest count** there are approximately 7 million.

C：But I'm sure you cannot possibly show all of them.

B：That's right. Some of them are in the process of being restored, some are in store for future showing and some are being shown in museums or exhibitions around the world.

C：I saw one exhibition in Beijing at the Capital Museum in the summer of 2006 but I was surprised not to see any Chinese objects. Why was that?

B：Simply because China has better art than we have! **No other reason**.

C：Were you not afraid that China might want some of them back? After all many Chinese art held abroad were looted by foreign armies.

B：The vast majority of the Museum's collections have been acquired legitimately and they are openly displayed **free of charge** to the 5 million visitors we have every year.

C：I know that the Greek government wants the return of its statues from the Parthenon.

B：The Elgin Marbles, **as they are more commonly called**, were purchased legally from the Ottoman Empire and rescued from further weather damage and held here on permanent display.

C：Is there any possibility of further British Museum exhibitions in China?

B: Yes, in 2007 we will be holding an exhibition that looks at the relationship between Britain and China in the 18th century.

C: Where does the British Museum get its money from to look after the building, buy new pieces and hold exhibitions abroad?

B: 70 percent of our money comes from the government and the rest comes from donations and interest on our investments.

C：中国游客　　B：大英博物馆主任

> * 埃尔金大理石雕：古代希腊帕特农神庙的部分雕刻与建筑残件，19 世纪时被英国贵族埃尔金伯爵运到英国，目前被收藏在伦敦的大英博物馆内。

C：感谢你带我参观大英博物馆。能给我讲讲它的历史吗？

B：好的。大英博物馆建于 1753 年，旨在让人们能够在一个地方同时看到来自世界各地的艺术品和古董文物。

C：是谁建立的呢？

B：是汉斯·斯隆爵士。他有 71,000 件收藏品，临死时他不希望自己死后这些收藏被卖掉或流散到各地，就以 2 万英镑的低价将全部藏品遗赠给了国家。

C：那你知道这里有多少件收藏品吗？

B：最近的数字表明大约有 700 万件。

C：但我肯定你们不可能把所有的收藏品都陈列出来。

B：是的。有一些正在修复过程中，有一些被保存起来为了将来陈列用，还有一些正在世界各地的博物馆或展览会上展出。

C：2006 年夏天我在北京首都博物馆看过一次展览，但很奇怪的是我没看到一件中国收藏品。这是为什么呢？

B：只是因为中国的艺术品比我们国家的要好！没别的原因。

C：你们有没有担心过中国可能想要回一些藏品？毕竟陈列在国外的很多中国艺术品都是由外国士兵从中国掠夺走的。

B：博物馆收藏的大多数藏品都是合法获得的，而且它们都是免费展出的，每年我们都有 500 万的游客参观。

C：我知道希腊政府就想把他们的帕特农神庙的雕像要回去。

B：人们通常把它称作"埃尔金大理石雕*"，这也是当年从奥斯曼帝国合法购买的，目的是避免其再遭受气候的侵蚀，后来就永久地陈列在此了。

C：大英博物馆有没有可能再到中国来举办展览呢？

B：有可能，2007 年我们将举办一个以 18 世纪中英关系为主题的展览会。

C：大英博物馆要维护建筑，购买新的展品以及在国外展览，那资金都是哪儿来的？

B：70% 的钱都是政府拨款，其它的是捐款和我们投资所得的利润。

- bequeath . . . to the nation　遗赠给了国家
- at the latest count　据最近的数据
- as they are more commonly called　通常被称为
- free of charge　免费
- no other reason　没有别的原因

88. Shakespeare

莎士比亚

C: *Chinese student*　　**E**: *English teacher*

C: I've been reading Shakespeare's *Romeo and Juliet* but I find it really **tough going** as the language is so difficult to understand.

E: That's true for native speakers too. I know that when I read one of his plays I am always glancing at the glossary and notes so that I can understand the words.

C: So how did Shakespeare become so popular if people can't understand what he wrote?

E: People in his time understand his plays because they **were meant to** be heard not read. It wasn't until seven years after his death that his plays were published in printed form.

C: But I read somewhere that Shakespeare invented about 2,000 new words. How did they understand these new words if they'd never heard them before?

E: Well some nouns he used as verbs, as adverbs and as adjectives. He also created new compound words such as "baby-faced" and "smooth-faced". He also brought into common use words that had appeared in the last half of the 16th century.

C: Perhaps it is the phrases he is most remembered for such as "To be or not to be, that is the question" and "Romeo, Romeo, wherefore art thou Romeo?"

E: Perhaps my favourite is "the milk of human kindness", but I'm sure everyone has their own favourite.

C: I know that some people don't think that Shakespeare wrote the plays. Why is that?

E: Primarily because he never went to university so some critics don't think that he received a high enough education to be able to write such great literature.

C: So if Shakespeare didn't write them, who did?

E: Various candidates have been put forward but perhaps the best is Edward de Vere, 17th Earl of Oxford (1550-1604).

C: Why is that?

E: In the sonnets and the plays there are frequent references to events that are paralleled in Oxford's life. Personally, I agree with the majority of Shakespearean academics who think Shakespeare was the author.

C: Well "a rose by another name would still smell as sweet"?

E: That's right. **One thing is for sure** and that is that the world's greatest plays have enriched the English language ever since and his plays are among the finest literature **the world has ever seen**.

C: 中国学生　　**E**: 英国老师

C: 我一直在看莎士比亚的《罗密欧与朱丽叶》，但我发现读起来真的很困难，因为文字太难懂了。

E: 对本国人来说也是一样难懂。我记得我读他的剧本时也总是翻看词汇表和注释，这样才能看懂词汇。

C: 那如果人们连他写的东西都看不懂，他又怎么这样受欢迎呢？

E: 莎士比亚那个年代的人们能明白他的戏剧是因为那些剧本是写给人听的而不是写给人看的。他的戏剧在他死后 7 年才被印刷出版。

C: 但我看别的地方写到莎士比亚创造了 2000 个左右的新词。如果那时的人们以前没听过这些新词，他们又怎能理解呢？

E: 是这样，他把一些名词用作动词、副词和形容词。他还创造了一些新的合成词，比如"生着娃娃脸的"、"脸上没胡须的"。此外，他还把 16 世纪后半期出现的词当成普通的词来用。

C: 让人铭记最深的也许是他的名句，如："生存还是毁灭，这是个问题"，以及"罗密欧，罗密欧，你为什么是罗密欧啊？"

E: 也许我最喜欢的还是"人性善良的乳汁"*这个说法，但我相信每个人都有自己最喜欢的语句。

C: 我听说有些人认为这些戏剧并不是莎士比亚写的。为什么会这么说？

E: 主要是因为他从没上过大学，所以有些评论家认为他没有接受足够的高等教育，也就写不出如此伟大的文学作品。

C: 那如果不是莎士比亚写的，会是谁写的呢？

E: 人们提出了很多个人选，但最可能的还是第 17 世牛津伯爵爱德华·德维尔（1550－1604）。

C: 为什么？

E: 十四行诗和戏剧中不断提及跟牛津生活相关的事。就我个人而言，我同意大多数的莎士比亚研究者的看法，认为莎士比亚才是原作者。

C: 嗯，"玫瑰换个名字闻起来还是一样香"，是不是？

E: 一点不错！可以肯定的一件事就是，从此以后，这些世界上最伟大的戏剧作品大大丰富了英语语言，莎剧被列入世界上迄今为止最优秀的文学作品之列。

- tough going　很难进行
- the world has ever seen　世界上现有的
- be meant to　用来做……用
- one thing is for sure　可以肯定的一件事

89. Sherlock Holmes

歇洛克·福尔摩斯

C: *Chinese student*　　*E*: *English teacher*

C: A friend told me that **detective stories** are a good way of learning English. Do you agree?

E: Yes I do because they are interesting and they also make you think about puzzles and how to solve them.

C: So **in that case** which detective stories would you recommend?

E: Sherlock Holmes stories by Arthur Conan Doyle are much loved here in China.

C: Why is that?

E: Maybe because he is an original character and because he is able to **tell from one look** exactly what a person does for a job.

C: So he uses observation and his intellect to solve crimes?

E: That's right. As he says in one of his films "Elementary, my dear Watson" as he solves another crime.

C: Are there any other famous sayings by him?

E: "When you have eliminated all which is impossible, then whatever remains, however improbable, must be the truth."

C: Which ones would you recommend for a newcomer to read?

E: *The Adventures of Sherlock Holmes* would be **a good place to start**.

C: He lived in London during the late 19th century?

E: His address was 221B Baker Street but that number does not actually exist. There is a bank at number 221 and any letters that you send to 221B will automatically go there as they have created that special address for Sherlock Homes fans all around the world.

C: Can you tell me anything interesting about Sherlock Holmes.

E: Well he smoked a pipe and wore a deerstalker hat and sometimes took the drug cocaine although at that time it was not illegal in England.

C: He sounds like a typical eccentric English gentleman.

E: Someone said that the funniest joke in the world involves him.

C: Oh, what was that?

E: He was camping in a tent with his friend Dr. Watson. It was late at night and Holmes asked him to look up and tell him what he saw. Watson said, "Well, I see thousands of stars." "And what does that mean to you?" asked Holmes. "Well, I guess it means we will have another nice day tomorrow. What does it mean to you, Holmes?" "To me, it means someone has stolen our tent."

C：中国学生　　　E：英语老师

C：一个朋友跟我说看侦探小说是学习英语的一种好方法。你同意吗？

E：是的，我同意，因为这些小说很有意思，也会促使你思考难题，想着如何去解决问题。

C：那你会推荐哪些侦探小说呢？

E：阿瑟·柯南道尔写的歇洛克·福尔摩斯的故事，在中国很受欢迎。

C：为什么？

E：也许是因为福尔摩斯是个原创人物，还因为他具备只看一眼就能判断出一个人的职业的能力。

C：所以他是通过观察和智慧来破案了？

E：是的。正如他在一部电影中又破了一个案子之后所说的："再简单不过了，我亲爱的华生。"

C：里面还有他说过的其它名言吗？

E："当你排除了所有的不可能之后，那么剩下的，不管有多么不可能，肯定就是真相了。"

C：对于初次接触这些书的人，你会推荐哪些呢？

E：一开始读读《歇洛克·福尔摩斯历险记》应该会不错。

C：福尔摩斯生活在 19 世纪末的伦敦，对吗？

E：他的住址是贝克街 221B 号，实际上这个号牌是不存在的。221 号是家银行，任何寄到 221B 的信件都会自动送到银行那里，因为他们为全世界的歇洛克·福尔摩斯迷们编造了那个特别的地址。

C：给我讲讲歇洛克·福尔摩斯的趣闻吧。

E：哦，他常抽着烟斗，戴一顶猎帽，有时候吸可卡因，尽管那在当时的英国并不违法。

C：听起来他好像是个典型的英国古怪绅士。

E：有人说世界上最滑稽的笑话都跟他有关。

C：哦，是什么笑话？

E：福尔摩斯跟他的朋友华生医生在一个帐篷里露宿。夜深了，福尔摩斯叫他的朋友朝上看，问他都看到了些什么。华生就说："哦，我看到了成千上万颗星星。" "那对你意味着什么呢？" 福尔摩斯问道。"哦，我猜这意味着明天我们又有个好天气。那对你又意味着什么呢，福尔摩斯？" "对我来说，我们的帐篷被人给偷走了。"

- detective stories　侦探小说
- in that case　这样的话
- tell from one look　一眼就看出
- a good place to start　从……起步会不错

90. The Beatles

甲壳虫乐队

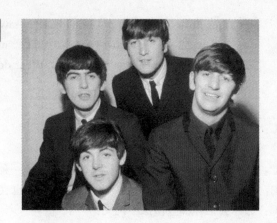

C：Chinese student　　*E*：English teacher

C：Who's your favourite band?

E：I would have to say The Beatles. Have you heard of them?

C：Who hasn't? They were the original boy band weren't they?

E：That's right. Four young men from Liverpool **caused a sensation** when they played in their local club called the Cavern. They created Beatlemania where girl fans went wild and would shout and scream.

C：What was so special about them?

E：They wore suits and had long hair and Paul, their lead singer was so handsome. But mainly it was their music.

C：So which of their albums would you suggest I listen to first?

E：You could try their latest album which was released in December 2006. It's called *Love* and is a reworking of some of their **greatest hits**.

C：Love seems to be what their music is all about. Did you know that every song from their first 5 albums was about love?

E：I know their first UK single was *Love Me Do* released in October 1962 so that does not surprise me.

C：Which of their albums do you like best?

E：I would have to say *Rubber Soul*. I could **listen to that all day**. The song writing partnership of Lennon and McCartney was the most successful in the world.

C：Yet they never wrote their songs together. One way to tell who wrote a song is to listen to who the main singer is.

E：They were the most successful band in the world from 1963 until 1970 when Paul McCartney left the band to pursue his own musical career.

C：It was really tragic the way John Lennon died, wasn't it?

E：Yes. He was signing autographs when a fan shot him 5 times in 1980. There's a memorial to him outside his home in New York.

C：And then George Harrison died of cancer and now there are only two Beatles left.

E：Ringo Starr and Paul McCartney. Paul's wife Linda died of cancer too. He remarried but

180

unfortunately that marriage ended after **lurid tales** of his wife's behaviour in her younger days emerged in the press.

C: I hope he finds true love at last. After all, their music has given us a lot of love, right?

E: Yeah, she loves me yeah, yeah, yeah!

C: 中国学生　　E: 英语老师

C: 你最喜欢哪一个乐队?

E: 我想应该是甲壳虫乐队*? 你听说过吗?

C: 怎么会没听说过呢? 他们是早期的男孩组合, 是吧?

> * 甲壳虫乐队: 又名"披头士"(Beatles), beat 是"搏击、跳动"的意思。甲壳虫乐队成立于 1960 年, 由利物浦青年约翰·列侬、保罗·麦卡特尼、乔治·哈里森、林里·斯达尔组成。列侬担任演唱和节奏吉它手, 麦卡特尼担任演唱和低音吉它手, 哈里森为主奏吉它手, 斯达尔任架子鼓手。甲壳虫乐队以其反正统艺术的风格、直指社会敏感问题的歌词, 以及挑战世俗的举止, 征服了各国青年。

E: 是的。来自利物浦的 4 个年轻人在他们当地一个叫做"深洞"的俱乐部表演, 由此掀起了一股热潮。他们引起了甲壳虫热, 女歌迷们都疯狂了, 她们狂喊着、尖叫着。

C: 他们有什么特别的地方?

E: 他们穿着西服, 留着长发, 领唱保罗非常英俊。但他们出名的主要原因还是他们的音乐。

C: 那你给我点建议, 先听他们的哪张专辑好呢?

E: 你可以试听一下他们最新的专辑, 2006 年 12 月发行的《爱》, 这是他们最轰动的一些歌曲经重新修订之后的合辑。

C: 他们音乐的主题好像都是与爱有关。你知道吗? 他们最初发行的 5 张专辑中, 每首歌都是关于爱情的。

E: 我知道他们第一个英国单曲唱片是《爱我吧》, 是在 1962 年的 10 月发行的, 所以我并不感到奇怪。

C: 你最喜欢他们哪张专辑?

E: 我想应该是《橡胶灵魂》。我能整天不停地听。列侬和麦卡特尼是世界上最成功的歌曲创作组合。

C: 然而他们从不一起作曲。要想知道一首歌是谁写的, 一种辨别方法就是听听主唱的歌手是谁。

E: 从 1963 年到 1970 年, 他们一直是最成功的乐队。直到 1970 年, 保罗·麦卡特尼离开了乐队去追求自己的音乐事业。

C: 约翰·列侬死得非常惨, 对吗?

E: 对。1980 年他在唱他自己写的歌时, 一个歌迷向他连续开了 5 枪。在他纽约的家门外还有一个纪念碑。

C: 后来乔治·哈里森也得癌症去世了, 现在甲壳虫乐队就只剩下了两个人。

E: 他们是林里·斯达尔和保罗·麦卡特尼。保罗的妻子琳达也死于癌症。后来他再婚了, 可不幸的是媒体大肆报道他妻子年轻时的一些耸人听闻的行为, 之后他们就离婚了。

C: 我希望他最终能找到真爱。毕竟他们的音乐给了我们很多的爱, 不是吗?

E: 是的, "她爱我, 耶耶耶!"(歌词)

■ cause a sensation 引起震动
■ listen to that all day 整天不停地听
■ greatest hits 最轰动的歌曲
■ lurid tales 耸人听闻的故事

91. Football

足球

F: *Football fan*　　**T**: *Tourist*

F: Welcome to Old Trafford, home of Manchester United.

T: Yeah, it's great to be here. I've heard so much about David Beckham. He used to play for Manchester United, didn't he?

F: That's right, but now he plays for Real Madrid.

T: I only know a little about him, but I know he's very handsome.

F: He certainly is. He's also married with three children.

T: I know he's married to Posh Spice who used to be with the Spice Girls.

F: That's right and he has three boys called Brooklyn, Romeo and Cruz.

T: Football is **England's national sport**, isn't it?

F: Yeah, we invented it. Rumour has it that Anglo-Saxons used the heads of captured Danes as footballs.

T: But what did they use as footballs when they ran out of heads?

F: Inflated pig bladders would you believe!

T: So football has always been popular in England, right?

F: Not quite. It was actually banned in 1477 because it interfered with young men learning to be archers.

T: Wow. I suppose national defence had to come first then. What about the modern game? How did that start?

F: It wasn't until 1863 that football **became as we know it now**.

T: Why? What happened then?

F: The rules of the game were formulated by a group of public school men and that led to the formation of football clubs and leagues.

T: The Premiership is supposed to be the best league in the world but England haven't won the World Cup since 1966. Why is that?

F: I think there are two reasons for that. First, there are a lot of foreigners who play in England which means less room for English players and secondly, we've never had a good manager.

T: I hope that will change in the future. Who do you think will win the Premiership?

F: It seems to be **a two horse race** between Manchester United and Chelsea.

T: It would be nice if a different team won this year. By the way, can you tell me what a "**hat trick**" means?

F: It means a player who scores three goals in a game.

F: 足球迷　　T: 游客

F: 欢迎来到曼联主场——老特拉福德。

T: 嗯。能来这里太好了。我听过很多有关大卫·贝克汉姆的事。他过去是在曼联队踢球吗？

F: 是的，然后为皇家马德里队效力。

T: 我只知道一点点关于他的情况。不过我知道他很帅。

F: 他的确很帅。而且他结婚了，还有3个孩子。

T: 我知道他娶了以前辣妹组合里的高贵辣妹。

F: 是的。他有3个儿子，分别叫做布鲁克林、罗密欧和克鲁兹。

T: 足球是英国的全民运动吧？

F: 没错，是我们首创的。据谣传，盎格鲁-萨克逊人曾经把被俘的丹麦海盗*的脑袋当作足球来踢。

T: 要是他们没脑袋踢了，又拿什么来当足球呢？

F: 用充了气的猪膀胱，不相信吧？

T: 所以足球在英国一直都很受欢迎，对吗？

F: 也不全是。实际上足球在1477年时曾被禁止过，因为它妨碍了年轻人练弓箭。

T: 哦，我想保家卫国是应该放在第一位的。那么现代的足球运动是从什么时候开始的？又是如何开始的呢？

F: 直到1863年足球才发展成为我们今天所看到的样子。

T: 为什么？那时候发生什么事了吗？

F: 一群私立学校的人制定了足球的比赛规则，这样就促使了各足球俱乐部和联赛相继成立。

T: 据说英格兰超级联赛是世界上最好的足球联赛。但英国自1966年后就再也没有赢得过世界杯，为什么呢？

F: 我想有两个原因。第一，有很多外国人在英国踢球，只给英国本土球员留下很小的发挥余地。第二，我们一直都没有一个好的组织者。

T: 我希望将来情况会有所改善。你认为谁能在本次英超中夺冠呢？

F: 曼联和切尔西队好像不相上下。

T: 如果今年有别的队能打赢的话就太好了。对了，你能告诉我"帽子戏法"是什么意思吗？

F: 那是指一个球员在同一场比赛中踢进了3个球。

> * 丹麦海盗：公元9世纪，丹麦海盗入侵英格兰。英格兰军队在阿尔弗雷德大王的带领下奋勇抵抗，最后双方签订和约，阿尔弗雷德统治英格兰南部，丹麦人退守北部。1016年，丹麦王子克努特占领了全英格兰。1042年，丹麦王朝灭亡，流亡的英国王室后裔爱德华王子回国执政。

- England's national sport　英国的全民运动
- become as we know it now　发展成为我们今天所看到的样子
- a two horse race　不相上下的比赛
- hat trick　帽子戏法

92. The Statue of Liberty

自由女神像

M: *Museum curator*   *T*: *Tourist*

T: Hello, I wonder if you could help me. Where do I find the USA exhibit?

M: Which part are you interested in?

T: The Statue of Liberty, I need to do some research about it.

M: It was presented by the people of France to the people of the United States in 1886 to honour the friendship between the two nations. Nowadays we consider it to be a symbol of liberty throughout the world.

T: Yes, and America couldn't have been liberated from Britain without the help of the French. Wow! It says here that more than 5 million people visit the statue every year. That's a lot of people.

M: It's a very popular symbol to many, nowhere else on earth is there a symbol that expresses the concept and ideals of personal freedom as dramatically.

T: What can you tell me about its size? How tall is it exactly?

M: The statue part is 115 feet tall and the pedestal is 89 feet tall. It weighs a whopping 225 tons!

T: That is huge. What's it made from? It often looks like stone in the pictures.

M: Actually, the statue is made from steel **coated with** copper and the pedestal is made from granite.

T: I see. Who was it designed by? I guess it must have been a French designer.

M: You're right. It was designed by Frédéric-Auguste Bartholdi, but the interior framework was designed by Alexandre-Gustave Eiffel, also designer of the Eiffel Tower.

T: So, it was an entirely French project, then?

M: Not entirely, the pedestal was designed by an American architect, Richard Morris Hunt. But many people **on both sides** of the Atlantic put money into her construction.

T: Perhaps it is fitting that hundreds of thousands of ordinary people contributed hundreds of thousands of dollars to her construction and that millions more contributed millions of dollars to ensure her continued existence.

M: Yes, she may have been created by the genius of a few visionaries, but the concept she represents speaks to **the hearts and minds** of ordinary men and women everywhere.

T: I hope that one day I can visit the museum at her base and **see her for real**.

M：博物馆馆长　　T：游客

T：你好，我想打听一下，哪儿能找到美国的展品？

M：你对哪方面感兴趣？

T：自由女神像*，我要对它做一些相关研究。

> * 自由女神像：位于美国纽约市曼哈顿以西的自由岛上。她手持火炬，矗立在纽约港入口处，迎来了自19世纪末以来到美国定居的千百万移民。1984年，自由女神像被列入世界遗产名录。女神像的钢铁骨架由设计巴黎埃菲尔铁塔的埃菲尔设计，雕像由法国雕刻家维雷勃杜克设计，并在巴黎完成。法国政府将这一标志自由的纪念像，作为庆祝美国独立100周年的礼物赠给美国。

M：它是1886年法国人民赠送给美国人民的礼物，目的是为了纪念两国之间的友谊。今天，我们把它看成是全世界自由的象征。

T：是的。如果没有法国的帮助美国是不可能从英国独立出来的。哇！这里说每年有500多万的游客来参观自由像。人还真是不少啊。

M：对很多人来说，它是个很受欢迎的象征。世界上没有任何一个标志如此突出地表达了个人自由的观念和理想。

T：你能跟我说说它的大小吗？它到底有多高？

M：雕像部分有115英尺高，底座有89英尺高，重达225吨！

T：那么大啊！它是用什么做的呢？在画里看上去像是用石头建的。

M：实际上，雕像是由钢镀上铜做成的，底座是大理石的。

T：我知道了。它是谁设计的？我猜肯定是法国人设计的。

M：你猜对了。它是由奥古斯梯·巴陶第设计的。内部结构是由亚历山大·居斯塔夫·埃菲尔设计的，他也是埃菲尔铁塔的设计者。

T：所以说它整个就是法国人设计建造的，是吗？

M：并不全是，它的底座是由一个美国建筑师理查德·茂里斯·亨特设计的。但最终建造时大西洋两岸的很多人都捐了钱。

T：也许更准确地说应该是成百上千的老百姓捐了数千美元建造的，而成千上万的人又捐了数百万美元来对它进行不断的维护。

M：是这样的。她可能只是由少数几个天才的幻想家创造的，但她所代表的理念却道出了世界各地每个普通男女的心声。

T：希望有一天我能到自由女神像底部的博物馆参观一下，并亲自看看雕像。

■ coat with　镀
■ the hearts and minds　心声
■ on both sides　两岸，两边
■ see for real　看看真品

93. Uncle Sam

山姆大叔

T: *Teacher*　　*S*: *Student*

T: It's nice to see you in the library doing some reading, what are you looking at?

S: I'm reading about *America and Uncle Sam*. Before I started this book I thought that Uncle Sam was a real person, perhaps the uncle of a president or something.

T: He is a popular U. S. symbol, usually seen in cartoons. He has long white hair, a beard and very interesting clothing.

S: Yes, he wears a swallow-tailed coat, a waistcoat, tall hat with a star, and striped trousers. Just like the American flag.

T: But do you know his appearance came from two other symbols in American folklore?

S: I know that, Brother Jonathan and Yankee Doodle. The name "Uncle Sam" was often used to describe the American government.

T: Very good. But do you know when this started and why?

S: It was in 1812, during the war. They said "Uncle Sam" because of the letters U. S. on the soldiers' uniforms.

T: That's right. But some people also say that the name came from Samuel Wilson, of Troy, N. Y. Wilson, whose nickname was Uncle Sam, was an inspector of army supplies.

S: Oh, because the army supply boxes also had U. S. printed on them. So he could have been a real person after all.

T: One story must be true, but I'm not sure which. Do you know what was the most well-known poster of Uncle Sam?

S: I think it was from the First World War. They used Uncle Sam, **pointing a finger at** the American people saying "We want YOU!" to encourage men to sign-up and become soldiers.

T: And a very effective **advertising campaign** it was too. Many young men **signed up** to **fight for their country** because of that poster.

S: I think that poster is perhaps the most famous American poster ever. Even more than the Hollywood movie posters you see outside cinemas.

T: I think you're right. In 1961 the American congress adopted Uncle Sam as the national symbol.

S: So nowadays Uncle Sam isn't just about war, like in the poster, he's the true symbol of the American people. I think it's special to have a cartoon as a national symbol, very different.

T: 老师　　S: 学生

T: 很高兴见到你在图书馆看书，看什么呢？

S: 我正在看《美国和山姆大叔》。看这本书之前，我还以为山姆大叔是个真实的人物，可能是某位总统或什么名人的叔叔。

T: 他是美国的大众化的象征，经常在漫画中可以看到。他留着白色长发，蓄着胡子，穿着有趣的衣服。

S: 是的，他穿着燕尾服、马甲，戴着一顶有星星图案的高帽子，穿着带条纹的裤子，就像美国国旗那样的。

T: 但是你知道吗？他的形象来自美国民间传说中的另外两个人物。

S: 我知道，是乔纳森兄弟和傻子扬基。山姆大叔经常被用来指美国政府。

T: 很好。不过你知道这个说法开始使用的时间和来历吗？

S: 是在战时的 1812 年。他们叫"山姆大叔"是因为士兵们制服上印的美国字母 U.S.。

T: 是的。但有些人也说这个名字代表着纽约州特洛伊城的塞缪尔·威尔逊。威尔逊的绰号就是山姆大叔，他是军队供应品的检查员。

S: 哦，是因为军需品的盒子上都印上了山姆大叔的名字。也就是说他可能是个真实的人物。

T: 总有一个说法是对的，但我也不知道哪一个是真的。你知道有关山姆大叔最有名的海报是什么吗？

S: 我想是与第一次世界大战有关。海报上山姆大叔用手指着美国人民说："我们需要你"，以此来鼓励国民入伍当兵。

T: 而且这个广告宣传真的很有效。很多年轻人都因为这个海报而参军入伍为国家而战。

S: 我认为这也是美国迄今为止最有名的一张海报，它甚至比你在影院外面看到的好莱坞电影海报还有名。

T: 你说得没错。1961 年，美国国会采用了山姆大叔作为美国的象征。

S: 所以今天的山姆大叔不仅跟战争有关，就像海报上的一样，而且他也是美国人民的真实象征。我认为用一个漫画人物做国家的象征还真是别出心裁，与众不同。

- point a finger at 用一个手指指着
- sign up 签约雇用，入伍
- advertising campaign 广告宣传
- fight for their country 为国而战

94. Hemingway

海明威

S1: *International student*　　**S2**: *Local student*

S1: I'm doing some research on American authors, could you help me?

S2: Sure, who are you researching?

S1: I'm thinking of doing Ernest Hemingway. I know a little about him already. Nature was an important part of Hemingway's life and work. That must be why he tried to **escape city life** as often as he could.

S2: As soon as he became successful he preferred to live in isolated places. All of the places he lived in after the big cities were convenient locales for hunting and fishing.

S1: While he was at school he wrote for the student newspaper, which led him to his first job at the Kansas *City Star*, a job which was arranged by his uncle.

S2: Did you know that when he was 18 years old he **tried to enlist in the army**? It was World War I at that time, but he wasn't allowed to join because of his **poor eyesight**.

S1: He joined the Red Cross instead as an ambulance driver, that's how he got to Europe. He was seriously wounded by an exploding mortar and in the army hospital he met a nurse, the nurse in his great novel *A Farewell to Arms*.

S2: After that, he went to work for another newspaper back home in America.

S1: Yes, he was the European correspondent, so he moved back to Europe.

S2: During the mid 1920s he wrote the most important works of 20th century fiction, both books of short stories, *In Our Time* and *Men without Women*.

S1: In four short years he went from being an unknown writer to being the most important writer of his generation, and perhaps the 20th century.

S2: His writing took him to Spain, Cuba, many places! Also, he was married many times.

S1: During the Second World War he returned to Europe to report, where he met another woman, his fourth wife.

S2: After that he began writing *The Old Man and the Sea*, another amazing book, and in 1954 he **won the Noble Prize for Literature**.

S1: Not long after, he became suicidal and in 1961 he took his own life.

S2: Such a shame, he was another tragic genius.

S1：外国学生　　S2：当地学生

S1：我在对美国作家做些研究，你能帮我忙吗？

S2：当然可以，你在研究谁？

S1：我正在考虑研究欧内斯特·海明威。我已经对他有了一些了解。他的生活和工作中最重要的部分都与大自然有关。那可能也是他为什么尽可能地逃离城市生活的原因。

> *《老人与海》：这部作品讲述了这样一个故事：老渔夫桑迪亚哥连续 84 天没有捕到鱼。第 85 天，老头儿在很远的海域意外地钓到了一条比船还大的马林鱼。老头儿和这条鱼周旋了两天，终于叉中了它，但也引来无数鲨鱼的争抢。老人奋力与鲨鱼搏斗，回到海港时，马林鱼只剩下一付巨大的骨架。作者通过老渔夫的形象表达了这样一个信念："一个人并不是生来要被打败的，你尽可以把他消灭掉，可就是打不败他。"这部作品还体现了典型的海明威风格，比如"冰山原则"，只表现事物的 1/8，使作品含蓄、耐人寻味；还有"电报式语言"，语言简洁凝炼。

S2：他成名之后就更喜欢生活在与世隔绝的地方了。他在大城市以外选择居住的地方都很适于打猎和捕鱼。

S1：他在上学时曾为学生报写稿，这使得他在堪萨斯城市《星报》获得了第一份工作。这份工作是他的叔叔帮忙安排的。

S2：你知道吗？他 18 岁时曾想过入伍。那是一战期间，但由于他视力不好而没被录用。

S1：后来，他加入了红十字会当了救护车司机，就这样他去了欧洲。由于被一个引爆的迫击炮炸成重伤，他住进了部队医院，遇到了一位护士。她就是他在《永别了，武器》里写的护士的原型。

S2：在那之后，他回到美国，为另外一家报社工作。

S1：是的，他是报社驻欧洲部的通讯记者，所以他又回到了欧洲。

S2：在 20 世纪 20 年代中期，他写出了 20 世纪最重要的作品，两部短篇小说集：《在我们的时代里》和《没有女人的男人》。

S1：在短短 4 年里，他从一个不知名的作家变成了他那个年代，也可能是整个 20 世纪最重要的作家。

S2：为了写作他去了西班牙、古巴和其它很多地方！此外，他还结过好几次婚。

S1：二战期间，他回到欧洲做报道，在那里他遇到了另外一个女人，他的第 4 任妻子。

S2：之后，他开始创作另一部名著《老人与海》*。1954 年他获得了诺贝尔文学奖。

S1：在那之后不久，他就想自杀，1961 年结束了自己的生命。

S2：真遗憾，又是一个悲剧式的天才。

- escape city life　远离城市生活
- poor eyesight　视力不好
- try to enlist in the army　想入伍
- win the Noble Prize for Literature　获诺贝尔文学奖

95. The Ivy League

常青藤联盟

Z: Zheng Hao   **L**: Luke

Z: I'm going to America in the summer and need some info.

L: Well, being an American myself I'd be happy to help.

Z: What can you tell me about the Ivy League? I know it's about football, but doesn't it include other sports too?

L: Yes, not only football, today it's known for its level of success of athletic scholarships while keeping high academic standards. The Ivy League **crowns champions** in more than 35 sports for men and women.

Z: I see, so for example, lacrosse, ice hockey, fencing, soccer, rowing, squash and many others.

L: That's right. The name Ivy League came from a journalist, Caswell Adams of the *New York Tribune* in 1937. It consists of eight top American universities, Brown, Columbia, Cornell, Dartmouth, Harvard, Pennsylvania, Princeton, and Yale.

Z: It's located on the campus of Princeton University, and is still known officially as the Council of Ivy Group Presidents, right?

L: Yes, and it continues to grow because of the great Executive Director, Jeffrey H. Orleans, who took the post in 1984.

Z: What about before that? How did it become so famous **throughout the world**?

L: In February 1954, what is more commonly accepted as the founding date for the Ivy League, the Ivy Group Agreement was changed and extended into all sports and to help intra-group competition.

Z: OK, so the basic intent of the original Ivy agreement was to improve and help college athletics, but not interfering with the real purpose of universities, which of course is education.

L: You've got it! **To be honest**, it comes from the American obsession with competition in both sports and learning.

Z: Ivy League members must be **exceptional people**, they have a rare spirit of competition and excellence. Ivy League teams have won many competitions over the years.

L: And the spectators love them, too. Watching an Ivy League game is wonderful, whether it's fencing, cross-country running, American football, basketball or lacrosse. They even have a golf team, at Yale University.

Z: What's that shield on your shirt? It looks familiar ...

L: Just one of the many Ivy League shields, I went to Columbia University, so I'm a real Ivy-Leaguer.

Z: 郑昊   **L**: 鲁克

Z: 我这个暑假打算去美国，想多了解些有关情况。

L: 好的，作为美国人，我很乐意帮你的忙。

Z: 你给我讲讲常青藤联盟的情况，好吗？我知道它与足球有关，难道不包括其它运动吗？

L: 不是的，不仅仅包括足球。如今众所周知的是它在保持较高学术水平的同时，还成功保持了相当高的体育运动成绩。常青藤联盟在不下35项男女运动项目上夺得冠军。

Z: 我知道，比如，长曲棍球、冰球、剑术、英式足球、划船、壁球和其它许多运动项目。

L: 是这样。常青藤联盟是1937年由《纽约先驱论坛报》的记者卡斯威尔·亚当斯发起的。它由美国8所高水平大学组成，分别是布朗大学、哥伦比亚大学、康奈尔大学、达特茅斯大学、哈佛大学、宾夕法尼亚大学、普林斯顿大学和耶鲁大学。

Z: 它设在普林斯顿大学的校园内，这里至今仍被认为是常青藤联盟常委会的正式办公地，是这样吗？

L: 是的。1984年伟大的执行董事杰弗里·奥尔良上任，由于他的努力，该联盟还在继续发展壮大。

Z: 在这之前的情况呢？它是怎么闻名全世界的？

L: 人们普遍认为1954年2月是常青藤联盟的成立日，此后更改了常青藤联盟协议，并把范围扩大到包括所有运动项目，以促进会内竞争。

Z: 好了，所以常青藤联合会最初的目标是提高和辅助大学体育运动，并不干涉大学的根本目的——当然就是教育。

L: 确实是这样。说实话，美国人迷恋体育和学习竞赛是成立该联盟的主要原因。

Z: 常青藤联盟的成员必须是与众不同的人，他们都有着罕见的竞争精神，都非常优秀。这几年来，常青藤联盟队在不少比赛中获胜。

L: 观众也很喜欢他们。观看他们的比赛感觉棒极了，无论是击剑还是越野赛跑，美式足球还是篮球，或是曲棍球。在耶鲁大学他们甚至还有一支高尔夫球队。

Z: 你衬衫上印的徽章是什么？看起来很眼熟……

L: 只是众多常青藤联盟徽章中的一种。我在哥伦比亚大学读过书，所以我算是个真正的常青藤联盟会员吧。

■ crown champion 获得冠军   ■ throughout the world 在全世界
■ to be honest 说实话   ■ exceptional people 与众不同的人

96. General Electric

通用电气公司

M1: Man 1   **M2**: Man 2

M1: I'm **filling out** a job application form, for an excellent job. I hope I **stand a chance**.

M2: What company is it for?

M1: General Electric or GE. They are a massive, Nobel Prize winning American company. Have you heard of them?

M2: Yes, of course! It's a very well known company. It was founded in 1876 by Thomas Edison and their first product was his light bulb invention.

M1: Actually it was called "The Edison Electric Light". And GE's first name was "The Edison Electric Light Company".

M2: I see. I know that in 1879 they invented the "Dynamo", which could power a whole neighbourhood's lighting.

M1: That's right, a very useful invention. Then, in 1890 they built their first lamp factory, so they began producing in large numbers.

M2: So, it was after that that General Electric was formed?

M1: Yes, in 1892, by merging the Edison Electric Company and the Thomson-Houston Company.

M2: That was when they **branched out into** X-ray machines, then. Also a very important discovery. And consequently, they began their research in a newly built lab. They also were the first to manufacture televisions, also another important thing in my opinion.

M1: You watch too much TV! They produced so many other things, including electric fans, steam turbines, planes, the first electric toasters . . .

M2: And they even got into commercial finance, to **provide loans to** small utilities. Then into broadcasting, with the first ever radio broadcast. Later, they made Trans-Oceanic Radio Communication, so that America could contact their allies overseas.

M1: They also were pioneers in electric trains that could pull heavy loads. Of course after that "Hotpoint" began.

M2: The Hotpoint range is still available, my washing machine is a Hotpoint. They were the first to produce fridges too, a design we sometimes still use today. In the 1930s they started making air conditioners, too.

M1: Did you know they invented microwaves in 1918? So long ago! That really revolutionised cooking. Nowadays everyone has one in their kitchen.

M2: From jet engines to news and information, GE can provide us with everything. What an incredible company to work for.

M1: I certainly think so, I hope I get the job.

M1：男人1　　M2：男人2

M1： 我正在填写一份求职申请表，是份不错的工作。我希望能把握住机会。

M2： 是什么公司？

M1： 是通用电气公司。他们是家规模宏大，得过诺贝尔奖的美国公司。你听说过吗？

M2： 是的，当然听说过。这是家很有名的公司。1876 年由托马斯·爱迪生创立，第一个产品是爱迪生发明的灯泡。

M1： 实际上这种电灯当时叫"爱迪生电灯"。通用电气公司的第一个名字叫"爱迪生电灯公司"。

M2： 我明白了。我知道 1879 年他们发明了发电机，可以用来为周围整个地区提供照明电力。

M1： 是这样，这项发明很有用。接着在 1890 年，他们建立了第一个灯泡厂，从此开始大量生产灯泡。

M2： 那之后就成立了通用电气公司，是吧？

M1： 是的，1892 年爱迪生电器公司和托马斯－休斯敦公司合并，在此基础上成立了通用电气公司。

M2： 那时他们扩大了规模，推出了 X 光射线机。这又是一项重要的发明。随后，他们开始在一个新建的实验室做研究。他们也是最早生产电视机的公司。我自己认为电视机也是一项很重要的发明。

M1： 你电视看得太多了。他们还发明了其它好多东西，包括电风扇、蒸汽涡轮、飞机、第一个电烤箱……

M2： 他们甚至还参与商业资金项目，向小型公用事业公司提供贷款。接着，他们跟第一个无线电广播公司合作搞广播事业。后来，他们又成立了一个越洋无线通信公司，使美国能够跟他们的海外同盟联系。

M1： 他们还是研制电动火车的领头羊，该火车能承载重物。当然，这是在"热点"系列之后才开始研制的。

M2： 有些"热点"系列产品至今还在使用。我的洗衣机就是一个热点产品。他们还是第一家生产冰箱的公司，这是一项我们今天仍在使用的发明设计。到了 20 世纪 30 年代他们又开始生产空调。

M1： 你知道吗？他们在 1918 年发明了微波炉？那是很久以前了！微波炉真的使烹饪发生了彻底的变化。现在每家厨房都放有一个微波炉。

M2： 从喷气发动机到新闻和信息，通用电气公司给我们提供了一切。能去这样一家公司上班，该有多好啊。

M1： 我当然也是这么认为的，希望我能得到这份工作。

■ fill out 填写　　　　　　　　■ stand a chance 把握机会
■ branch out into 业务扩展，推出　　■ provide loans to ... 向……提供贷款

97. Bill Gates

比尔·盖茨

H：*Henry*　　*L*：*Leslie*

H：Let's **look up** Bill Gates, I think he is probably the richest person in the history of the universe.

L：Let's see ... Bill Gates, founder of Microsoft, born in 1955. He's pretty young, then. I hope I'm as rich as him when I'm his age.

H：You've got no chance! You're too lazy to become a billionaire. He started studying at Harvard University in 1973, but he **dropped out**. That sounds more like you!

L：It was at Harvard that he met Paul Allen. Gates and Allen worked on a version of the programming language BASIC, that was the basis for the MITS Altair, the first microcomputer available.

H：So, dropping out in his junior year **worked out well** for him because that's when he set up Microsoft. Microsoft helped to make the computer easier to use with its developed and purchased software, everyone wanted to use it.

L：But Microsoft is a monopoly, I don't think that should be allowed in business and I think many people agree with me. Bill Gates has certainly **had his critics over the years** concerning the way he does business.

H：It's because he is an aggressive businessman, he gets what he wants using every tactic available.

L：Wow! In 2006, his wealth was estimated at $ 53 billion, I can't even imagine that much money. I wonder what it would look like if it was all in cash.

H：What people forget is that although he is an aggressive businessman, he is also very kind-hearted. He often donates considerable amounts of money to charity and has even set up his own charitable foundation.

L：Yes, he and his wife Melinda, who he has 3 children with, created the foundation in 2000. They donate more than $ 1 billion each year.

H：In 2005 he received an "honorary" knighthood from the Queen of England, a KBE Order for his services in reducing poverty and improving health in the developing countries of the world.

L: It's the second highest order given out. He can't be a "Sir" though, because he isn't British. I think he deserved it, he does so much good work.

H：亨利　　L：莱斯利

H：咱们查查比尔·盖茨吧。我觉得他可能是世界有史以来最富有的人。

L：我们来看看……比尔·盖茨，1955 年生，微软公司的创始人。他很年轻嘛。希望我到他这个年纪时也能跟他一样富有。

> * 荣誉爵士勋章：英国王室授予的爵位封号分为 7 级，包括贵族与平民两大部分。贵族爵位（peerages）分为公爵（Duke）、侯爵（Marquis）、伯爵（Earl）、子爵（Viscount）和男爵（Baron）5 个等级；另外两种封号为准男爵（Baronet）与骑士（Knight），属于平民，而非贵族；每一种勋位又分为不同的等级。公侯伯子男称 Lord（爵士），准男爵及骑士称 Sir（勋爵）。英女王每年两次授爵颁勋，每次分封达上千人。众多富人名人得到了这一殊荣，如足球明星贝克汉姆、导演斯皮尔伯格、美国前总统老布什、"甲壳虫"乐队成员麦卡特尼，还有两届 007 肖恩·康纳利和罗杰·摩尔等。

H：没机会啦！你太懒了，成不了亿万富翁。比尔·盖茨 1973 年在哈佛大学读书，但后来退学了。听起来很像你嘛！

L：在哈佛大学，他遇见了鲍尔·艾伦。他们一起研制 BASIC 计算机程序语言编译器，这是微型仪器和遥感系统公司牛郎星计算机运行的基础，是当时可用的第一台微型电脑。

H：所以，在大三的时候，退学对他来说是个不错的决定，因为正是那时他创办了微软公司。该公司利用自己开发和购买的软件，使电脑用起来容易多了，每个人都想用。

L：但微软是个垄断企业。我认为在这一行不应该搞垄断，而且我想很多人都和我的看法一致。最近几年，比尔·盖茨的经营方式肯定遭到了不少批评。

H：那是因为他咄咄逼人，利用一切手段得到他想要的东西。

L：哇！到 2006 年，他的财富估计达到了 530 亿美元。那么多钱我连想都不敢想。如果这些钱都是现金，不知道会是什么样子。

H：别忘了，比尔·盖茨除了是个有进取精神的商人之外，还是个慈善家。他经常向慈善事业大量捐款，还成立了自己的慈善基金会。

L：是的，他和妻子梅林达在 2000 年创办了基金会，他们有 3 个孩子。他们每年的捐款都超过 10 亿元。

H：2005 年，因为他为世界发展中国家的脱贫和健康事业所做的努力，英国女王授予他荣誉爵士勋章*。

L：那是英国的二等高级帝国勋爵士头衔。不过他不能做爵士，因为他不是英国人。但我觉得这个头衔对他是当之无愧，他做了那么多善事。

■ look up　查找，查查　　　　　■ drop out　中途退学
■ work out well　结果不错　　　 ■ have his critics over the years　最近几年遭到批评

98. Hollywood

好莱坞

K: *Kerry*   **A**: *Ashley*

K: Are you reading about gossip again?

A: Hollywood gossip. What's wrong with that?

K: You should be studying, not reading rubbish.

A: I am studying, it's all about the history of Hollywood.

K: Sounds interesting, I know something about that. It's the movie capital of the world, the home of the "Silver Screen".

A: But before Hollywood was Hollywood, it was Rancho La Brea and Rancho Los Feliz. In 1886, H. H. Wilcox bought an area of Rancho La Brea that his wife then **christened** "Hollywood".

K: He bought the area to make a place for rich mid-westerners to spend their winter holidays, not to make movies.

A: In 1911, the Nestor Company opened Hollywood's first film studio in an old **tavern** on the corner of Sunset and Gower. That's how it all began.

K: So, because of the new industry being created Hollywood would have to develop into more than just a small community. It wasn't long before nearly all the homes along the Boulevard were replaced by commercial buildings linking the three corners.

A: Right, people needed to work there. Also people need to have fun there, banks, restaurants, clubs and movie palaces **sprang up** during the 1920s and 1930s. They also need grand houses for the stars.

K: At this time movie stars actually lived in Hollywood? Of course nowadays they would get mobbed everyday if they lived there, so they moved out to Beverly Hills.

A: During the 1960s more and more businesses started to move out of Hollywood, and the nightclubs and bars moved to the west. Hollywood today is a diverse, vital, and active community **striving to** preserve the elegant buildings from its past.

K: But most of the movie industry is still there, right? But I guess the outward appearance of the neighbourhood has changed. How are they protecting the buildings?

A: In 1985，the Hollywood Boulevard commercial and entertainment district was officially listed in the National Register of Historic Places. This will protect the neighborhood's important buildings so that Hollywood's past can be seen in the future.

K: Great! So when you finally have enough money to visit everything will still be there，just the way it used to be.

K：克利　　**A**：阿希里

＊好莱坞：从1912年起，许多电影公司在好莱坞落户，著名的电影公司有：米高梅公司（Metro Goldwyn Mayer，简称MGM）、派拉蒙公司（Paramount）、二十世纪福克斯公司（20th Century Fox）、华纳兄弟公司（Warner Brothers）、雷电华公司（Radio Keith Orpheum，简称RKO）、环球公司（Universal）、联美公司（United Artists）、哥伦比亚公司（Columbia Pictures）。

K：你又在看那些小道消息了？

A：是好莱坞的花边新闻。有什么不对吗？

K：你应该好好学习，而不是看这些垃圾。

A：我是在学习，这些都是关于好莱坞的历史的。

K：听起来蛮有意思，这方面我也知道一些。好莱坞是世界影视之都，银幕之家。

A：但在好莱坞成为好莱坞之前，那里是拉布里尔达牧场和洛斯菲利兹达牧场。1886年，H. H. 维尔克斯买下了拉布里尔达牧场的一块地，他的妻子后来把那里取名为"好莱坞"。

K：他买那块地是为了给富有的中西部美国人提供一个冬季度假的场所，而不是为了制作电影。

A：1911年，内斯特公司在日落-高尔街角的一个老酒馆创办了第一家好莱坞电影演播室，此后就有了好莱坞＊。

K：所以，由于好莱坞有了新的行业，这里不再是个小社区。不久之后，好莱坞大道上几乎所有与三个街角相连的住房都被商业大厦取代了。

A：是的，人们需要在那里工作，也需要在那里放松享乐。20世纪20年代到30年代间，银行、旅馆、俱乐部和电影院纷纷建起，这里还要为明星提供豪华的住宅。

K：那时候，明星都住在好莱坞吗？当然，现在他们要是住在那里的话肯定会被影迷们蜂拥围观，所以他们都搬到了比弗利山庄去住。

A：到了20世纪60年代，越来越多的公司开始迁出好莱坞，夜总会和酒吧也纷纷搬到了西部。好莱坞作为一个多姿多彩、生气勃勃、精力充沛的社区，现在正努力想保留它过去优雅的建筑。

K：但大多数电影公司还在那里发展，是吧？不过我可以猜到当地社区的外观肯定发生了变化。现在他们是怎么保护这些建筑的？

A：1985年，好莱坞大道上的商业和娱乐区已在历史古迹国家注册处正式登记入册，这将有助于保护当地社区的重要建筑，这样将来人们还可以看到好莱坞辉煌的过去。

K：太好了！那就是说当你终于攒够了钱去那里参观的时候，那里的一切还会保留在原地，就跟过去一样。

■ spring up　纷纷建立　　　　■ christen ...　给……命名
■ travern　小酒馆　　　　　　■ strive to　努力

99. NBA

美国职业篮球联赛

M1: *Man 1*　　**M2**: *Man 2*

M1: There's a good NBA game on TV tonight, shall we watch it?

M2: That depends ... who's playing?

M1: The Houston Rockets and Miami Heat. You know, Yao Ming plays for the Rockets so we have to watch.

M2: Do you have any idea who invented basketball or the NBA? Someone must have made up the rules.

M1: I do know, yes. A Canadian man, Dr. James Naismith created the game of basketball from 13 original rules. It's played a little differently nowadays, but the principle is still the same.

M2: It was first played in Canada? I'm sure I read somewhere that the first game was played in 1946 in Toronto.

M1: That's right, the first game was between the Toronto Huskies and the New York Knickerbockers. At that time the game was pretty boring, though. They didn't introduce the 24-second clock until after.

M2: The 24-second clock and of course an accompanying limit on the number of fouls a team could commit in a quarter. This created **the game we know and love today**.

M1: So, the NBA became more and more popular after that. When it started in Canada, most children grew up playing ice hockey and didn't really like basketball, but **over the years** it has changed considerably.

M2: Is the NBA one organisation or is it made of many **put together**?

M1: Like most pro sports leagues, the NBA is a confederation of separate organizations that compete yet must also cooperate.

M2: This kind of confederation wouldn't be able to survive and become more popular without outstanding leadership at the top. Also, you said earlier that the rules have changed, how so? What are the current rules we follow today?

M1 : There are 12 rules that we must follow today including court dimensions, players, definitions, scoring, violations and free throws.

M2 : The referee controls the game using some very interesting hand signals. There must be a manual for the **hand signals** that must be followed, so that everyone can learn them. How many teams are there altogether?

M1 : It started out having just 8 teams, but now it has 30. But of course, my favourite will always be the Rockets.

M1 : 男人 1   M2 : 男人 2

M1 : 今晚有一场精彩的 NBA 联赛，我们一起看吧？

M2 : 看情况吧……谁跟谁比赛？

M1 : 是休斯敦火箭队对迈阿密热队。你知道，姚明在火箭队，所以这场比赛我们一定要看。

M2 : 你知道是谁发明的篮球或组建的 NBA 吗？肯定有人制定了比赛规则。

M1 : 是的，我还真知道，是加拿大的詹姆士·奈史密斯博士。他自创 13 条比赛规则，发明了篮球运动。今天的篮球打法和过去比有一点点不同，但规则没变。

M2 : 首次篮球比赛是在加拿大举行的吗？我敢肯定在哪里看到过说第一场比赛是 1946 年在多伦多举行的。

M1 : 没错，第一次比赛是多伦多的爱斯基摩队对纽约的尼克博克斯队。不过，那时的比赛相当没意思。后来他们引进了 24 秒钟进攻时限。

M2 : 除了 24 秒进攻时限，还有一条附加限制规则，是为了限制球队在 15 分钟里犯规的次数。这样就形成了我们今天所熟悉和喜欢的篮球比赛。

M1 : 所以，自那以后 NBA 就变得越来越受欢迎了。篮球比赛开始在加拿大举行时，大多数的孩子都玩曲棍球，并不怎么喜欢篮球，但这些年来情况发生了很大的变化。

M2 : NBA 是一个组织还是由多个组织组合而成的呢？

M1 : 就像大多数职业运动联盟一样，NBA 是一个独立的组织联盟，相互竞争也相互合作。

M2 : 如果没有优秀的领导阶层，这样的联盟就不能存活下去，也不会变得更加受欢迎。还有，刚才你说的一些规则已经变了，这是怎么回事？我们今天遵守的是什么样的规则？

M1 : 现在我们所遵守的有 12 条规则，包括球场规格、球员数量、解说、计分、违规和罚球。

M2 : 裁判用一些非常有趣的手势信号来控制球赛。肯定有一本大家必须遵守的手势信号手册，这样人人都可以学习。NBA 一共有多少支球队？

M1 : 开始的时候只有 8 支球队，现在有 30 支。当然我最喜欢的一直都是火箭队。

■ the game we know and love today 我们今天所熟悉、喜欢的篮球赛
■ over the years 这些年以来   ■ put together 集合
■ hand signal 手语，手势信号

199

100. Cowboys

牛仔

S1: Student 1　　**S2**: Student 2

S1: I want to write about something which is truly American, what do you think? A president or a businessman?

S2: Neither, you should write about cowboys. They are a true symbol of the USA.

S1: Like in the movies?

S2: No, the life of a cowboy was **anything but glamorous**—it entailed hard work and long, lonesome hours.

S1: What about the clothes? Do they really wear jeans, cowboy boots and Stetson hats?

S2: Cowboy clothing is an everyday part of their wardrobes. Today they are remembered in "Spaghetti Westerns", movies and TV shows which **started a craze** during the 1950s and 60s. Some are still popular today, but most people's attraction shifted to space travel, maybe because of the moon landing in 1969.

S1: Many country and western songs **try to capture** the true cowboy spirit. This fascination with the "Old West" is still popular today. I think lots of Americans like country and western music. But you think movies, music and television tells us nothing about the true cowboy?

S2: Yes, but music especially has made cowboys more and more popular. The cowboy's real job isn't singing though, it's looking after cattle. Hence the name "cowboy".

S1: The cowboy's reign in the Wild West was quite short, about 30 years, why are they such a big part of American history?

S2: Well, when the Civil War ended, many of the soldiers had no home to return to and started drifting to the West on horseback.

S1: I see, then ranch owners hired these hard working men as ranch hands and they were the first cowboys.

S2: And when the time came to sell the beef, the hands would **round-up** the cattle from the open prairie and take them to market.

S1: So why was their reign in the Wild West so short?

S2: It was short because the West stopped being wild. Barbed wire was invented and soon it was almost impossible to roam around freely as they had done before.

S1: So as Western America developed, the cowboys' jobs became less and less. Nowadays no one thinks of these original cowboys, only the ones we see in the movies.

S1: 学生 1   S2: 学生 2

S1: 我想写点真正属于美国的东西，你认为该写些什么呢？写总统还是商人？

S2: 都不好，你应该写美国牛仔。他们才是真正能代表美国的象征。

S1: 就像电影里演的那样吗？

S2: 不是，牛仔的生活一点也不诱人——他们必须承受繁重的劳动和长期的寂寞孤独。

S1: 那衣服呢？他们是真的都穿牛仔服、牛仔靴，戴宽边帽吗？

S2: 牛仔服就是他们的日常服饰。今天他们留给人们的记忆仍然是他们在意大利式西部片*中的形象。正是这些影视作品在上世纪五六十年代引发了一阵热潮。直到今天有些这样的影片还是很受欢迎，但后来大多数人把注意力转移到了太空旅行，这大概是因为 1969 年的登月事件吧。

S1: 很多乡村音乐和西部歌曲都试图表现真正的牛仔精神。这种对"老西部"的迷恋至今仍然还很流行。我觉得很多美国人都喜欢乡村音乐和西部音乐。可是，你认为电影、音乐和电视并没有表现出真正的牛仔，对不对？

S2: 是的，尤其是音乐，它们让西部牛仔变得越来越有名。不过，牛仔真正的工作并不是唱歌那么轻松，而是照看牛群，所以他们才被叫做"牛仔"。

S1: 牛仔在美国蛮荒的西部活动的时间并不长，大约是 30 年。为什么他们在美国历史上那么重要呢？

S2: 是这样，内战结束时，很多士兵都无家可归，于是他们就骑着马漂泊到了西部地区。

S1: 我知道了，那里的大牧场主就雇佣这些勤劳的人做牧场的帮手，他们也就成了最早的牛仔。

S2: 到了出售牛肉的时节，这些劳工们就从空旷的大草原把牛群集拢到一起，把它们赶到市场。

S1: 为什么牛仔在蛮荒的西部活动的时间那么短呢？

S2: 那是因为西部不再荒凉了。此外，人们发明了带刺的铁丝网，这样牛仔再也不可能像以前那样自由自在地四处游逛了。

S1: 所以随着美国西部的发展，牛仔的工作变得越来越少。现在人们知道的不是这些最初的牛仔，而是我们在电影中看到的那些人物形象。

■ anything but glamorous 一点没有魅力   ■ start a craze 掀起一阵热潮
■ try to capture 试图记录   ■ round-up 聚拢

图书在版编目（CIP）数据

英语畅谈世界文化 100 主题：英汉对照／（英）斯德克（Stirk，N.）著；
许卉艳，周维译．–北京：外文出版社，2007
（英语国际人）
ISBN 978-7-119-04741-6

Ⅰ．英… Ⅱ．①斯… ②许… ③周… Ⅲ．①英语 – 汉语 – 对照读物
②文化史 – 世界 Ⅳ. H319.4：G

中国版本图书馆 CIP 数据核字（2007）第 023637 号

英语国际人
英语畅谈世界文化 100 主题

作　者	Nick Stirk
翻　译	许卉艳　周　维

选题策划	蔡　菁
责任编辑	王　欢
封面设计	红十月设计室
印刷监制	冯　浩

ⓒ 2007 外文出版社
出版发行　外文出版社
地　　址　中国北京西城区百万庄大街 24 号　　邮政编码　100037
网　　址　http：//www.flp.com.cn
电　　话　（010）68995964/68995883（编辑部）
　　　　　（010）68995844/68995852（发行部）
　　　　　（010）68320579/68996067（总编室）
电子信箱　info@flp.com.cn/sales@flp.com.cn
印　　制　北京佳信达艺术印刷有限公司
经　　销　新华书店/外文书店
开　　本　小 16 开　　　　　　　　　印　张　13
印　　数　0001—8000 册　　　　　　字　数　183 千字
装　　别　平
版　　次　2007 年 4 月第 1 版第 1 次印刷
书　　号　ISBN 978-7-119-04741-6
定　　价　25.00 元